e-PROFIT

High Payoff Strategies for Capturing the E-Commerce Edge

Peter S. Cohan

AMACOM

American Management Association

New York • Atlanta • Boston • Chicago • Kansas City • San Francisco • Washington, D. C.
Brussels • Mexico City • Tokyo • Toronto

Special discounts on bulk quantities of AMACOM books are available to corporations, professional associations, and other organizations. For details, contact Special Sales Department, AMACOM, a division of American Management Association, 1601 Broadway, New York, NY 10019.
Tel.: 212-903-8316. Fax: 212-903-8083.
Web site: www.amanet.org

This publication is designed to provide accurate and authoritative information in regard to the subject matter covered. It is sold with the understanding that the publisher is not engaged in rendering legal, accounting, or other professional service. If legal advice or other expert assistance is required, the services of a competent professional person should be sought.

Library of Congress Cataloging-in-Publication data has been applied for and is on record at the Library of Congress.

Printing number

10   9   8   7   6   5   4   3   2   1

To Robin, Sarah, and Adam

Contents

List of Illustrations

Preface

One of the most important questions about e-commerce is whether it is a real, lasting business phenomenon or a passing fad. There is ample evidence to support both positions.

The most compelling argument in its favor is the extremely rapid growth rate of companies whose sole business is e-commerce. Amazon.com with its 250 percent annual revenue growth, its several hundred million worth of losses, and its $18 billion market capitalization comes to mind as an example.

Amazon.com is growing so fast because it offers such a compelling value proposition to its 10 million (and growing) customers in comparison to its land-based competitors. Simply put, the 100 million Americans (and more worldwide) with Internet connections can shop intelligently, and place an order for any one of 1.4 million books from the comfort of their homes 24 hours a day, seven days a week, and expect, in most cases, to have that book delivered to their door steps within two or three days.

But Amazon.com is also losing huge amounts of money as it pursues its vision of being the WalMart of the Web. This is one of the factors that makes people question the viability of e-commerce over the long run. There is a real question about whether Amazon.com can continue to incur such huge losses as it moves into an increasingly broad array of new markets beyond the inherently low-margin book business from which it started.

It is Amazon.com's market capitalization that is perhaps the most attention-grabbing. With a market capitalization of $18 billion, Amazon.com is worth more than its two largest land-based competitors—Barnes & Noble and Borders—combined. Despite the 40 percent drop in its stock price since its April 1999 high, Amazon.com's market capitalization suggests that a very powerful economic phenomenon is underway. This is despite the obvious disconnect between Amazon.com's horrendous profit performance and its extraordinary market capitalization.

Despite all the hype surrounding e-commerce, a surprisingly small number of companies are actually conducting e-commerce. Of the several hundred land-based companies that I contacted for this research, only a handful were willing to discuss their e-commerce strategies. Companies begged off because their strategies were at such early stages of development that they had not even been presented to their boards. Other managers I contacted were concerned about tipping their hands to their competitors. Another, possibly more comprehensive survey, suggested that only 25 percent of traditional companies were engaged in any form of e-commerce as of August 1999. This anecdotal evidence of low levels of e-commerce suggests that e-commerce could be a passing fad.

As I began to examine this apparent disconnect between the hype and the reality surrounding e-commerce, it became apparent that there was something going on beneath the surface that was impeding the progress of e-commerce. This book is an exploration of how to remove the road blocks that inhibit the progress of e-commerce. I discovered quite a few of these road blocks during the research for this book—fear of change being the most important one. But I also discovered companies that have been able to overcome that fear—and considerable short-term pain—to profit quite substantially from their willingness to cannibalize their core business to provide a better (e-commerce–enabled) deal for their customers.

About This Book

This book guides managers through the process of overcoming the fear of change and embracing the benefits of e-commerce for customers, employees, and shareholders. To do this, I first examine the compelling economic evidence of the growth of e-commerce and its benefits for streamlining the business relationships between a company and its customers, suppliers, and employees. I deconstruct some of the highest payoff e-commerce applications, and identify the principles of using e-commerce to create competitive advantage.

After reviewing these compelling economic arguments, I dig into the fears that companies have about changing their ways of doing business. I show how companies are getting their CEOs on board, how they are managing the change process to create effective e-commerce strategies, and how they create cultures that can sustain the benefits of change into the future.

I conclude by exploring the role of senior management in translating the vision of e-strategy into a concrete reality. To do this, I examine how senior managers participate in the design of e-commerce architectures. I continue by discussing the most effective techniques for evaluating e-commerce suppliers and negotiating contracts with them. Finally, I conclude by exploring how the most successful companies manage their e-commerce projects so that they can quickly enjoy the benefits of e-commerce even as they continue to adapt their systems and processes to the ever-changing demands of their customers.

Acknowledgments

This book could not have been written without the help of many people. I am grateful to all the professionals whose insights helped shape my thinking for this book, including Todd Adams (*Milwaukee Journal Sentinel*), Richard Bentz (Hershey Foods), Larry Carter (Cisco System), Bob Chaffin (GM), Bob Clanin (UPS), Bob Culver (Cabot Corporation), William Farrell (Fannie Mae), Mark Hoffman (CommerceOne), Jeff Henley (Oracle), Brad Sharp (Sterling Commerce), Guy Tallent (Chase Manhattan), Steven C. Van Wyk (Morgan Stanley Dean Witter), and Robert Zahler (Shaw, Pittman, Potts & Trowbridge). Justin Fox, Joann Coviello, and Dawn Gorski (Fortune Conferences), Kavin Moody (Babson College), and Dr. Richard Schroth (The Wharton School) were great pleasures to work with during the Fortune Conference *Revolutionizing Corporate Finance With Technology*.

I also appreciate the help of my colleagues Bruce Henderson (Matrix USA), Jeff Coburn (Coburn & Company), Geoff Fenwick (The Balanced Scorecard Collaborative), Tom Lynch (Lazard Freres Capital Partners), Peter Laino (Monitor Clipper Partners), Jake Wesner (Perot Investments), Mordechai Fester (Cisco Systems), Jay Spahr (BankBoston), Howard Seibel, and Eric Stang. I am very grateful for the support and encouragement throughout this project of Ray O'Connell of AMACOM Books who first suggested the idea for this book, and sagely guided me through its creation.

Finally, I would like to offer special thanks to my wife, Robin, who patiently tolerated the seemingly endless weekends of writing and revisions.

1

Introduction: e-Profit

There was $74 billion worth of electronic commerce (e-commerce) conducted in 1998, a figure which is expected to grow to $1.2 trillion by 2002. Despite such dramatic growth forecasts—or perhaps because of them—managers maintain a high degree of skepticism about the role of e-commerce in our economy. For example, many comparisons have been made between Internet stocks and previous speculative fads, from the bowling stocks of the 1960s to the Dutch tulip-bulb craze of the 16th century. The difference with the Internet is that neither bowling nor tulips ever had the power to transform the economy.

The Internet is changing communications and commerce. Because it is changing so quickly, many managers underestimate its transforming power. Here is one historical analogy. In the early 1960s, when Haloid Xerox first developed photo-copying, analysts computed the size of the market by multiplying the number of secretaries in the U.S. by the average number of letters they typed by the average number of carbon copies they made. It did not occur to these analysts that everybody would end up Xeroxing every document, leading to a market many thousands of times bigger.

The Internet is misunderstood because it arrived as a commercial phenomenon in roughly 1995, when Netscape introduced its first commercial Web browser. By comparison, the automobile developed much more slowly. For example, the commercial sales of automobiles began in 1895. It would be twenty-one years before windshield wipers were invented, nineteen years before the traffic signal and forty years before the parking meter.

The Internet has developed far more quickly. In April 1999, 55 percent of all of Charles Schwab's transactions were conducted online. Amazon.com grew to become the third largest bookseller in the United States in only three years. Intuit's Quicken Mortgage originated $375 million in mortgages in six months. The Web helps people comparison-shop and exchange ideas globally. People in business and academia use e-mail as their preferred form of communication.

Even if the magnitude of future e-commerce is grossly overestimated, there is no question that e-commerce is an important business phenomenon. Despite the tremendous hype surrounding e-commerce, there are actually not that many companies currently conducting it.

Companies are beginning to ask themselves some fundamental questions about e-commerce. The answers to these questions are likely to determine how widely companies end up embracing e-commerce:

- What is e-commerce?
- Which e-commerce projects have the highest payoff and why?
- How should managers evaluate e-commerce projects?
- How does e-commerce improve a company's competitive position?
- How can managers change their organizations in order to implement the highest payoff e-commerce applications have to offer, and sustain the benefits?
- What role should managers play in the design and development of e-commerce systems architectures?
- What is the role of senior managers in implementing these e-commerce systems?

What This Book Is about and Why You Should Read It

This book is about helping managers to profit from the transition to e-commerce. The book is for managers of companies of all sizes. For managers of large companies, the book will help identify high-payoff e-commerce applications, reposition their companies to compete against Internet-only competitors, manage the organizational change process, and drive the implementation of the highest-payoff e-commerce applications.

Managers of Internet-only companies will find this book useful by providing insights into the strategies and management approaches that their land-based competitors will attempt to use in order to compete with them. Internet-only competitors will find it useful to understand how larger companies are coming to grips with the competitive and organizational challenges that e-commerce forces the large company executives to face.

This book accepts the notion that e-commerce is a force that is not likely to fade as previous management fads. This is not to say that e-commerce will not change dramatically and unpredictably in the future. However, this book is based on the assumption that all companies will eventually be forced to rethink their strategies, management structure, and business operations in light of the economic benefits that e-commerce enables.

This is not to say that such corporate transformation will be easy. In fact, this book assumes that most companies will find the transformation to be a very difficult one. Many will not be able to accomplish it. In industry after industry, we observe three kinds of companies. The first kind of company is an e-commerce "pure play." The Internet-only company is able to challenge the land-based companies and adapt much more quickly to changing competitor strategies, new technologies, and evolving customer needs.

There are actually two kinds of land-based companies. The first kind is able to recognize that continued market leadership depends on the ability to cannibalize its business ahead of competitors. As a result, this first kind of land-based company is willing to take the short-term pain that such self-cannibalization demands. The second kind of land-based company is hoping that e-commerce will go away or that e-commerce simply does not apply to their industry. This second type of land-based company is the one less likely to survive.

This book has been written to help all three kinds of companies to profit from the ongoing change process of e-commerce. It is important to note that e-commerce actually forces companies to accept that they must always be in the process of becoming. Companies must become better at creating value for customers. New technologies provide the foundation on which such superior value propositions can be built. Competitors challenge the relationship between customers and their current suppliers by deploying new business models based in these new technologies. And customers—recognizing the increased bargaining power that e-commerce enables—are increasing their demands for quality, service, and value.

To help managers deal with these challenges, this book has much to offer. It presents many case studies from well-known companies such as Cisco Systems, General Motors, Barnes & Noble, Amazon.com, and Microsoft. It also develops case studies from less well-known organizations such as Toronto Hospital, DARPA, Eastman Chemical, and Homebid. com. From these case studies, the book develops principles of effective management and describes methodologies for such important processes as:

- Picking high payoff e-commerce applications
- Developing "e-strategy"
- Conducting financial evaluation of e-commerce projects
- Getting the CEO "on board" with e-commerce
- Managing the organizational change induced by e-commerce, creating a culture that sustains change
- Designing the e-commerce architecture
- Evaluating e-commerce suppliers

- Managing successful contract negotiations with e-commerce suppliers
- Implementing the e-commerce system

To introduce managers to this world of ongoing self-transformation, Chapter 1 continues by describing the research on which this book is based. Chapter 1 then introduces five important concepts that executives can use to help them profit from the transition to e-commerce. Chapter 1 concludes by describing how the remainder of the book expands on these findings and frameworks.

Research

This book explores these questions based on research conducted over the course of a one-year period. The idea for the book came from an open forum called *E-Commerce and the CFO*, in which I participated during three Fortune Conferences entitled *Revolutionizing Corporate Finance With Technology* in February and March 1999. This open forum was held in Chicago, San Francisco, and New York, with roughly 180 CFOs and other senior financial executives. These executives supplied their e-commerce questions to Fortune before the conference. A moderator posed the questions listed above to three or four panelists selected for their expertise in e-commerce software and Internet business strategy.

I was a panelist in each of the three conferences, serving in the role of "Internet Business Strategy Expert." Given the early stage of the evolution of the use of the Internet in business, such a title is, at best, provisional.

My credentials in this area come from having spent five years running a firm that provides strategy consulting services to companies that compete in the Internet business, and companies that use Internet technology to enhance their profits. At the Fortune conference, I was billed as the author *of Net Profit: How to Invest and Compete in the Real World of Internet Busi-*

ness (San Francisco: Jossey-Bass, 1999). *Net Profit* defines nine distinct Internet business segments, analyzes the industry structure of each segment, and identifies the competitive strategies that the most successful companies use to dominate their markets. *Net Profit* provides a framework for investors to evaluate Internet company investments, a way for Internet business managers to develop winning strategies, and a method for non-Internet business managers to develop strategies that use the Internet to enhance their companies' competitiveness.

While this open forum received the highest performance ratings of the Fortune conference, the answers to the questions made it clear that there was absolutely no consensus. Ray O'Connell of AMACOM suggested that a book focused on these questions would be useful to CFOs, and I agreed to write it.

To address these questions, I conducted interviews and reviewed articles and books. Several of the senior financial executives who participated in the Fortune conference agreed to be interviewed for this book. While their interviews yielded valuable insights, many of the senior financial executives did not wish to participate in the research. A few disclosed the reason that they chose not to be interviewed—they did not wish to reveal their freshly hatched e-commerce strategies to their competitors.

Fortunately, the companies that agreed to participate in the research represent a wide cross-section of American industry. Senior financial executives in industries such as newspapers, automobiles, financial services, mining, and many others did agree to participate.

While this book began with a focus on helping financial managers, the research process revealed that because of the newness and strategic significance of e-commerce, it is much more helpful to think about e-commerce from the perspective of the CFO as a member of the executive management team, rather than as the chief accountant or chief treasurer. Therefore, this book is focused on dealing with strategic issues from the perspective of the senior management team of a company.

Key Concepts

To help senior executives deal with the challenges of e-commerce, this book presents five key concepts that are designed to answer the five most essential questions that e-commerce raises for senior executives. Table 1-1 outlines these questions and concepts.

Each of these concepts is introduced below.

Strategic Balance Sheet Analysis

With the advent of e-commerce, financial executives are finding that the return on capital is higher from investing in intangible assets than in tangible ones. As a result, financial executives need a way to pinpoint the intangible assets with the greatest potential to increase their companies' shareholder value. Strategic balance sheet analysis is such a process.

Strategic balance sheet analysis consists of three steps. First, a company must identify its intangible assets. Then the

Table 1-1. Key questions and concepts of e-commerce.

Strategic Issues	Key Concept
What are our intangible assets, and how can e-commerce help unlock their value?	Strategic Balance Sheet Analysis
What opportunities for market-share gain does e-commerce create for us, and how does e-commerce threaten our competitive position?	Competitive Opportunity and Threat Assessment
What risks does e-commerce introduce into our company, and how can we address these risks?	E-Commerce Risk Evaluation
How can e-commerce transform the stock market's assessment of our company's value?	Enterprise Value Assessment
How can our management team prioritize potential e-commerce projects to guide the allocation of capital and people?	E-Commerce Portfolio Analysis

company must conceptualize e-commerce applications that can extract value from these intangible assets. Finally, the company must estimate how much these e-commerce applications will add to the company's profits.

As Figure 1-1 illustrates, companies that are successful at using technology are finding that their intangible assets contribute to the huge gap between their market capitalization and the book value of their equity.

As Figure 1-2 indicates, the e-commerce applications and the sources of incremental shareholder value tend to vary with the specific type of intangible asset.

Customer Relationships

The figure lists four of the many types of intangible assets that e-commerce can convert into increased shareholder value. Once a company has established initial customer relationships, the Web is an efficient way to sell additional products

Figure 1-1. Strategic balance sheet analysis framework.

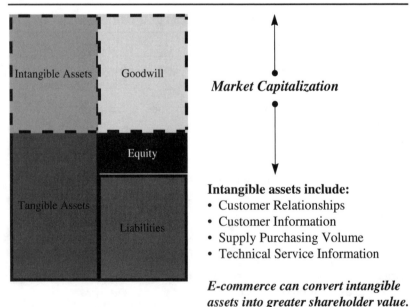

Intangible assets include:
- Customer Relationships
- Customer Information
- Supply Purchasing Volume
- Technical Service Information

E-commerce can convert intangible assets into greater shareholder value.

Figure 1-2. E-commerce applications by intangible asset class.

Intangible Asset	E-Commerce Application	Sources of Value
Customer Relationships	Web-Based Selling	Increased Revenues; More Efficient Order Fulfillment
Customer Information	Personalization	Increased Revenues per Customer
Supply Purchasing Volume	Electronic Procurement	Volume Discounts; More Efficient Administration
Technical Service Information	Web-Based Self-Service	Lower Technical Service Costs

to existing customers. Two benefits of using the Web in this way are increased revenues and lower incremental selling costs. A third benefit is that the Web can help streamline the order-fulfillment process, particularly for complex products, by using artificial intelligence to guide customers through a process of ordering product configurations that can be manufactured. As we will see, Cisco Systems has used this approach to selling over the Web, adding more than $500 million to its profits in the process.

Customer Information

Customer information is another intangible asset that e-commerce can convert into added shareholder value. Web-based personalization allows consumer marketers to use the Web to learn about a consumer's preferences and interests. When a consumer makes a purchase, the marketer can then use knowledge of these preferences to recommend additional items that people with similar interests have purchased. With personalization technology, such recommendations have a very high chance of being followed. This leads to dramatic increases in sales per customer. Levi Strauss' Web site uses this personalization technology from San Francisco–based Andromedia, and has found that its customers accept 76 percent of the recommended additional items.

Supply Purchasing Volume

Many multidivisional companies purchase large volumes of supplies at the division level. Since these companies do not centralize purchasing, each division forges unique contractual arrangements with suppliers. In many cases, each division buys the same item from different suppliers. As a consequence, these companies leave money on the table by not purchasing these items from a single corporate location, and not negotiating volume discounts with a preferred supplier. Electronic procurement is a Web-based application that enables companies to capture these volume discounts while streamlining the administration of the purchase process. Large companies such as General Electric are implementing electronic procurement systems. By doing so, GE is saving $1 billion on its $5 billion worth of corporate office supply purchases annually.

Technical Service Information

Companies that sell complex products typically offer technical service. Most companies that provide technical service keep records of each interaction between the technical service professionals and the customer. In many companies, these records are kept in file drawers. As a result, if a customer in one country has a particular technical problem with a product, it is unlikely that the customer service representative in that country will be familiar with all the solutions to that problem that may have been developed around the world. Therefore, there is a risk that the technical service may spend hours or days devising a solution to a problem that may have already been solved elsewhere within the company.

Web-based technical self-service enables customers to tap into the cumulative technical service experience of their vendor. It enhances customer satisfaction because technical problems are solved faster. It saves the vendor money by limiting the need to hire as many additional technical service people as a company grows. It also saves the vendor the cost of printing and mailing updated technical brochures and software patches to customers. Cisco's Web-based technical self-service application saved more than $100 million in the latter category alone.

While each company must follow its own process of strategic balance sheet analysis, these examples should provide financial executives with a feeling for how successful users of e-commerce have proceeded.

Competitive Opportunity and Threat Analysis

While financial executives are finding that strategic balance sheet analysis is a useful way to get started in thinking about how best to deploy e-commerce, this analysis should not be conducted in isolation.

As Figure 1-3 illustrates, the Internet can change the structure of many industries. A new company that uses the Internet to create competitive advantage can grow much faster than the average participant in that industry. An incumbent company, growing at an average rate, faces an adaptation gap. The adaptation gap is the difference in growth rate between the incumbent and the new entrant. If the incumbent adapts its business model effectively, it can accelerate its rate of growth and sur-

Figure 1-3. Competitive adaptation gap analysis.

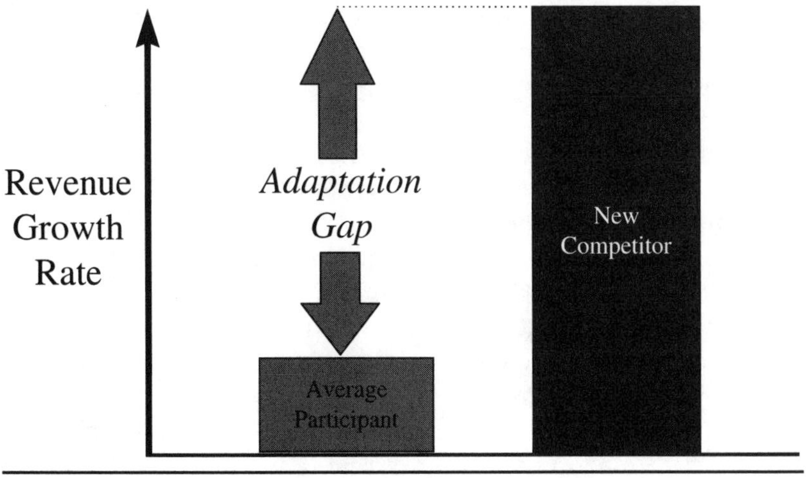

Revenue Growth Rate

Adaptation Gap

New Competitor

Average Participant

vive the onslaught of the new competitor. If the incumbent adopts a wait and see attitude, it may be too late to adapt.

The book-selling industry is one example of this phenomenon. Amazon.com sells books, CDs, and videos over the Web. While Amazon.com has been growing at more than 100 percent per year, Barnes & Noble and Borders are growing at less than 10 percent annual rates. The stock market has rewarded Amazon.com with a market capitalization that is greater than the sum of Barnes & Noble's and Borders' combined market capitalization. Barnes & Noble chose to adapt, somewhat slowly, through a two-pronged strategy. First, Barnes & Noble began to sell books over the Web itself. Second, Barnes & Noble attempted to purchase Amazon.com's chief book supplier, Ingram Book Group. This proposed acquisition was terminated in 1999 following pressure from the Federal Trade Commission. It remains to be seen whether Barnes & Noble will be able to accelerate its revenue growth and impede the progress of Amazon.com. As I noted earlier, executives must find ways to enhance the value of the company's intangible assets. The competitive adaptation gap analysis suggests that executives must also analyze the strategies of new competitors, like Amazon.com, who can use the Internet to put the company at a substantial competitive disadvantage. In fact, executives should also develop ideas for e-commerce applications that can put the company in a position to accelerate its growth rate relative to these new entrants. Executives should also consider strategic moves that can position the advantages of the incumbent company against the weaknesses of the new entrant.

While the majority of incumbent companies are likely to wait until a new entrant has established a presence, in every industry there will be a few companies that will take the initiative (and the risk) necessary to implement game-changing e-commerce applications ahead of their peers. Executives in these companies must create competitive opportunities.

As Figure 1-4 suggests, there is an important sequence of activities that must be performed to identify valuable competitive opportunities. First the company must talk to customers in order to identify specific unmet needs with the industry's products. Amazon.com found that customers wished that there were a more efficient way to search, select, and take delivery of books. Office Depot found that small businesses were looking for a much more efficient way to select, take delivery, and pay for office supplies.

The next step in the analysis is to study competitors to understand where they would be vulnerable if they chose to offer a product that satisfied the customers' unmet needs. Amazon.com found that traditional bookstores could not stock all the titles in print, nor could they create an efficient way of matching a consumer's interests with all the possible books in print. Office Depot found that many competing office super-stores would be reluctant to sell over the Web because the Web channel would compete with in-store, catalog, direct marketing, and telephone sales forces. These incumbent methods of

Figure 1-4. Competitive opportunity analysis.

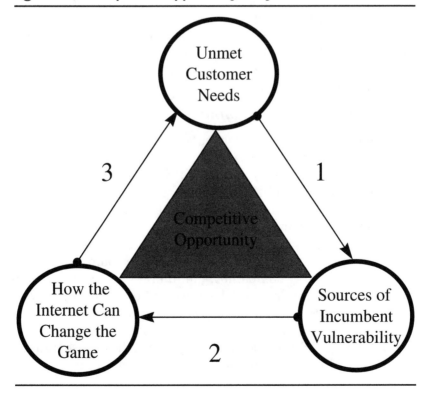

office supply distribution would not welcome the additional internal competition from a Web site.

The final step in the competitive opportunity analysis is to think of ways that the Internet can change the game to favor your company. More specifically, the challenge is to imagine a way that your company can use the Internet to satisfy unmet customer needs in a way that will be difficult for competitors to copy. Amazon.com realized that selling books over the Web would enable consumers to select from a larger set of books more efficiently and take convenient delivery at a competitive price. Furthermore, given the high relative costs, lower selection, and relatively inefficient search process of traditional book stores, Amazon.com would enjoy a sustainable competitive advantage.

Office Depot is hoping to achieve significant sales growth by using the Web as a parallel channel for distributing office supplies. It remains to be seen how effectively Office Depot's Web-based selling of office supplies will work. Nevertheless, Office Depot's experience represents a credible demonstration of the value of competitive opportunity analysis for an incumbent company seeking to take the initiative in its industry.

E-Commerce Risk Evaluation

The financial executive is particularly concerned about how e-commerce initiatives identified through the previous analyses may increase the risk of loss to the company. In many cases, executives' fear about the additional risks that e-commerce introduces into the company is as great as the absence of tools to help evaluate and manage such risks.

As Figure 1-5 demonstrates, e-commerce introduces three new kinds of risk into the company. While fraud has always been a problem for companies, the Internet creates the potential for an unscrupulous purchasing agent to create bogus Web-based suppliers. If the company is not aware of the fraud, the unscrupulous purchasing agent can create false transactions with the bogus Web-based supplier and use these false transactions to steal from the company. One solution to this problem is to use authentication technology.

Figure 1-5. E-commerce risk evaluation framework.

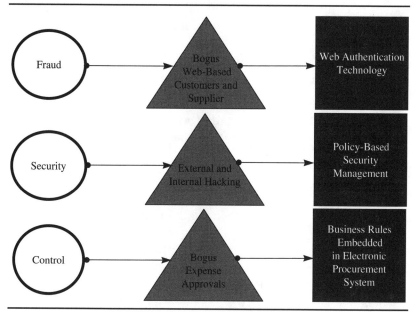

While information security has always been a concern, e-commerce opens up the risk of information security breaches to a larger number of individuals both inside and outside the company. To combat these information security problems, the policy-based network security management products offered by software manufacturers enable companies to secure their information assets from theft and tampering in an integrated fashion.

Finally, e-commerce introduces new control problems. For example, an electronic procurement system streamlines the administration of the purchasing process. There is a danger that this streamlined process will open up opportunities for employees to obtain bogus approval for the purchase of valuable products and services.

Many electronic procurement system vendors offer companies the ability to embed business rules regarding approval of purchases into the electronic procurement system, thereby sustaining managerial controls.

Despite these technologies, the e-commerce risks are real. Executives must evaluate them diligently and take a cautious approach to the adoption of the technologies outlined above. We will examine in greater detail the procedures that executives can follow to identify the risks of e-commerce, and take steps to protect their companies from losses.

Enterprise Value Assessment

The research for this book reveals that there is nothing new about the method of financial analysis that executives apply to e-commerce projects. However, as Figure 1-6 suggests, e-commerce applications present opportunities for financial executives to consider factors in their financial evaluations that are typically associated with mergers or stock buybacks, not information technology projects. In other words, some e-commerce projects can significantly boost shareholder value.

Executives attempt to quantify the cash flows associated with each e-commerce project. The costs of the project are typical of other information technology projects, although often the cost of the hardware and software is less than that of the Web consulting services. Furthermore, the time frames for sys-

Figure 1-6. Enterprise value assessment.

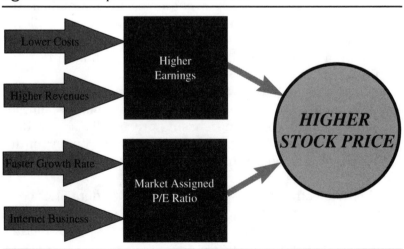

tems development should be dramatically shorter because in many cases, e-commerce applications are intended to be introduced to the market quickly and subsequently modified, based on user feedback.

Nevertheless, the real benefits to the company that must be measured have to do with two factors that influence growth in a company's stock price. The first factor is the extent to which the e-commerce project enhances the company's profits by lowering costs and/or increasing revenues. The second factor that is particularly powerful in the case of e-commerce applications is the extent to which the application increases the price/earnings ratio that the market assigns to the company's earnings.

Certain e-commerce applications can cause the market to assign a much higher P/E ratio to the company's expected earnings. Dramatic examples of such applications have become increasingly common. For example, when Zapata Corporation, a maker of fish extract, announced that it was going to purchase Internet companies, its stock promptly doubled. While such extreme examples are not likely to apply to traditional companies, they do indicate the extent to which companies are able to improve their market capitalization through investment in Internet subsidiaries. We will explore the specific steps required to make the sorts of investments in e-commerce applications that can both create value for customers and sustain high shareholder returns.

E-Commerce Portfolio Analysis

Once executives have completed the foregoing analysis, there is a need to integrate all the potential e-commerce applications and choose the ones that the company will build. In order to make this choice, executives need a framework that appropriately weighs the right factors and compares each potential e-commerce application using the same factors. Figure 1-7 illustrates how such a framework might be deployed for a hypothetical set of five potential e-commerce applications.

While the data has been developed for purposes of illustration, the Figure 1-7 is useful for explaining the methodology

Figure 1-7. E-commerce portfolio analysis framework.

RANKED PROJECTS	Competitive Shield	Minimize Risk	Customer Value Add	Stock Value Add	Overall Score
WEIGHT	25	25	20	30	100
Project A	125	125	100	150	500
Project B	100	75	80	120	375
Project C	75	100	60	90	325
Project D	25	50	40	60	175
Project E	50	25	20	30	125

Key: 6 = best project in category; 1 = worst. Figures in table are weighted scores.

used to evaluate a set of potential e-commerce applications. There are four evaluation criteria in this case. *Competitive shield* means how much the potential e-commerce project protects the company from loss of market share to competitors. *Minimize risk* refers to the extent to which the project is conceived to limit the loss to the company from fraud, security breaches, or weak controls. *Customer value add* measures the extent to which the project will cause the company to do a better job of satisfying unmet customer needs. *Shareholder value add* refers to the extent to which the potential e-commerce application will enhance the company's stock price.

The weights are an attempt to measure the relative importance of these four criteria in evaluating the potential e-commerce projects. This example places the least weight on customer value add and the most weight on shareholder value add. Each project is force-ranked on each criterion, and the weighted score is included in the table. The weighted scores are added, and the projects are ranked in descending order of weighted score. This ranking may help companies with limited budgets to decide which e-commerce projects to fund, and which to defer or cancel.

Overview of This Book

The remainder of this book uses these five frameworks to address executives' questions regarding e-commerce. Part I focuses on financial and strategic evaluation of e-commerce. Part II shows how executives manage the change induced by e-commerce. And Part III provides a road map for building the e-commerce infrastructure.

Part I includes Chapters 2, 3, and 4. Chapter 2 explores the evidence of high payoff e-commerce applications. It describes the methods that executives are actually using to determine the costs and benefits of e-commerce applications. It presents case studies of some of the most successful e-commerce applications, including Cisco System's Cisco Connection Online. Based on these case studies, the chapter presents ten principles that characterize the most successful e-commerce applications. The chapter concludes by examining some less successful e-commerce applications, and highlighting three common e-commerce application pitfalls and how to avoid them.

Chapter 3 first looks at what CEOs and CFOs are doing with e-commerce, and the factors that are driving their thinking. Then the chapter scrutinizes the success measures that were used in IBM's successful e-commerce projects. Next Chapter 3 examines Healtheon/WebMD, a dramatic case of how the stock market is assigning value to intangible assets. Based on the general trends of e-commerce adoption and the specific case studies, Chapter 3 concludes by introducing a new method of conducting financial evaluation for e-commerce projects.

Chapter 4 begins with a case study of how e-commerce has altered the sources of competitive advantage in the book-selling industry by profiling the competitive dynamics between Amazon.com, Barnes & Noble, and its online subsidiary bn.com. The chapter then uses this case to develop key principles of e-commerce and competitive advantage. Chapter 4 concludes with a ten-step methodology that applies these principles to help managers use e-commerce to create competitive advantage.

Part II includes Chapters 5 through 8. Chapter 5 starts off by looking at some general statistics that gauge the trend in senior executive attitudes toward e-commerce. Next, Chapter 5 examines a framework that executives can use to identify which of four types of organization they belong to with respect to the CEO's attitude toward e-commerce. Then, the chapter examines case studies of each of these types of organizations in order to explore the issues that face senior executives seeking to take advantage of e-commerce. Chapter 5 concludes by outlining a process for getting the CEO engaged in building a new "e-strategy" that enables the company to maintain its competitive position against Internet-only competitors.

Chapter 6 explores how companies evaluate potential e-commerce applications. Chapter 6 organizes thinking about this topic by discussing the different intellectual constraints faced by self-reinventors versus the change avoiders. The chapter then explores two cases that exemplify the different approaches to evaluating e-commerce applications: Citigroup, a self-reinventor, and Merrill Lynch, a change avoider. From these cases, Chapter 6 describes specific principles for evaluating e-commerce applications. Chapter 6 concludes by outlining a process for evaluating potential e-commerce applications that incorporate these principles.

Chapter 7 describes four different kinds of change processes depending on the source of the e-commerce strategy, and the extent to which that strategy alters the company's basic business model. Then Chapter 7 examines cases from Microsoft, Merrill Lynch, and Provident American that expose the anatomy of these change processes. The chapter then extracts principles for successful e-commerce–driven change management. Chapter 7 concludes by outlining a methodology that financial executives can use to help guide their organizations in a change process that will help their organizations to realize the expected returns from e-commerce.

Chapter 8 explores the management techniques that work most effectively for sustaining change induced by technology by presenting two brief cases from Digital Equipment Corporation (DEC) and Microsoft. Chapter 8 then uses these brief cases to develop principles for sustaining change and principles for inhibiting it. The chapter continues by presenting the case of Hewlett-Packard (HP) and the InkJet printer market to illustrate how a large, successful company like HP can adapt— going from being a change inhibitor to a change sustainer.

Chapter 8 concludes by presenting the implications for managers seeking to sustain the change induced by e-commerce.

The book concludes with Part III, "Building the Infrastructure," which includes Chapters 9 through 12. Chapter 9 defines what is meant by e-commerce architecture. Then it describes how companies can partner with ISPs to experiment with e-commerce in a way that does not put their entire business at risk, while also enabling the business to learn. The chapter continues by exploring how Eastman Chemical and Weyerhaeuser established e-commerce architectures for their electronic procurement systems. Chapter 9 continues by describing two e-commerce architectures, one from Charles Schwab and the other from eBay, to demonstrate effective and ineffective handling of e-commerce architecture. Next, Chapter 9 develops six principles for designing e-commerce architectures. Chapter 9 concludes with a methodology that senior managers can use to design effective e-commerce architectures.

Chapter 10 presents two case studies of e-commerce supplier evaluation. The first case study focuses on the evaluation of five e-commerce application software packages. This case study will help managers gain insights into the specific characteristics of an effective e-commerce software evaluation process. The second case study illustrates the process that the Defense Advanced Research Projects Agency (DARPA) used to evaluate suppliers of Virtual Private Networks (VPNs) for its intranet. This case helps demonstrate the complexities of evaluating the purchase of network services. Following each case, Chapter 10 develops a set of lessons on how best to conduct e-commerce vendor evaluation. Chapter 10 concludes by presenting a methodology that senior managers can use to help build and administer a process for evaluating e-commerce suppliers.

Chapter 11 begins by outlining the vision for a successful purchase negotiation outcome. The chapter continues by outlining the risks that managers must anticipate and overcome in order to achieve this vision. Chapter 11 presents four mini-cases of successful and less-than-successful contract negotiations (Horizon Healthcare, Children's Hospital of Los Angeles,

Whirlpool, and Toronto Hospital), to illustrate these concepts in greater detail. Chapter 11 concludes by outlining a methodology that managers can follow to translate their vision for e-commerce into a successful purchase negotiation process.

Chapter 12 helps to address these issues. The chapter begins by outlining the most important elements of successful e-commerce project management. It continues by presenting four cases of companies that have managed e-commerce projects (United Airlines, Allied Signal, American International Group, and Homebid.com). Chapter 12 continues by highlighting several principles that managers can follow to increase their chances of success in managing e-commerce projects. It concludes by presenting a methodology that managers can follow to implement e-commerce projects successfully.

ⓔ   ⓔ   ⓔ   ⓔ

For your company, the potential economic benefits of e-commerce are great. Let's explore together how you can capture these benefits for your customers, employees, and shareholders!

PART I

Winning the Economic Case for E-Commerce

2

The Evidence on High-Payoff E-Commerce Applications

E xecutives are paid to cast a cold eye on new technologies—unless the company can use these technologies to generate a return that exceeds their cost of capital. Our research has found that large organizations are finding that traditional capital budgeting methods are difficult to apply to projects that employ Internet technology. Despite the difficulty of applying such traditional investment evaluation disciplines, there are a few very successful e-commerce applications. The results of these applications are measured by their measurable impact on companies' profits.

This chapter presents the results of our research into e-commerce applications. It describes the methods that executives are actually using to determine the costs and benefits of e-commerce applications. It presents case studies of some of the most successful e-commerce applications, including Cisco System's Cisco Connection Online. Based on these case studies, the chapter presents ten principles that characterize the most successful e-commerce applications. The chapter concludes by examining some less successful e-commerce applications, and highlighting three common e-commerce application pitfalls and how to avoid them.

E-Commerce Demands New Methods of Project Financial Evaluation

E-commerce forces executives to adopt a nontraditional approach to measuring the payoff of a project. In traditional financial analysis, managers project the cash out- and inflows associated with a project. Discounting for the time value of money, managers calculate the net present value (NPV) of the project. If the net present value of the project is positive, then managers should fund the project because it will generate value for the company in excess of the cost of the capital required to fund the project. If the net present value of the project is negative, managers should decline to fund the project because it will subtract from the company's value.

If managers attempt to apply this traditional approach to analyzing e-commerce projects, they run into some practical difficulties. While the cash outflows associated with the project may be quantifiable, it is virtually impossible to estimate the cash inflows that the project will generate. In the case of e-commerce for service provision, the future "cash inflows" are estimates of the number of people that will not need to be hired because the e-commerce application will perform a traditional process more efficiently. In the case of e-commerce for selling and distribution, the "cash inflows" may be measured in terms of the value of not falling behind competitors who are pursuing e-commerce initiatives. As a result of the serious challenges involved in estimating the cash inflows associated with many e-commerce initiatives, executives are forced to make up a new way of measuring the payoff that will lead to the decision regarding whether or not to fund a proposed e-commerce initiative.

The experience of many companies studied for this book suggests that executives are developing such measurement approaches. What emerges from the research is a new attitude on the part of executives toward both the cash in- and outflows associated with e-commerce projects.

Many executives view the cash outflows of an e-commerce initiative to be relatively small. In fact, the relatively low cost of getting a Web site running makes it easier to get approval for e-commerce projects. A consistent theme in the research for this book is that executives view e-commerce as a new frontier where there are no established ways of doing things. The implications of this observation for evaluating project costs is that executives in established companies appear comfortable spending a relatively small amount of money to learn and experiment. With the experimentation come ideas for modifications to the original e-commerce project. These modifications also cost a relatively small amount of money, and result in an ongoing cycle of modest spending that generates useful insights for how to improve the e-commerce application. So the financial evaluation of the cash outflows for an e-commerce project has evolved into a process of quantifying the costs of a sequence of small learning experiments.

Similarly, the financial evaluation of the cash inflows from an e-commerce site has evolved into a process of estimating the likelihood that using the Internet to solve specific operating or competitive challenges facing the company would ultimately translate into some form of quantifiable value at an undetermined point in the future. This is a far cry from the traditional process of estimating future cash inflows and discounting them back to the present using the appropriate annuity discount factor. Nevertheless, executives have accepted such fuzzy justifications for projects based on the insistence of CEOs who believed that e-commerce provided the most effective and fastest way to solve pressing business challenges.

The Highest-Payoff E-Commerce Application: Cisco Connection Online

Although it is difficult to obtain specific figures on the cost of Cisco Systems' Cisco Connection Online, the company estimated in 1999 that CCO had added $1 billion to Cisco's profits. Furthermore, Cisco generated 80 percent of its sales, or $12 billion worth of revenue from CCO. Based on the research conducted for this book, it is likely that CCO is the single highest payoff e-commerce application in the world. What is CCO? How was it started? How did it evolve? What is the source of its value to Cisco Systems?

CCO is a Web site that performs two primary functions for Cisco Systems' customers. CCO lets customers find online solutions to technical problems with their Cisco products. CCO also lets customers place and track the progress of orders for network equipment. CCO was started by mid-level Cisco managers who found that they were able to use the Internet to solve basic business problems. These mid-level managers were successful at selling the notion of e-commerce to Cisco's senior management team. As a result, e-commerce evolved into a corporate crusade for Cisco Systems.

According to *Fortune*, Chris Sinton, a Cisco marketing staffer, was the inspiration for CCO. Sinton was responsible for distributing marketing materials to customers including technical brochures and even coffee mugs and golf tees, all of which customers had to pay for. Sinton's idea of using the Internet to sell these items ultimately evolved into the e-commerce engine that drives Cisco Systems' $175 billion market capitalization.

Sinton was one of the lowest-tech people at Cisco. However, he did understand customers. He knew they did not like wasting time phoning and faxing in orders, and ordering hats and mugs from printed, inaccurate price lists. Sinton solved these customer problems by selling his golf tees and brochures on the Internet. The result was that demand for souvenirs quintupled, and ten times as many people requested technical material as before.

As Sinton was experiencing positive results from his Internet selling efforts, managers from other parts of Cisco were discovering their own ways of using the medium. These experiments were not forced on the organization by top management. Typically, a department manager would commission a small number of engineers, working on a limited budget, to explore how much they could achieve with a new idea.

By gaining the interest of marketing people two levels above him, Sinton was allotted fifteen minutes to introduce his concept of

Internet selling at a meeting of senior executives. He praised the other Internet projects taking place within Cisco, and urged the executives to use these projects as the catalyst for a new approach to doing business. Sinton argued that selling its products over the Internet would enable Cisco to save money and enhance customer service.

While Sinton was the first to introduce Cisco's top management to the concept of using the Internet to change its approach to doing business, Cisco's first Internet project came in its Technical Assistance Center, which provides after-sales service. Due to the complexity of the network equipment, customers must stay in contact with their supplier. As a result, the quality of after-sales service is an important factor in the customer's network equipment purchase decision.

By 1994, the Technical Assistance Center (TAC) faced a staffing problem. Service engineers are trained and scarce. However, at Cisco they spent much of their time addressing minor product malfunctions or helping customers order software. As a result, there was not enough time to deal with difficult technical challenges. The inability to meet the growing need for customer service threatened to impede the growth of Cisco's sales of routers and switches.

Brad Wright, TAC's manager, thought that the solution to this bottleneck would be to automate routine customer service solutions on the Internet, and let buyers serve themselves. With the backing of Doug Allred, the head of all sales and support services, Wright assigned several of his engineers to develop programs that could answer customer service questions online. The system would translate a network engineer's imprecise inquiry (e.g., "Cannot connect to remote server") into a standard description of a familiar problem. Then the system would provide the most likely explanations onscreen. This would allow the engineer to avoid wasting time. Within ninety days, Wright's engineers had installed the answers to the most frequent questions on the Web. They also wrote a program that let customers choose and download software.

Customers were happy to substitute playing phone tag with customer service people from 9 to 5 with effective twenty-four–hour service on the Internet. Calls and faxes diminished. While Cisco's sales increased fourfold between 1995 and 1998, its engineering support staff doubled, to 800. Without automated sales support, Cisco estimated it would have needed to hire at least 1,000 additional engineers. Cisco estimated that the system saved $75 million a year, plus an additional $250 million per year by distributing support software over the Internet rather than transferring it to disks and mailing them to customers. While it is difficult to quantify, the system also enabled Cisco to make billions in additional sales because it was able to keep up with the demand for additional customer service.

Cisco's use of the Internet to solve business problems was not limited to technical service and sales. In early 1995, Linda Thom Rosiak, the head of customer service, was concerned about Cisco's ordering process. Rosiak was dissatisfied with the time and effort required to transfer orders from Cisco's customers to its manufacturing plants or its suppliers.

The delays were the result of errors in the orders, which arrived by fax. Cisco custom-builds all its products. Each has about twelve major elements, including memory, power supply, software, and cables. Cisco offers choices for each, but many of the combinations do not work together. For example, customers frequently chose insufficient memory to handle their choices of software. Another problem is that customers found the prices for 13,000 parts in thick catalogs contained inaccurate information. Forty percent of the time, Cisco received orders with the wrong prices or configurations. Cisco responded to the errors by faxing them back to the customers.

Frank Santafemia, head of network installations for Sprint, found the process a disaster. Sprint, like most of Cisco's customers, schedules delivery of the products that are used by the systems that it builds and operates for its corporate clients. Santafemia would fax incorrect purchase orders back and forth. In the interim, Sprint would need a router to build the project. These errors delayed Sprint's jobs for weeks.

Rosiak realized that putting the sales process on the Internet would eliminate errors. Customers could complete their projects much faster, and Cisco would avoid the cost of hiring new people to identify errors.

Peter Solvik, Cisco's chief information officer, assigned Rosiak several of his department's engineers to help design programs linking customers to Cisco. Solvik saw that if Cisco could use the Internet for technical support, it could use the Internet for every step in selling and servicing Cisco's products. The first program that Solvik's engineers designed, called Status Agent, let customers track the progress of their orders online. The next involved posting the prices of all Cisco products. The third was so significant that it required the support of top management.

Around this time, a venture capital firm had introduced Solvik to Calico Technology, a startup company that made software for selecting compatible parts for complex machines like routers. Solvik convinced Cisco CEO John Chambers to allow him to spend the several million dollars required to buy Calico. Chambers was persuaded by Solvik's argument that online configuration of its products would make Cisco more customer-friendly.

In 1996, Cisco began offering routers and switches over CCO. Customers preferred picking out prices and configuring products electronically. They simply click onto a program called Configuration Agent, which walks them through the components that go into a router. If they choose an inappropriate combination of circuit boards, for example, the program generates an error message, and guides them to an acceptable choice. Once customers select a workable configuration, its current price appears.

Resellers use CCO because it allows them to take delivery of their equipment, and finish their jobs much more quickly. At Sprint, it used to take sixty days from the signing of a contract to complete a networking project. Now, due in part to ordering Cisco equipment online, it takes thirty-five to forty-five days. Sprint has also been able to reduce its order-processing staff from twenty-one to six, allowing the other fifteen employees to work instead on installing networks, a business that has doubled at Sprint since 1996.

Cisco is also saving money by hiring fewer order-processing workers. Rosiak employs 300 service agents. She would need 900 without the help of CCO. The difference represents roughly $20 million in annual savings.

Cisco's sales are growing by 30 percent a year, much more quickly than those of rivals such as Cabletron and Nortel Networks. Resellers who used to place orders with several vendors now purchase network equipment mainly from Cisco, due to the convenience and speed of CCO. Santafemia notes that the increased speed of working with one vendor is leading Sprint to work on an increasing number of projects where Cisco supplies all the equipment.

While Cisco estimates that CCO has added $500 million to its profits, Chris Sinton has benefited as well. Sinton is now a member of Cisco's top management, overseeing the operation and design of CCO. Sinton points out that he just knew the Internet could be a portal to Cisco's business. History will also record his contribution: The white paper he wrote in 1995 on the future of e-commerce is now preserved in the Smithsonian Institution archives.[1]

As Figure 2-1 indicates, the growth in Cisco's e-commerce revenues exceeded 315 percent per year from the first quarter of 1997 to the third quarter of 1998.

Principles of High-Payoff E-Commerce Applications

The CCO case contains ten important principles for successful e-commerce applications. Surprisingly, these principles suggest that general management behavior is a significantly more

Figure 2-1. Quarterly growth in Cisco e-commerce revenue
(Q1 1997 to Q3 1998).

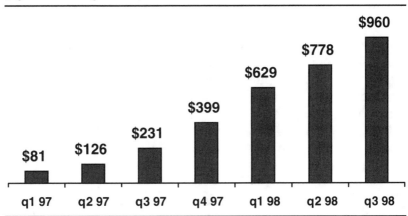

important driver of e-commerce success than specific technical skills.

Here are the ten most important principles for e-commerce success:

e **Management must create an environment that en-
courages people at all levels to engage in frugal experimentation.** The CCO example indicates that the
idea of using the Internet to solve business problems originated
at the first-line management level in three distinct Cisco departments. While it is simple to suggest that companies encourage
this sort of experimentation, in practice many organizations
choke off such initiatives before they can receive the support that
they need to make a difference. What is clear from the Cisco
example is that senior management encouraged such initiatives,
and provided them the technical and economic support that they
needed to be implemented across the company. Cisco's spurring
of lower level experiments is a principle that occurs repeatedly
among the most successful e-commerce initiatives.

While the payoff of General Motor's BuyPower Web site has
yet to be quantified (at least publicly), the origin of the site was
not at the corporate level but in its California regional office. The
West Coast division was experiencing below-average sales re-

sults, so the division manager decided to try a different marketing approach, called the California Marketing Initiative. This approach initially included the creation of a dealer-based kiosk for car buyers. Eventually, the kiosk evolved into a Web site that let consumers visualize individually tailored versions of vehicles and look at their pricing. As a result of the Web site and the accompanying marketing programs, California's sales results improved dramatically. As a result, the Web site and the related marketing programs were rolled out across the West Coast division, which includes California, Arizona, Nevada, Oregon, and Washington. Then, GM management agreed to roll out the Web site nationwide, creating what is now its BuyPower Web site.[2]

e *Management must place enhanced customer satisfaction at the top of the corporate hierarchy of values.* Each of the three Internet experiments that led to the emergence of CCO were focused on solving a problem that threatened the strength of the customer relationship with Cisco. Because Cisco placed such a strong emphasis on improving customer satisfaction, it seemed natural to the three department managers to look for ways to use the Internet to accomplish that end. The Sinton initiative was intended to make it easier for customers to purchase technical literature and marketing trinkets. The Wright initiative was intended to solve customers' technical problems more efficiently (and to eliminate a speed bump on Cisco's growth path). The Rosiak initiative was intended to eliminate a source of dissatisfaction in the product-ordering and supply process. In Cisco's case, success in e-commerce offers an ancillary benefit: By showing potential customers how valuable e-commerce can be, Cisco hopes to increase the sales of its e-commerce enabling products.

Cisco is not the only company that adheres to this principle. As Amazon.com's Jeff Bezos points out, online 70 percent of a company's resources should be devoted to creating a great customer experience, and 30 percent should be spent communicating it. According to *Business Week*, Furniture.com, a startup company in Worcester, Massachusetts, is following Bezos's advice. Furniture.com's digital aid offers a possible glimpse into the future. Visitors to Furniture.com's Web site type in style preferences, and within seconds, a company representative is available to the customer, ready to communicate—via Web chat or Netphone—about the personalized showroom that has just been created and sent to the customer's computer. From there, buyers can choose among furniture colors, fabrics, prices, and dimensions.

After the sale, customers are "adopted" by Furniture.com's sales representatives, who e-mail or phone customers to identify complaints or offer a new fabric-coordinated accessory. The result of this process is that while shoppers who use the personalized showroom take 20 percent longer, their orders average 50 percent larger. CEO Andrew Brooks says Furniture.com can afford to spend more on service because doing business over the Web is less expensive. Brooks notes that e-commerce shifts bargaining power from sellers to buyers. As a result, customer service becomes the most critical success factor.[3]

While customer service is increasingly important to e-commerce success, the cost of delivering e-service is much lower. For example, *Business Week* cites a Forrester Research study of financial institutions, which points out that Web service costs companies an average of four cents per customer for a simple Web page query, while a live phone call costs $1.44. Shifting service to the Internet could let companies handle 33 percent more service requests at 43 percent of the cost.[4]

e *Management must encourage an effective working partnership between IT and the business units.* Cisco's CCO initiative benefited from the effective working relationship between its IT department and the business units. The example of Rosiak working with Solvik's engineers to design the Status Agent program demonstrates the benefits of such an IT/business unit partnership. In less successful environments, there is a legacy of disharmony between IT and the business units that hamper the development of e-commerce.

e *Managers must think in nontraditional ways to conceive effective e-commerce applications.* The successful CCO e-commerce applications were all the result of taking a nontraditional approach to solving a problem that related to the scarcity of information processing capability. For example, Wright's initiative was intended to address Cisco's need for a greater capacity to understand and resolve customers' technical problems. The traditional approach to this problem would have been to simply try to hire more technical service people.

Wright recognized that an adequate supply of such people was simply not available. So he needed to develop a way of providing the additional information processing capacity without hiring so many new people. Wright understood that much of the technical service people's time was spent answering fairly routine questions, which he could automate. The automation of these solutions raised productivity, and enhanced the intellectual challenge of the remaining technical service peoples' work. The nontraditional solution paid off.

Such nontraditional thinking is not limited to high-tech Cisco. For example, according to *Information Week*, in 1999 an online steel-industry marketplace called E-Steel was introduced. One barrier to such a marketplace has been the traditional fear of competitors' accessing strategic information.

E-Steel has a potential solution to that problem. E-Steel uses *profiling* software from Broadvision to deliver customized content and pricing to registered steel buyers based on parameters specified by the supplier. General price lists are not posted. According to Chris Hanan, VP of business development at E-Steel, building trust depends on allowing buyers and sellers to mirror their existing business relationships on the Web. As a result, E-Steel members do not lose control over their information.

E-Steel will charge sellers a transaction fee of less than one percent on all purchases initiated on the site, though payments between trading partners will occur offline. The site will also sell advertising and provide industry and trade news, job listings, and stock data. Despite the ancillary data, Hanan emphasizes that E-Steel's emphasis is commerce first, and content second.

E-Steel, backed by outside investors, is a more typical independent industry marketplace, such as PlasticsNet in the plastics industry. E-Steel is more ambitious than its competitors, aiming to create a market for all kinds of steel products, not simply surplus inventory.

Steel company executives are beginning to become more comfortable with e-commerce. At a November 1998 meeting of the Steel Service Center Institute trade group, 96 percent of steel industry CFOs said they use the Internet. In November 1997, this percentage would have been 30 in Hanan's opinion. Hanan's efforts have contributed to a level of Internet penetration in the steel industry sufficient to justify thinking about it as a business-to-business tool.[5]

Nontraditional thinking is required to make e-commerce succeed. Often, the older the business practices within an industry, the more difficult it will be to overcome industry inertia. At the same time, the traditional practices may include more process inefficiencies—the elimination of which could produce tremendous cost savings that could jolt traditional players out of their old ways of doing business.

e *Management must recognize that experiments in e-commerce require less rigorous up-front financial analysis.* The lower cost and enhanced speed of Internet development projects should particularly encourage financial executives to empower first-line managers to take the initiative rather than wait for corporate level approval of every e-commerce experiment. As in all things, balance is important. But Internet technology permits a greater proliferation of experimentation and creativity. A related element of e-commerce experimentation is that Cisco did not feel compelled to invest heavily in calculating the estimated financial benefits of the experiment. First, it would have been impossible at the early stage to develop reasonable estimates. Second, the effort involved in making such estimates would have been rather costly themselves in terms of delaying the start of the experiment.

e *Management must adopt a pioneering spirit in its e-commerce efforts.* Cisco's CCO initiative is an early and compelling example of the notion that figuring out how best to use the Internet is uncharted terrain. At this point, there are no established rules for what works and what does not work that can be safely generalized across companies. Each company must be willing to discover for itself how best to use the Internet to solve its own business problems. Cisco figured out ways to use the Internet that had literally never been done before. Even Cisco's senior management had not thought about all the possible ways that the Internet could help the company's business. Nevertheless, armed with its desire to create the future of internetworking and a willingness to listen to effective new ways to enhance customer satisfaction, Cisco's management created the appropriate working environment to spur the development of CCO.

Similarly, GM saw itself as entering uncharted territory as it built its BuyPower Web site. At GM, the proponents of the Web site appeared to have a somewhat greater pioneering spirit than many GM senior managers. Nevertheless, the fear of falling behind competitors and not adapting to evolving demographics was sufficient to spur GM senior management into backing the Buy-Power initiative.[6]

 Effective e-commerce applications come from understanding significant sources of organizational and customer pain. Rosiak's in-depth understanding of how Cisco's order-fulfillment process was misfiring contributed immensely to the success of the e-engineering of that process. Because she was able to trace customer frustration and Cisco's operational inefficiencies to specific process bottlenecks, she was able to focus her creative efforts on fixing the right problem. Using the Internet to eliminate a major source of pain is highly likely to generate a big payoff.

There are many other examples of companies using the Internet to lance the boil of organizational pain. According to *Business Week*, Pfizer now transmits electronic versions of its drug applications to Washington, D.C., for Food & Drug Administration approval. Before its Web-based document transmittal system was in place, Pfizer trucked tons of paper to regulators. Furthermore, if regulators had a question, Pfizer needed to manually search the pages to provide an answer. By managing documents on the Web, Pfizer reduced the old one-year approval timetable nearly in half.

In the future, Pfizer's drugs will move through the development process even faster. Pfizer's researchers now use the Web to search libraries of technical data and collaborate on new drug development. So Pfizer is continuing its efforts to use the Internet to eliminate sources of the costly delay in its drug development process.[7]

Before an e-commerce application "goes live," it is essential that the front- and back-end systems are integrated and tested. While Cisco experimented with several e-commerce applications, its front- and back-end systems were fully integrated and tested before Cisco began to use CCO for live customers. Most companies are very reluctant to deploy an e-commerce system if there is a perceived risk that system flaws will undermine customer relationships that the company has cultivated over a long period.

Another example of this from *Information Week* is the Compumotor division of manufacturer Parker Hannifin. Compumotor's "extranet" for handling orders for industrial automation system products was used by customers beginning in December 1998. The extranet was delayed by an entire year to deal with response time, server upgrade, and integration challenges. Compumotor's IS manager Bud Parer noted that setting up e-commerce is not easy or fast. Parer found that performance and scalability were the biggest issues. Since Compumotor decided to use the extranet to operate its business, the company decided to delay deployment of the system until it had acceptable response time and accurate data.[8]

Compumotor's extranet handles orders for 12,500 products, warranty and nonwarranty repair-status queries, and many other transactions from sixty-five distributors, thirty-five factory representatives, twenty direct customers, and fifty internal employees. To improve performance, Compumotor upgraded its Hewlett-Packard server, and moved part of its Oracle database to a Sun Microsystems UltraSparc server to share the load. Compumotor devoted four worker-months to designing and integrating the extranet applications' Active Server pages, with 90 percent of the coding time spent on data availability and accuracy. Parer made all this additional effort because he was reluctant to make guesses in light of the central importance of the extranet to running Compumotor's business.

 E-commerce applications must be marketed aggressively to reach critical mass. Cisco built its Web site and then invested heavily in telling the world about the system. For Cisco, the marketing achieves two objectives: It brings customers to the site, and it tells potential customers about the benefits of e-commerce, the implementation of which involves the purchase of Cisco's products. An analysis of Amazon.com's income statement indicates that 70 percent of its revenue is spent on marketing through "traditional" media such as TV, radio, and newspapers. Because it is relatively inexpensive to build a Web site, more companies build them. As a result, the need to differentiate a company's site in order to build a sufficient level of traffic is intensified. Fortunately for established companies with a strong brand in traditional media, the incremental cost of differentiating a Web site is smaller than it would be for a startup company.

How to Avoid Low-Payoff E-Commerce Applications

Not all e-commerce applications are as successful as the ones cited above. Nevertheless, the examples of less-than-successful e-commerce initiatives can provide useful lessons about some of the pitfalls that executives may need to overcome. Here are three such examples.

ANX (Automotive Network Exchange)

One such example is ANX (Automotive Network Exchange), an auto industry extranet. ANX was announced in 1997 with great fanfare. According to *Information Week*, as of January 1999, only fifteen manufacturers had begun using ANX. When it was launched in 1997, major U.S. automobile manufacturers were leading ANX proponents. They believed that the extranet would provide 10,000 manufacturers with a standard virtual private networking (VPN) platform to exchange order and inventory data, engineering designs, and other information via Computer Aided Design (CAD) files, groupware (such as Lotus Notes), and e-mail.

Karl Schohl is ANX manager at the Automotive Industry Action Group (AIAG), the industry organization coordinating the ANX effort. Schohl notes that AIAG is not satisfied with the fifteen. Schohl says that another fifteen companies are preparing to go online. However, thirty companies is far short of the number needed to make ANX an effective industry-wide program.

Bhaskar Kakulavarapu is IS manager at United Technologies Automotive (UTA). UTA has 400 engineers using ANX worldwide to exchange CAD files, do file transfers, exchange warranty data, and even run mainframe applications. According to Kakulavarapu, ANX is not going as quickly as he had hoped. Nevertheless, he is optimistic about its progress.

Kakulavarapu points out several technical, legal, and organizational hurdles that must be overcome. He notes that there are continuing problems with the ability to send files among different network technologies of ANX participants. In addition, an agreement is not yet in place to address contingencies such as what happens should ANX's service levels fall below preset standards.

Another obstacle, Kakulavarapu says, is convincing industry suppliers that they can collectively gain by sharing some of their best practices with competitors. In his view, people are reluctant to share their benefits with their competitors.

Ames Research Center

ANX is one of several less-than-successful examples of e-commerce. According to *Business Week*, NASA's Ames Research Center in Moffett Field, California, spent $100 million building a Web-based collaborative engineering system to help accelerate development of the space station. Since the project lacked the technology infrastructure to handle the task, some valuable data was lost including the plans for the Saturn V rocket.[9]

CIBC

While technology can be a source of e-commerce failure, so can a slow-moving corporate culture. John Thorp, vice-president of DMR

Consulting Group, suggests that for many older executives, converting to e-business is like changing their religion. One example of such resistance is from an electronic purchasing application at Canadian Imperial Bank of Commerce (CIBC) in Toronto. When CIBC initially installed its electronic procurement application, purchasing agents did not grasp the purpose of the new Web-based system for ordering supplies. They attempted to press suppliers for price cuts when the point was for all employees to buy from an electronic catalog so that CIBC could earn volume discounts. CIBC was able to resolve the problem by offering the purchasing agents tailored incentive bonuses.[10]

Here are three important pitfalls that contribute to the failure of e-commerce initiatives and how to avoid them:

e **Avoid investing in e-commerce initiatives where the vision for the technology is clearer than the economic benefit to participants.** In high technology projects, it is quite common to find that the enthusiasm for a new technology overwhelms other considerations. The ANX project is a good example. The proponents of ANX were so excited about the efficiency gains from automating document and file transfer among industry participants that they completely overlooked many important success factors.

The problem of putting the technology before the economic benefit to participants is particularly pronounced in retailing. For example, Office Depot built a Web site in 1998 to sell office supplies. Prior to its e-commerce initiative, Office Depot already had three sales channels: direct sales, telephone sales, and in-store sales. These three channels felt threatened by the e-commerce initiative because they were afraid it would siphon away commissions as people increasingly used the Web to purchase office supplies. It took the absolute insistence by Office Depot's CEO that e-commerce was critical for the company's survival to persuade these long-standing channels to support the Web site's development.

To avoid these "competing channel" pitfalls, managers should make sure that all constituents to an e-commerce project are involved from conception to implementation. By including all constituents *and incorporating their goals and concerns* into the solution, it is likely that this first pitfall can be avoided.

■e **Avoid the deployment of untested e-commerce technologies.** Because e-commerce is so new, it is quite difficult to find a set of e-commerce technology suppliers that offer innovative products that have been extensively proven in the field. Even if it *is* possible to find suppliers of individual technology components whose products are innovative and tested, there is always a danger that these technologies will not work together effectively in the company's overall e-commerce system. This may have been the problem with the Ames Research Center project.

To avoid this pitfall, managers should either work with highly reputable e-commerce systems integrators, or methodically test their systems in a simulated production environment before deploying them. By working with experienced and reputable e-commerce systems integrators, it is often possible to reap the benefit of other organizations' e-commerce experiences. By thoroughly testing the integrated e-commerce application before rolling it out, it is generally possible to identify and overcome many technical problems before too much time or money has been spent. Nevertheless, one of the reasons that e-commerce hype exceeds its reality is that there are very few companies that wish to host the pioneers' arrows in their collective backs.

■e **Avoid skimping on communication, training, and adjustments to compensation systems that are inherent in a new e-commerce application.** E-commerce projects demand e-engineering. Just as reengineering involves radical rethinking of how an organization works, and its supporting structures, so does e-commerce involve fundamental changes in the way work is done. Managers risk the kinds of problems that took place in the CIBC case if they underestimate the need for communication, training, and adjustments to compensation systems. To avoid such pitfalls, managers should make sure that they develop a clear plan for communicating and training the people who will facilitate the e-engineered work process. If making the new process work involves changing job responsibilities and compensation systems, these changes should be made explicitly before the e-commerce system is rolled out. By taking these organizational considerations into account as part of the e-engineering process, it is likely that this third pitfall can be avoided.

Conclusion

Traditional capital budgeting approaches to e-commerce do not make much sense. Although some companies have enjoyed significant payoffs from e-commerce, these payoffs were not calculated and planned for *a priori*. Rather, the payoffs from e-commerce are realized through a series of tightly budgeted experiments targeted at solving discreet business problems. The highest-payoff e-commerce applications share a number of characteristics. Conversely, less-than-successful e-commerce applications provide managers with useful object lessons in specific pitfalls to be avoided.

Notes

1. Shawn Tully, "How Cisco Mastered the Net," *Fortune,* August 17, 1998 [http://www.pathfinder.com/fortune/1998980817/cis.html].
2. Author interview with Joe Chrzanowski, GM Chief Information Officer of Vehicle Sales Service and Marketing, April 1999.
3. Marcia Stepanek, "You'll Wanna Hold Their Hands," *Business Week*, March 22, 1999 [http://www.businessweek.com/datedtoc/1999/9912.htm].
4. Ibid.
5. Clinton Wilder, "E-Commerce—Old Line Moves Online—Steel, Auto, and Other Established Manufacturers Are Turning to Web Commerce to Open New Markets and Redefine Existing Ones," *Information Week,* January 11, 1999.
6. Chrzanowski, op. cit.
7. Steve Hamm with Marcia Stepanek, "From Reengineering to E-Engineering," *Business Week,* March 22, 1999 [http://www.businessweek.com/datedtoc/1999/9912.htm].
8. Jeff Sweat and Clinton Wilder, "Changing the Rules—Online Business Is Challenging—And Changing—The Rules of Commerce," *Information Week,* August 24, 1998 [http://www.techweb.com/se/directlink.cgi?IW K1998082450020].
9. Hamm with Stepanek.
10. Ibid., [http://www.techweb.com/se/directlink.cgi?IWK1999011150013].

3

Financial Evaluation of E-Commerce

For executives, conducting a financial evaluation of an e-commerce project is a unique undertaking that involves answering some challenging questions. For example, what factors are driving the evaluation process that executives use to evaluate e-commerce? How have some of the most successful e-commerce applications defined their success? How does the stock market assign value to e-commerce? Based on all these findings, what is the best way for managers to conduct the financial evaluation of e-commerce?

To answer these questions, Chapter 3 first looks at what CEOs and CFOs are doing with e-commerce and the factors that are driving their thinking. Then the chapter scrutinizes the success measures that were used in IBM's successful e-commerce projects. Next, Chapter 3 examines Healtheon/ WebMD, a dramatic case of how the stock market is assigning value to intangible assets. Based on the general trends of e-commerce adoption and the specific case studies, Chapter 3 concludes by introducing a new method of conducting financial evaluation for e-commerce projects.

An Executive Perspective on Why E-Commerce Counts

Executives are dipping their toes in the water of e-commerce—not diving in. According to a *Harris/Business Week* poll of 308 large-company executives, most companies are using the Web to distribute product information, advertise, or support customer service. Just 45 percent of executives said their companies actually sell to customers on the Internet. Most of the rest do not sell over the Web, and have no intention of starting. The most common reason for not selling over the Web was cited in Chapter 2: Executives see electronic commerce as conflicting with another sales channel. The majority of companies with no plans to go online are also concerned about security. For those companies that *do* sell over the Internet, most reach a broader base of customers, communicate with suppliers more easily, and save on transaction costs.[1]

These findings are worth examining here because they shed light on how best to count e-commerce's impact on a company from the perspective of the financial executive. For example, the results in Figure 3-1 suggest that the more superficial an Internet application, the more likely companies are to adopt it.

Conversely, the more the Internet application forces companies to change their fundamental approach to doing business, the less frequently the application is used. This result suggests an important insight about where senior executives are with respect to their thinking about how to use the Internet—it is an *experiment* and it is *defensive.*

Most companies are trying to learn about the Internet by using it to do something that will not upset the organization's business too much if the Internet application breaks. In other words, if an online product information system breaks down, the company can always resort to sending out paper brochures to customers. Conversely, if an Internet-based selling process breaks, there is a real danger that the company could deeply anger its customers and thus harm its business in an irreversible manner.

Figure 3-1. Percentage of companies using the Internet by application (June 1998).

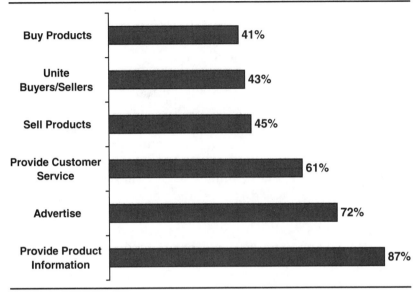

But companies are also worried about how competitors will use the Internet. Given the amount of publicity that Amazon.com has received, it is highly unlikely that any executive could not be aware of the threat that the Internet can pose for traditional business models. Many executives are hoping that their business will not be "Amazoned." Nevertheless, a substantial minority of executives is sufficiently aware of the power of the Internet that it is not comfortable completely "burying its head in the sand." As a result, many companies strike a balance between doing nothing about the Internet and radically transforming their business model to take advantage of it. This middle ground is reflected in the high percentage of companies that use the Internet for product brochures and advertising.

Over time, it is likely that these numbers will change so that an increasing share of the companies are using the Internet for fundamental business processes such as buying and selling. For executives, this means that many e-commerce applications are measured now in terms of the cost to design, build, and maintain them, and the savings that they produce in terms of fewer printed and mailed product brochures. As an increasing proportion of companies begin to use the Internet to perform more fundamental tasks such as selling or buying, the financial measures of the projects will become broader and more difficult to estimate. Nevertheless, research suggests that only 27 percent of executives who currently do not sell over the Internet have any intentions of doing so in the future. Of the remaining, fully 64 percent have no plans to sell online, and 9 percent have not made up their minds.

As Figure 3-2 illustrates, the companies that do not currently sell online are concerned that the Internet will create a conflict with their existing sales channels. As I discussed in Chapter 2, channel conflict is a fundamental problem that companies have dealt with in the past after the advent of new technologies. For example, when companies realized that they

Figure 3-2. Percentage of companies not selling online by reason (June 1998).

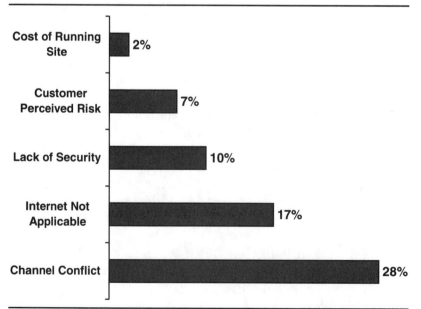

could advertise on TV and take orders with toll-free 800 numbers, similar channel conflict issues arose. The key challenge for senior management is to recognize that what sustains the company is investing to create superior value for customers.

To that end, the Internet may represent a strategic inflection point. Management can defer investment and hope that the Internet does not change the industry structure. Or management can take the initiative and force the company to push ahead with online selling, even as it acknowledges the discomfort that the channel conflict will cause internally.

For the senior executive, the strategic decision to move ahead with online selling creates the need for a way to generate financial analysis that quantifies e-commerce's incremental benefits and risks. To that end, executives will need to quantify the extent to which revenues generated online will cannibalize the revenue from existing channels, create new revenues by tapping into new customer groups, or a combination of the two.

Similarly, as senior executives decide to push forward with online selling, they will need to recognize that adding a new distribution channel will require new sales compensation formulas. For example, if a salesperson generates a business relationship with a new customer, and that new customer subsequently reorders the company's products online, senior management must decide what the salesperson's commission on the online sales should be. For the executive, these commission issues can enter into the cash flow analysis of the e-commerce project. The commission issues also factor into ongoing budgeting and reporting matters as well.

Senior executives perceive that the most significant benefits of online selling are reaching customers directly and reaching a broader base of customers. As the results in Figure 3-3 suggest, senior executives think online selling is more useful as a way to increase revenues than as a way to reduce costs.

While these executive opinions are imprecise, they also create analytical challenges. For example, in evaluating a potential e-commerce project or subsequently measuring its impact, executives must attempt to quantify the benefits of dealing with customers directly. Some of the benefits, such

Figure 3-3. Perceived benefits of online selling by degree of benefit (June 1998).

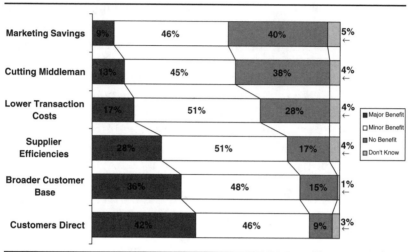

as eliminating the costs of an intermediary, may be easier to quantify. Other benefits, such as increasing knowledge of customer needs and purchase behavior could help to increase the effectiveness of marketing and new product development efforts. While these benefits are real, they are difficult for financial analysts to quantify.

Similar considerations affect the financial evaluation of the other potential benefits of online selling. For example, while the Internet may help the company reach a broader customer base, it is difficult to estimate how many additional customers will buy from the company due to the Internet, and what the annual revenues for each of these customers might be. Furthermore, the new customers that the Internet enables the company to reach may have different needs and product preferences than the company's traditional customers. If so, meeting these new needs might force the company to incur additional costs that should be included in the financial evaluation.

Despite the analytical challenges associated with quantifying the value of e-commerce, there was a marked increase in its adoption between 1998 and 2000. For example, according to a March 1999 survey by the *Financial Executives Institute and Duke University* of 371 companies, by 2000, 56 percent will sell their products over the Internet, accounting for an average of 8 percent of a company's total revenue. In 1998, just 24 percent of companies reported Internet sales, representing an average of 5 percent of total sales.[2]

While this doubling of online sales over two years is impressive, it masks important differences by industry. As Figure 3-4 illustrates, high technology, communications, and media will be by far the most significant adopters of online selling by 2000. By contrast, mining and construction companies are anticipated to lag the averages dramatically. Executives in the industries that are most likely to adopt online selling will become the most sophisticated financial analysts of e-commerce projects. Executives in other industries may have an opportunity to draw the expertise of these executives as they begin to adopt online selling further into the future.

These differences in potential adoption of online selling by industry may be related to differences in e-commerce distri-

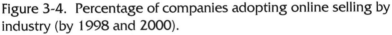

Figure 3-4. Percentage of companies adopting online selling by industry (by 1998 and 2000).

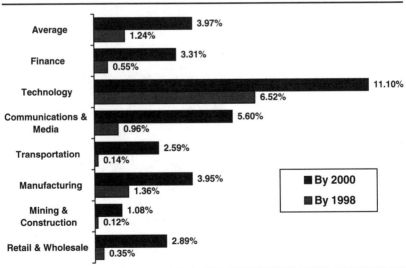

bution costs by industry. Consider these examples from the Organization for Economic Cooperation and Development (OECD) report *The Economic Impact of Electronic Commerce,* cited by *The Industry Standard:*

- *Airline Tickets.* The cost of distributing an airline ticket through traditional means is $8, whereas Internet-based airline ticket distribution costs $1, an 87 percent savings.
- *Bill Payment.* The cost of paying a bill via the traditional system costs between $2.22 and $3.32, whereas Internet-based bill payment costs between $0.65 and $1.10, a savings between 67 and 71 percent.
- *Term Life Insurance Policy.* The cost of distributing a term life insurance policy through traditional means is between $400 and $700, whereas Internet-based term life insurance policy distribution costs $200 to $350, a 50 percent savings.
- *Software.* The cost of distributing software by traditional means is $15, whereas Internet-based software distribution costs between 20 and 50 cents, a 97 to 99 percent savings.[3]

As financial executives in different industries attempt to quantify e-commerce benefits to their companies, they should consider the broader impact of e-commerce on the economies of developed nations. According to the OECD, e-commerce will result in improved productivity, tighter inventories, and improved customer service. For example, the OECD estimates that business-to-business e-commerce will cause a one-half to two-thirds of a percentage point reduction in costs in five OECD countries.

In addition, the OECD estimates that e-commerce could facilitate between $250 and $350 billion in reduced inventory costs. Furthermore, the report estimates that e-commerce could facilitate just-in-time (JIT) inventory systems' ability to link suppliers, improve demand forecasting, and replenish products leading to a cut in U.S. inventories between 20 and 25 percent.

Finally, the report expects that customer service costs, which usually account for 10 percent of a company's operating expenses, will be reduced from 10 to 50 percent through the use of a Web customer service interface to reduce errors. Furthermore, the e-commerce ordering process has been shown to cut the time to process orders by 50 to 96 percent.[4]

These data provide a context that can help financial executives perform financial evaluation of e-commerce initiatives for their companies. The key insight from this analysis is that financial executives should understand how e-commerce can transform the company's underlying business processes. This transformation should result in cost savings and increased revenues. But in order for financial executives to do an effective job of analyzing the payoffs from e-commerce, they must participate in the formulation of the e-commerce strategy so that they understand how the new system will alter the company's economic structure.

Measuring a Successful E-Commerce Project

While an executive perspective on e-commerce provides a useful context, financial executives need to understand how companies have created and measured a successful e-commerce project. A comprehensive survey of e-commerce financial evaluation techniques might be useful; e-commerce is at too early and *experimental* a stage in its evolution to make such analysis meaningful. Therefore, we rely here on anecdotal evidence. Readers should see how they can apply the lessons from these anecdotes to their own organization.

IBM followed the lead of Cisco Systems, and cobbled its own shoes to help show potential customers the economic benefits of e-commerce. According to *CFO Magazine*, IBM began to realize in the mid-1990s that there was tremendous potential to use the Internet as a means of streamlining its accounts payable process. By January 1999, IBM had achieved some dramatic improvements in HR payments and vendor processing productivity. As Tables 3-1 and 3-2 indicate, IBM measured the benefit of its e-commerce application in both process and financial terms.[5]

Table 3-1. Performance improvements from IBM's HR Payments
E-Engineering.

Performance Measure	Before	After	% Improvement
Expense Reports per Full-Time Equivalent (FTE)	14,450	78,862	446%
Pay Distribution per FTE	43,200	72,810	68%
Error Rate for Travel & Entertainment (T&E) Transactions	7.0%	0.5%	93%
T&E Cost as a Percentage of Revenues	0.06%	0.01%	83%
Process Cost per Expense Report	$23.00	$2.02	91%
Payroll Cost as Percentage of Revenues	0.20%	0.01%	95%
Process Cost per Pay Distribution	$5.75	$1.77	69%

How were these performance improvements achieved? For the
HR payments e-engineering project, IBM adopted the following practices:

- Standardized payroll cycles and calendars—weekly for
  hourly employees, and semimonthly for salaried employees.
- Employed a single common employee information database
  for both HR and payroll.
- Direct-deposited paychecks for 94 percent of employees.
- Used automated time-collection tools and sophisticated algo-
  rithms to verify time.
- Developed, communicated, enforced uniform T&E policy.
- Processed all T&E expense reporting through single system.
- Replaced cash advances with corporate-sponsored credit card
  program.
- Used T&E expense data to negotiate discounts with vendors.

Table 3-2. Performance improvements from IBM's Vendor
Payments E-Engineering.

Performance Measure	Before	After	% Improvement
Computer Applications Used	12	1	92%
Procurement Error Rate	34%	9%	74%
Procurement Cost as a Percentage of Purchased Cost	1.8%	0.9%	50%
Process Cost per Invoice	$1.50	$1.02	32%
Percentage of Suppliers Accounting for 90% of Purchases	11%	9%	18%

The vendor payments e-engineering process achieved its results by adopting the following best practices:

- Used a procurement card.
- Moved approvals and data validations up front.
- Developed online catalogs and online requisitioning.
- Treated purchasing and accounts payable as one process.
- Extended integrated information systems to suppliers.
- Involved suppliers in new-product development and value-chain analysis.
- Integrated purchasing, payables, and receiving computer applications.
- Used electronic commerce and electronic data interchange.

Since the details of these applications are useful for financial executives, we will explore IBM's practices in greater depth and conclude this section with an assessment of the implications of IBM's strategy here for e-commerce project financial evaluation in general. According to Robert Hughes, IBM national accounts payable services manager, the accounts payable e-engineering project was prompted by his department's receipt of a million invoices per year from its smaller suppliers. Hughes realized that IBM should practice what it preached: Use e-commerce to let its smaller suppliers send IBM their invoices electronically.

In 1998, IBM formed a team made up of Global Services (IBM's business service organization), procurement, and accounts payable to develop a customized electronic invoice. IBM used Forms Exchange, a component of the Global Services network, to accomplish this objective. Now, IBM's smaller suppliers (95 percent of its vendors) use a standard Internet connection and a Web browser to access IBM's Web site, fill out the forms, and submit them electronically.

IBM converted the Web-based forms into EDI documents, and routed them through its EDI system to accounts payable, where they were treated as if they were standard EDI transactions from IBM's larger vendors.

IBM's accounts payable department also required its employees to use paper purchase orders to buy products and services ranging from internal catering services to software. IBM had twelve separate systems for dealing with vendors, and no connection between procurement and accounts payable.

If an IBM employee wanted to buy an office chair, that person would make the request of the procurement department. Procurement then went to IBM's suppliers, picked a chair, issued a paper purchase order, and the chair was shipped. The paper invoice from the supplier later went to accounts payable. Often, the invoice did not match the purchase order, was coded inaccurately, or arrived late. So only 66 percent of invoices were paid when first received. The others required more information. Frustrated employees often skipped the procurement process altogether to get supplies.

Changing the process first required procurement and accounts payable to do something not done in the past: Communicate. In early 1997, IBM formed a team of the appropriate people from accounts payable and purchasing. IBM brought in some suppliers and employees to join the team. The team asked the suppliers and employees for ideas on what the team could do to make it easier and more cost-effective for them to accomplish the objectives of the procurement process.

Ultimately, the twelve general procurement and accounts payable systems were integrated into one system. The paper requisition process was replaced by an online system, which helped reduce errors and speed up the process. IBM also expedited its process by eliminating levels of corporate approval, and by increasing expense authorization limits. IBM also established a data warehouse of purchase order and payment data.

These process improvements helped procurement save $1 billion for IBM. Now, 91 percent of invoices are paid when first received, and cost-per-invoice has dropped from $1.50 to $1.02. IBM's assistant controller Joseph Martin notes that IBM now has a very efficient system with common processes.

Another benefit of the change is that IBM uses its purchasing volumes to negotiate lower unit costs for procured items. This was achieved by the team's decision to replace paper purchase orders for under $200, high-volume orders with employee purchase cards. Employees use the cards to make purchases without authorization with an online catalog.

Automated buying currently represents 80 percent of IBM's procurement transactions. For the remaining 20 percent of IBM's higher-priced orders, a contract form with preapproved authorization and standard terms and conditions has been developed. This new procedure cuts the time for placing contracts from nine months to one. By the year 2000, IBM expects electronic procurement to reduce the cost to process an order by 80 percent. Hughes estimated that every $1 saved in procurement was equivalent to $7 in revenue in terms of its impact on profit. Hughes believes that his group has helped create a seamless requisition-to-payment process, making it easy and flexible for the employee to procure goods and services, and for the vendor to send IBM electronic invoices and receive payment.

IBM also took a team-based approach to its employee disbursements system. Tony Angelo, IBM project executive for worldwide employee disbursements, worked with IBM's human resources department in 1996 to improve employee disbursements. Prior to 1996, IBM's Human Resources (HR) department would develop a new compensation policy, and Angelo's department would need to figure out how to administer it. However, since IBM's HR department determines employee benefits, salary increases, and frequency of increases, Angelo wanted to work more closely with HR.

Angelo also wanted a more streamlined approach. In the 1980s in the United States, Angelo had eight payroll systems and locations in the U.S. alone. Depending on their location, some employees were paid weekly, some biweekly. Now IBM has one system. All IBM's regular employees are paid on a semimonthly basis, and temporary employees on a weekly basis. IBM saves money by minimizing the number of times it runs the payroll over the course of the year. The new system helped cut payroll costs by 95 percent, and reduced per-pay-distribution costs from $5.75 to $1.77.

IBM also used technology to cut T&E (travel and entertainment) expenses. T&E expenses are the costs of processing and payment of employee expense accounts. In the early 1990s, IBM had twenty-five U.S. locations processing T&E expense reimbursements. In 1993, it consolidated them into one centralized system. As a result, processing T&E costs dropped by 83 percent, and the process cost per T&E expense report fell from $23.00 to $2.02.[6]

The IBM example demonstrates the way financial managers should be thinking about how to conduct the financial analysis of e-commerce. Financial executives should take note of several aspects of IBM's approach. IBM combined measures of process improvement with financial measures. By combining these two categories of measures, IBM was able to understand how best to achieve financial benefits and to pinpoint the specific operational levers that would generate these financial benefits. Simply put: IBM measured both the specific financial improvements of its e-engineering projects as well as the means to change its work processes to achieve these financial benefits. In addition, financial executives should note that IBM was willing to combine a number of different technologies to achieve business benefits. For example, IBM used procurement cards, a data warehouse, and the Internet as different means to achieve different, but related, business objectives.

How the Stock Market Assigns Value to Intangible Assets

IBM's successful e-commerce initiatives demonstrate the quantifiable value that e-commerce can offer a company. As any observer of Internet IPOs will recognize, there appears to be a parallel universe for assigning value to intangible assets.

There is probably no more dramatic example of how this parallel universe operates than the May 1999 acquisition of WebMD by Healtheon. Healtheon, at the time of the acquisition, was a publicly traded company that offered health payment services to connect doctors, hospitals, insurers, and consumers over the Internet. WebMD was a privately held company that provided medical information and transaction services to physicians, and operated a consumer healthcare Web site. The combined company, Healtheon/WebMD aimed to dominate the online healthcare market by offering a single portal to allow doctors and patients to conduct transactions and obtain medical information. The merger between the two companies also involved investments from Microsoft and others that would lead to Healtheon/WebMD being the featured healthcare content provider on Microsoft Network (MSN), Excite, Lycos, and CNN.

While the description of the business combination may seem prosaic, the financial aspects of the transaction set new records for the magnitude of the gap between demonstrated financial performance and stock market valuation. Healtheon exchanged 1.82 shares of its stock for each of WebMD's 54 million shares. Based on Healtheon's May 21, 1999 closing price of $105 per share, Healtheon paid $10.3 billion for WebMD. While this was the largest Web-related merger as of May 1999 in terms of value, what was even more astonishing was that WebMD had generated a *mere $75,000* worth of sales and a net loss of $13.9 million. Another interesting fact is that Healtheon's stock began that week at $56 per share. After the merger was announced, Healtheon's stock rose as high as $120 per share before closing the week at the aforementioned $105.

It is difficult to imagine a more compelling example of how the stock market is assigning value to intangible assets since WebMD's tangible net worth was probably close to zero at the time of the merger. In Chapter 1, I discussed the idea that the stock market is assigning value to intangible assets. Here are the intangible assets of the Healtheon/WebMD deal:

• *Big market.* Investors assign more value to companies that are targeting big markets. As Healtheon's chairman Jim Clark pointed out, the market for healthcare was about $1 trillion. Due to the tremendous process inefficiencies in the payment of health claims, Clark estimated that the Internet could cut out at least $250 billion worth of inefficiencies from that process.

• *Market leadership.* Investors assign the most value within an industry to the company that is perceived as the clear market leader. Analysts discussing the deal hailed the combined companies as the clear market leader in the health services industry. Given the small size of the company, it is hard to imagine such market leadership could be insurmountable. However, in Internet business, the perception of market leadership can become reality if it is repeated often enough in the press. Ultimately real customers and partners begin to act on the perception that the company is the market leader. This action can transform the perception of market leadership into a reality.

• *Partnerships.* Investors also judge businesses and organizations by the company they keep. If companies have leading partners, it helps create the perception of leadership. In the Healtheon/WebMD merger, Microsoft, E*Trade, CompuServe, Excite, Lycos, CNN, and DuPont had announced significant partnerships, and in some cases, investments in the combined company.

- *Strong management.* Jonathan Arnold, the 29-year-old CEO of WebMD, was appointed CEO of the combined company. Arnold was an extremely compelling salesperson who had started and sold a remote heart monitoring company soon after graduating from college. Arnold's entrepreneurial track record and strong leadership skills made him an excellent choice to lead the company.

How much of the $10.3 billion could be assigned to each of these intangible assets is unknown. However, it is clear that without all four, the value of the company would be much less.

An Approach to E-Commerce Financial Evaluation

The remainder of this chapter describes an approach to e-commerce financial evaluation. This process enables financial executives to gauge the costs and benefits of proposed e-commerce projects in a rigorous way. The process also lets financial executives gain a thorough understanding of not only the concrete financial effect of the proposed e-commerce project, but its intangible risks and benefits as well. For example, the process mapping phase of the process will help highlight potential control and audit security risks in the proposed e-commerce project. Financial executives can use this process to alter the proposed e-commerce project to minimize or eliminate these risks.

Many of the analytical techniques that IBM used to conduct financial evaluation of its accounts payable reengineering projects can be employed for e-engineering. Here is a seven-step process that financial managers can follow to conduct an e-engineering project financial analysis:

 Diagram the current business process. In order to assess the value of an e-engineering project, management must understand how that project will enhance the company's cash flows. The assessment of this enhancement depends on having a baseline to which the e-engineered process can be compared. In order to create such a baseline, financial managers must take responsibility for the development of a map of the company's current way of performing the process that is to be e-engineered. Without the financial manager's involvement, it is difficult to be certain that the company can develop an understanding of the costs and time consumed in the current process. And without that understanding, the benefits of an e-engineered process cannot be quantified.

The foundation for understanding the company's current process is a diagram that maps the specific steps in the process from its start in one department to its conclusion, however many organizations later. To conduct this process mapping, the company must build a team that crosses the departments and organizations that actually conduct the entire process. When IBM reengineered its procurement process, for example, it found that the accounts payable and purchasing departments needed to work together. Undoubtedly, IBM also involved its suppliers and employees in the process redesign as well.

Once the team has been built and its objectives are clear, an independent party—possibly a management consultant—should participate in mapping out the process to be reengineered. While there are numerous process mapping methodologies, the team should select one that helps to identify how specific processes act on information and documents at different levels of the organization. The intent is to pinpoint opportunities for improvement by identifying errors that are the result of handoffs from one department to another, which involve the rekeying of data that could simply be entered into an online system once and then be available to all process participants. The process mapping is also intended to help managers quantify the amount of time and cost that is involved in the creation of a unit of work, such as the production of an employee payment or the sale and fulfillment of a customer order.

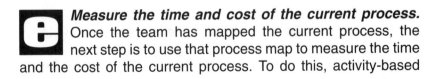 **_Measure the time and cost of the current process._** Once the team has mapped the current process, the next step is to use that process map to measure the time and the cost of the current process. To do this, activity-based

costing is a particularly useful approach. Managers can interview the people who perform these activities to find out how much time they spend on a particular process step. The managers can access personnel records to identify the fully loaded annual cost of those employees and their total annual work hours. With these statistics, the manager can calculate a costing rate for that employee's time.

By cumulating the cost per employee of each process step, financial managers can then develop an estimate of the total cost of performing the current process for a specific unit of output. Once the manager has developed the analysis of the cost of the process for each unit of output, the total annual cost of the process can be calculated by applying the unit process cost to the total number of units produced per year by the organization.

The purpose of all this measuring is to develop baseline statistics. Statistics should be developed for the current process's operating and financial performances. The IBM case provides good examples of both kinds of statistics. The procurement example tracked operating performance statistics such as the number of expense reports processed by accounts payable employees as and the process error rate. The procurement example also tracked the total process cost per item purchased and the total cost of the items procured. Ultimately, the generation of such baseline statistics is the most important deliverable of this second step.

Map out the e-engineered process. By conducting the first and second steps of this e-commerce project financial evaluation process, the team can generally identify many improvement opportunities. Studying cases of successful e-engineering projects and using a general understanding of how the Internet can enable more efficient business processes, the team can envision ways of using the Internet to achieve significant improvements in the measures developed in step two.

Unless this vision is mapped out in some detail, it becomes difficult for the financial manager to develop an accurate estimate of the operational and financial benefits of the e-engineered process. Therefore, it is essential for the team to develop a map that details its vision for the e-engineered process. This process map should detail how the new process will work, including such details as how information will initially be collected, how the information will be shared, and how process customers will ultimately be able to accomplish their objectives. In generating the map of the new process, the team should use the map of the current process as a basis for comparison. While the new process should incorporate significant improvements over the old process, it should be drawn in sufficient detail to be as useful in step four (below) as the process map developed in step one was for step two (above).

e   *Estimate the time and cost of the e-engineered process.* In general the e-engineered process should enable the process customer to accomplish more without human intervention. For example, as we saw in the case of Cisco's CCO in Chapter 2, there are many service questions that customers would rather be able to answer themselves whenever they experience the need for answers to technical questions. An e-commerce application certainly can provide such benefits.

Such benefits must then be translated into the same terms as were developed to measure the current process. To follow along with the CCO example, the financial managers should estimate how the new process would change the number of technical service questions that could be resolved per technical service person, how the new process would alter the average time to resolve a technical service question, or how the new process would affect the company's overall customer satisfaction rating. In addition, financial managers would need to estimate how the new process would change such financial measures as the cost to resolve a technical service question or the overall technical service department budget as a percentage of revenues.

These measures would be developed using the same activity-based costing techniques outlined in step two. In this case, financial analysts would measure the time and cost to perform the e-engineered process per unit of output. The costs would again be estimated by calculating a costing rate for each employee involved in the various steps of the e-engineered process, and applying this rate to the time to perform each activity.

Managers will also find it useful to compare the statistics

developed through this process to some of the process-improvement benchmarks presented earlier in this chapter from the OECD. If the activity-based cost-approach to estimating the performance benefits of the e-engineered process yields results that are much greater than or less than the OECD benchmarks, there may be an opportunity to double check the assumptions and calculations.

e ***Develop a plan for the e-engineering project.*** In Part III, we will examine a more detailed version of the concept of the e-engineering project plan. To conduct a thorough cash flow analysis of the potential e-commerce application, the financial manager must participate in the process of developing a plan for implementing the proposed project. This plan must include the significant project phases from concept development to system testing and installation. For each phase, the project plan should include detailed information about the specific action steps that make up each project phase.

For costing purposes, the project plan should estimate the amount of time that internal and external project participants will devote to each action step. In addition, the team should make clear what the project participants will deliver at the end of each phase. Finally, in developing a project plan for costing purposes, the team should estimate the specific timing of the project activities. For financial analysis purposes, the timing of expenses can make a significant difference in the present value of the proposed e-commerce project.

e ***Calculate the cost of the e-engineering project.*** Using the e-engineering project plan as a guide, the team should endeavor to convert the time estimates for each phase in the plan to specific costs. The time of internal resources can be converted using the costing rates that I discussed earlier. The time of external resources should be calculated using their billing rates. Other project costs such as the cost of additional hardware, software, and telecommunications connections should be included in the e-engineering project cost-estimate at the time when cash for these resources is actually expended.

Prepare an integrated cash-flow analysis of the e-engineering project. Steps one through six provide a foundation on which to base the integrated analysis of the cash flows resulting from the e-engineering project. Each potential e-commerce project will have unique elements. Nevertheless, the sources and uses of cash from the proposed project are likely to fall into four categories:

1. *Incremental Cash Inflows from Additional Revenues.* While the examples used in this chapter focus on cost reduction benefits, many e-commerce applications such as Cisco's CCO end up generating substantial additional revenues. Existing Cisco customers generally order new products via CCO. Thus the incremental cash flow from such e-commerce–related revenues should be estimated on an operating profit basis—subtracting from the e-commerce revenues the related cost of goods sold and the CCO-related operating costs.

2. *Incremental Cash Inflows from Reduced Costs.* The examples I used in this chapter illustrate how to measure the incremental cash inflows from reduced costs. In the IBM example, the cash-flow analysis should have reflected reductions in the cost of, for example, processing T&E forms resulting from the new process. The analysis of the cash-flow benefits from reduced costs should include all related process improvements. In the IBM case, the use of a data warehouse to aggregate purchase information enabled IBM to negotiate lower prices from suppliers. In this case, the new system resulted in more than $1 billion in savings to IBM that were attributable to the new system. Just this savings alone undoubtedly helped pay for IBM's new system many times over.

3. *Incremental Cash Outflows for Building the Proposed E-Commerce System.* As I noted earlier, the analysis of the cost of building the proposed system should be based on a rough project plan. If so, the plan should reflect the costs of internal and external project staff members. These costs should be included in the cash-flow model at the time that the cash is expended. Additional costs for hardware, software, and telecommunications services

should be included as well at the appropriate time. Finally, the team should include the cost of training employees and customers (where appropriate) in using the new system. If the system will entail reducing headcount, then severance costs should be included in this cash-flow category.

4. *Incremental Cash Outflows for Operating the New System.* To the extent that the ongoing operation of the system involves incremental costs above the cost of operating the old system, these costs should be included as cash outflows here. Such incremental operating costs might cover upgrading software, maintaining the accuracy of data, adding to the communications capacity of the system to accommodate growth in its use, and modifying the system's functions to adapt to changing user needs.

As with other capital budgeting analyses, the last step in the process is to calculate the net-present-value of the project. This is accomplished by discounting the net cash flows in each year of the project by the appropriate annuity discount factor to account for the riskiness of the project and the timing of the cash flow.

Depending on the complexity of the project, it may be useful for financial managers to think of a specific e-commerce project as being one in a series of future projects. For particularly strategic projects, this sort of thinking would cause managers to look at the first e-commerce project as providing a platform for future projects. For example, at Cisco, the project to streamline the customer service process created a technical platform upon which Cisco was able to build its e-commerce capability.

If senior management is thinking along these lines, then it may be useful for financial managers to model a series of e-commerce projects as a decision tree. Each branch off the original project would have a certain probability (probably less than 100 percent) of actually happening. Similarly, each subsequent project would have its own cash-flow analysis. In this case, financial managers would calculate the expected value of the series of e-commerce projects by multiplying the probabilities by the individual project cash flows. Since these probabilities would reflect the riskiness of each individual project, the discount rate used to calculate the net-present-value would be the risk-free rate (normally the long-term treasury bill rate, currently between 5 and 6 percent.)

Conclusion

Executives need a way to conduct a rigorous financial evaluation of potential e-commerce projects. This evaluation must be rigorous so that management can rely on the analysis to make an intelligent decision on whether or not to proceed with a proposed e-commerce project. Given the very rapid development cycles and relatively low costs of many e-commerce applications, financial executives also need an e-commerce project financial evaluation process that can be completed efficiently. This chapter has outlined a seven-step process that relies heavily on process mapping and activity-based costing techniques to provide the foundation for detailed e-commerce project cash-flow analysis. This seven-step process balances the need for rigor and speed in a way that executives will find useful.

Notes

1. Keith Hammonds, "Weaving the Web Into Corporate Strategy," *Business Week,* June 22, 1998 [http://www.businessweek.com/1998/25/b3583001.htm].
2. Financial Executive Institute and Fuqua, "CFO Survey: Company Internet Sales and Purchases Jump; Few Price Increases, Stronger Earnings Ahead," *PR Newswire,* March 29, 1999 [http://www.prnewswire.com/cnoc/exec/menu?310650].
3. Maryann Jones-Thompson, "Spotlight: The Economic Impact of E-Commerce," *The Industry Standard,* April 26, 1999 [http://www.thestandard.net/metrics/display/0,1283,881,00.html].
4. Ibid.
5. Russ Banham, "IBM Seeks the Solution Within," *CFO Magazine,* January 1999 [http://www.cfonet.com/cgi-bin/vdkw_cgi/xec75e7f839/search/2446472/18].
6. Ibid.

4

How E-Commerce Creates Competitive Advantage

I t is too early to tell whether e-commerce produces sustainable competitive advantage. The research for this book indicates that e-commerce is producing clear changes in the competitive landscape. In some industries, companies that had been leaders have already lost significant ground to upstart e-commerce companies. In other industries, e-commerce is hardly making a dent in the current industry structure. Two things are clear, however. First, managers in all industries are afraid that their business could be the next one to be "Amazoned." Second, these same managers feel that they lack reliable methods for assessing what e-commerce means to their companies' competitive position, and what they should do about it.

This chapter provides managers with a way to address these concerns. The chapter begins with a case study of how e-commerce has altered the sources of competitive advantage in the book-selling industry by profiling the competitive dynamics between Amazon.com, Barnes & Noble, and its online subsidiary bn.com. The chapter then uses this case to develop the key principles of e-commerce and competitive advantage. Chapter 4 concludes with a ten-step methodology that applies these principles to help managers use e-commerce to create competitive advantage.

Book Selling and the Internet

In the last four years, no Internet company has received more attention than Amazon.com. While part of this attention may be the media appeal of Amazon.com's founder, Jeff Bezos, the more fundamental reason for Amazon.com's prominence is that there is no more dramatic example of the power of the Internet to utterly transform an entire industry. One measure of this impact is that two years from the date of its initial public offering, Amazon.com's stock market capitalization was *6.3 times* that of its two biggest bricks-and-mortar competitors, Barnes & Noble and Borders, combined.

Success on this scale raises a number of managerial issues. How much of this stock market performance is grounded in business fundamentals? What are the sources of advantage that drive Amazon.com's relative performance? How have Amazon.com's bricks-and-mortar competitors responded to the assault from Amazon.com? How effective have these responses been? What is Amazon.com doing about these competitive responses? How is the future likely to play out? I will now address these issues in turn.

Performance Fundamentals

One of the axioms of Internet business is that traditional approaches to valuing stocks are not effective. Nevertheless, it is useful to demonstrate how these traditional methods break down by trying to apply them. For example in May 1999, at 159x, Amazon.com's ratio of market capitalization to shareholders' equity was far greater than that of Barnes & Noble (3.5x) and Borders (1.5x). While some of this valuation difference may be a result of investors' irrational exuberance, it may also be due, in part, to the inability of our accounting methods to quantify the value of all of Amazon.com's assets.

Anecdotal evidence suggests that part of Amazon.com's stock market valuation advantage could be due to its much more rapid growth. As Figure 4-1 demonstrates, Amazon.com's market capitalization to revenue ratio was *33 times* that of Barnes & Noble's, while

Figure 4-1. Market capitalization/revenues (5/7/99) and revenue growth rate (1997 to 1998) for Amazon.com, Barnes & Noble, and Borders.

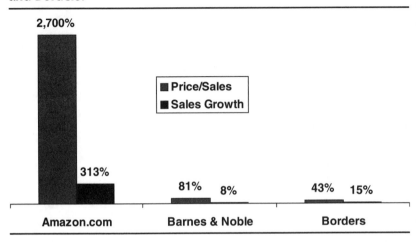

Amazon.com's revenue growth rate was *39 times* Barnes & Noble's. In Chapter 1, I noted that the stock market seems to assign a value to intangible assets that are not quantified by traditional accounting methods. We will examine later in this case some of Amazon.com's sources of competitive advantage. Many of these advantages derive from Amazon.com's ongoing efforts to improve the quality of its customers' experience. Traditional accounting would not reflect accurately the value of this intangible asset.

The stock market also appears to be rewarding Amazon.com for another intangible asset—the relative absence of barriers to growth in its business model. Amazon.com's growth is limited by the ability of its computer systems to adapt effectively as customer demand grows and product lines are expanded. Amazon.com's growth also depends on its ability to hire and develop a sufficient number of capable staff members. Nevertheless, these barriers to growth take much less time to overcome than those of its bricks-and-mortar competitors.

Barnes & Noble and Borders traditionally needed to add stores along with people and more adept computer systems in order to achieve additional growth. The cost of these stores constitutes a significant speed bump impeding growth. As Figure 4-2 illustrates, Amazon.com's most significant advantages over the bricks-and-mortar model of book selling are its absence of retail stores and its twenty-seven-times-wider selection of books and other items delivered with fewer than one-tenth the number of the employees of Barnes & Noble.[1]

Sources of Competitive Advantage

While these measurable attributes suggest some of Amazon.com's sources of advantage, the fundamental sources of Amazon.com's competitive advantage emerge from an understanding of the company and its origins. As we will see, Amazon.com's growth is a result of effective branding (both to consumers and to investors), the relative convenience of its service, and the ability to personalize the Amazon.com experience to each of its millions of customers.

Jeff Bezos, Amazon.com's founder, came up with the idea for

Figure 4-2. Retail store square feet (000s), employees, and number of titles (000s) for Amazon.com, Barnes & Noble, and Borders (1998).

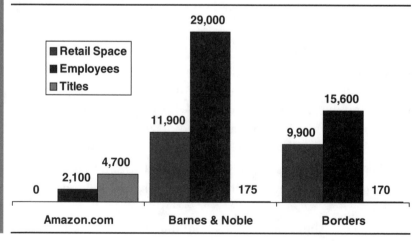

selling books online while he was working as a senior vice president of D. E. Shaw, a New York–based investment management firm. According to *Wired*, Bezos was assigned to come up with profitable ideas for selling over the Internet. Bezos concluded that online book selling would be a good business because two of the United States's largest book distributors already had electronic lists.[2]

Bezos realized that no single book store could carry a comprehensive inventory of the books in print. The distributors who carried thousands of titles acted as the warehouse for most stores, particularly smaller booksellers. When customers asked a store for a book it did not have in stock, they filled the customer's order through one of the two largest distributors—Ingram or Baker & Taylor. These companies' inventory lists were digitized in the late 1980s. The online inventory lists would enable Bezos to offer books online through the company he envisioned creating.

David Shaw, Bezos' boss, was not willing to invest in the idea. Bezos told Shaw that he wanted to start a company based on this idea because he was afraid he would later regret not taking advantage of the opportunity to get in at the beginning of the Internet's 2,300 percent annual growth rate. Bezos and his wife then drove across country to Seattle to start the company. Bezos typed the business plan on his computer while his wife drove. But before he left for Seattle, Bezos convinced one of the programmers he had met through his investigations for D. E. Shaw, Shel Kaphan, to become his first employee.

Kaphan and a contractor named Paul Barton-Davis built a prototype of the Amazon.com Web site in a converted garage of a rented home in Bellevue, Washington. Bezos raised the first $1 million of seed capital from fifteen wealthy individual investors. At one point, a single venture capital firm in the Seattle area wanted to purchase the entire million-dollar round, but demanded a 50 percent discount on Bezos' valuation. Bezos refused, and the venture firm passed, in part because they believed Barnes & Noble would quickly crush Amazon.com.

The naming of Amazon.com was based on the importance of its relative size. According to *Upside*, Bezos equated Earth's biggest river and Earth's biggest bookstore. Bezos reasoned that the Amazon River was ten times as large as the next largest river, which was the Mississippi, in terms of volume of water. Twenty percent of the world's fresh water was in the Amazon River Basin, and Amazon.com had six times as many titles as the world's largest physical bookstore.[3]

To deliver on this vision of huge relative size, Bezos and Kaphan started work on their Web site. They programmed the site to sound a bell every time the servers recorded a sale. Amazon.com was launched in July 1995, and the bell started ringing—so often that within a few weeks, the noise had become unbearable and they disabled it. Every week, the revenues went up. By the second or third week, Amazon.com was generating revenues of $6,000 or $10,000 per week. By the end of early September 1995, revenues were $20,000 a week.

Amazon.com's success is the result of the cumulative effect of many sources of competitive advantage. Amazon.com's sources of advantage include the location of its warehouses, its focus on continuously enhancing its customer's experience, its rigorous approach to hiring, its extreme frugality, its approach to corporate development, and the way it manages executive time.

Warehouse Locations

Bezos realized that not all activities should be conducted online. For example, Bezos decided that Amazon.com should own its own warehouses, so that it could maintain quality control over the packaging and shipping of orders, which he saw as an opportunity to enhance the Amazon.com customer experience. This allowed Amazon.com to combine orders for books from multiple publishers—or orders that include, say, a book, a CD, and a video—into single packages. It also gave Amazon.com employees who pack orders a chance to check for defective goods. In its music department, for example, Amazon.com replaced cracked or broken CD jewel cases.

The reason for locating in Seattle was not to be near a technology hub. It was to be near one of the distribution facilities of Ingram, Amazon.com's largest book supplier. Bezos recognized that this proximity to distribution facilities would allow for quicker turn-around on deliveries. Furthermore, since Washington had a relatively small population, the pool of potential customers from whom Amazon.com would be required to collect sales tax was smaller. Similarly, Amazon.com located its second warehouse in Delaware, which not only has no sales tax, but is also a good base for serving East Coast customers. Amazon.com's third and most recent ware-house is near Reno, Nevada. This location enables Amazon.com to originate deliveries close to the huge California population, while remaining outside California's tax-collection borders.

Enhancing Customers' Experiences

Bezos also focused on ways to enhance Amazon.com customers' ex-periences. He altered the Web site to make it easier to understand, streamlining the ordering process and responding immediately to each customer question. As Bezos noted, Amazon.com wants people to feel as though they are visiting a place rather than a software ap-plication.

Bezos recognized that every business must deal with scarcity, and in the case of Amazon.com, this scarcity is screen real estate. Despite these limitations, Bezos makes Amazon.com entertaining. For example, rankings tell shoppers how well each book is selling. Dedicated collectors of rarities appreciate Amazon.com's attention to detail. Using the music keyword-search function, for example, users can pull up a listing of the six CDs offered by Amazon.com that feature the "oud," a traditional Middle Eastern stringed instrument.

Hiring

Bezos was extremely selective about hiring. According to *Wired*, Bezos would interview candidates himself. Then, in hiring meetings, he would probe every other interviewer, occasionally constructing elaborate charts on a whiteboard detailing the job seeker's qualifications. If Bezos identified any doubt, rejection usually followed. One Bezos motto was that every time Amazon.com hired a new employee, he or she should raise the bar for the next hire, so that the overall talent pool was always improving.[4]

Frugality

Amazon.com is loath to spend on things that do not add value. According to *Upside*, Amazon.com's 1998 offices in downtown Seattle were located in a drab four-story cube called the Columbia Building. Amazon occupied all four floors, above and behind the dry cleaner, print shop, and Indian restaurant on the street level. Amazon.com also leased space in two other equally inexpensive commercial buildings nearby.[5]

Bezos has desks made from doors. The wood and the brackets cost about $70, and the labor is about $60. Bezos built the first four himself, but now hires carpenters to come in and build them seventy at a time. Bezos also refuses to spend money on office equipment such as monitor stands and extra chairs. Monitors are propped up on telephone books. Chairs for meetings are "borrowed" from those who leave them unguarded.[6]

Corporate Development

Bezos spends hours thinking about the future. He looks for ideas, explores his own site, and sometimes just surfs the Web (particularly on Mondays and Thursdays, which he tries to keep unscheduled). Bezos also catches up on e-mail, wanders around and talks to employees, and sets up meetings that are not part of the regular calendar.

He also gathers new ideas from other Amazon.com employees

who are similarly searching for growth opportunities. Amazon.-com's August 1998 purchase of Junglee, then a Silicon Valley–based company that produced product comparison software for Web shoppers, came about when Amazon.com treasurer Randy Tinsley approached Bezos in late April 1998, and argued on behalf of the acquisition. After a half-hour debate during which Tinsley allowed that Junglee might resist a sale, Bezos told Tinsley to forget about the acquisition. Two hours later, Tinsley called Bezos back to say he had called Junglee anyway, and that the management there was actually interested.

Amazon.com continues to use its stock as valuable currency to make acquisitions and to expand into new product lines. For example, in April 1999, Amazon.com purchased three companies that would enhance its ability to offer personalized products and services to its customers. Amazon.com has also been expanding the products it offers from books to gifts, CDs, videos, and online auction services to compete with eBay.

One example of how Amazon.com expands through internal development is its June 1998 move into selling CDs online. According to *Upside*, Amazon.com created an online CD purchase process that borrows techniques developed for its online book-selling capability. For example, the online CD site uses one-click shopping. This means that for repeat customers, Amazon.com stores shoppers' shipping addresses. When shoppers find something they want to buy, they just click one button. During the focus groups when Amazon.com was testing this feature, shoppers thought the process was too easy. As a result, Amazon.com put a phrase on the thank-you screen that says, "Yes, you are done!" Amazon.com also uses collaborative filtering to look at a customer's purchases and make recommendations.[7]

For its music site, Amazon.com also created content to help people make purchase decisions. Amazon.com recognized that in order to buy music easily, people need reviews, explanations, and sound clips. Amazon.com hired a staff of freelance editorial people to write

750,000 words worth of reviews for its music site. Amazon.com's reviews are designed to help people make purchase decisions—and they are not all positive. Some of them suggest that a particular CD is not the artist's best work, and recommend trying another CD that better represents the artist.

While Amazon.com tried to make the online site into a music store, it was also an encyclopedia of music. For example, an artist's page, shows who influenced the artist, and includes cross-links to all of those artists. Amazon.com also has lists of essential works. There are fourteen categories of music and 280 subcategories. The site also categorizes music by instrument. Although the listing is subjective, Amazon.com gets a significant amount of online feedback. If a listing of essentials is not appropriate, Amazon.com is likely to receive large numbers of angry e-mails in a short period of time. Amazon.com will use the feedback to change the list of titles until the angry e-mails diminish.[8]

Time Management

Bezos and his top executives manage their time as a strategic resource that must be aligned with the company's objectives and strategies. According to *Wired*, every three months, Bezos sits down with his assistant, Kim Christenson, to examine and analyze his calendar for the quarter just passed. He wants to know how much time he has devoted to each of the dozen or so categories to which Christenson has assigned every meeting, phone call, or trip. The categories include recurring activities such as recruiting, as well as one-time items such as the launch plans for Amazon.com's U.K. and German sites.[9]

In order to avoid becoming Amazon.toast, Bezos spends time defending against challenges by Barnes & Noble to Amazon.com's book business. In particular, Amazon.com faced a potential threat to its supply chain in Barnes & Noble's purchase of Ingram, the book distributor that has been an essential source of Amazon.com inventory. Bezos knew that Ingram was for sale, but he passed on the opportunity. Getting items into customers' hands quickly is an important part of the Amazon.com experience, and Bezos needs to retain good relationships with the company's distributors. Over the longer term, Amazon.com's initiatives to build direct relationships with publishers could solve the problem of Barnes & Noble's acquisition of Ingram. Bezos predicted that by 2000, Barnes & Noble will not consider Amazon.com a direct competitor. While Bezos is trying to invent the future of e-commerce, Bezos feels that Barnes & Noble is merely defending its turf.

Competitive Response

To its credit, Barnes & Noble did not take Amazon.com's success standing still. Barnes & Noble has taken two strategic countermeasures. First, Barnes & Noble established its own Web site. Bn.com is a separate legal entity from Barnes & Noble. Bn.com was taken public in June 1999. Second, Barnes & Noble announced its intention to purchase Ingram, Amazon.com's book wholesaler, in November 1998 for $600 million. As I noted, Amazon.com clearly viewed this intended purchase as a threat to its supply lines. However, the deal was not approved by the Federal Trade Commission, and Barnes & Noble withdrew its bid. If the deal had been approved, Amazon.com could have faced a short-term threat to its ability to fulfill customer book orders efficiently.

Therefore, bn.com may represent the more profound long-term threat to Amazon.com. While Barnes & Noble launched its Web site in March 1997, awkwardly naming it barnesandnoble.com, its initial success was quite limited. According to *U.S. News & World Report,* Barnes & Noble began a major renovation of its Web site in May 1998, making it 2.5 times faster and quadrupling the number of links off the home page. Barnes & Noble also changed the color scheme of its site from forest green to teal and khaki after extensive consumer testing found the colors "stimulating" yet "pleasant." The result of this effort was that visitor count increased nearly twofold, and barnesandnoble.com became one of the top fifty most-visited Web sites for the first time. Barnes & Noble's problem was that Amazon.com grew even faster. In fact, Amazon proceeded to double its lead, with 8.7 million visitors in February 1999, compared with 3.4 million for barnesandnoble.com.[10]

Barnes & Noble's competitive arsenal in its battle against Amazon.com was strengthened in October 1998 when Bertelsmann AG announced a $200 million investment in bn.com. According to *Red Herring*, Bertelsmann AG is the third largest media group in the world, controlling the record company BMG Entertainment and the leading U.S. book publisher, Random House. Bertelsmann is also America Online's partner in Europe, and has a similar partnership with Lycos Europe.[11]

The most significant threat to Amazon.com from the Bertelsmann investment in bn.com is Bertelsmann's control of worldwide radio, TV networks, and print media properties. The deal provided bn.com with cash and access to media properties that would help promote the Web site in the U.S. and Europe.

Despite the importance of promotion—Amazon.com's biggest expense item is marketing and sales—it still remains to be seen whether bn.com can compete effectively. Reports indicate that Amazon.com responds more quickly to Web sites' requests to join its traffic-driving affiliate program. Amazon.com has also spent more aggressively to gain exclusive access to highly visible portions of the largest Web portals.[12]

Despite the potential threat, Amazon.com dramatically outperformed bn.com. Amazon.com generated sales of $609 million in 1998, while bn.com generated $62 million in that year. At one-tenth the size of Amazon.com, bn.com will need to make dramatic strategic moves in order to achieve its goal of online book market dominance. Amazon.com's current market share online has been estimated at between 65 and 80 percent.

Increased competition for Amazon.com is also taking place in the online music retailing business. Large online music retailers N2K and CDnow merged in 1998. The combined entity has approximately a 45 percent share of the online music market. And the competition from these online music retailers could be further exacerbated by the emergence of a new online music transmission standard, MP3, that could enable artists to sell their music to the public without creating CDs, thereby bypassing the record companies, the bricks-and-mortar CD retailers, and online CD retailers.

Amazon.com also faces competition in the online video retailing market. For example, in 1998, online video retailer reel.com was purchased by Hollywood Video, the second largest video retailer in the United States. Hollywood's financial backing is likely to make reel.com into a serious threat to Amazon.com in this market.

Finally, while Amazon.com entered the online auction market to compete with eBay, so did Yahoo!. The point is that mobility barriers—the ease with which companies can move into related fields—are very low for the leading online consumer retailers.

Amazon.com Counterattack

Amazon.com launched an immediate counterattack on Bertelsmann. This counterattack took the form of an intense Amazon.com media blitz in Germany, a country where Bertelsmann enjoys a strong market position. Specifically, Amazon.com announced a German bookselling service in October 1998, and also placed full-page advertisements in various German magazines.

In April 1999, Amazon.com announced a plan intended to reduce its dependence on Ingram, as a defensive move against Barnes & Noble's proposed purchase. According to *Publisher's Weekly*, Amazon.com is leasing a distribution center in Coffeyville, Kansas. The new center is a 460,000-square-foot space that will be converted into 750,000 square feet. This move will double Amazon.-com's existing capacity. The distribution center houses books, CDs, videos, and other products. Amazon.com's dependence on Ingram has dropped from 60 percent of its book inventory to 40 percent. This percentage should shrink further once the Kansas center is in use later in 1999. Ingram has distribution capability of two-million square feet, slightly more than the 1.3 million Amazon will have when the expansion is complete. The new warehouse in Kansas will allow also allow Amazon.com to cut delivery time to Chicago, St. Louis, Dallas, and Minneapolis.[13]

The Future

While these tactical moves should make a difference, ultimately, the winner of the battle between Amazon.com and bn.com will be the one who understands that customer experience on the Internet matters most. The reason that customer experience matters most is that word of mouth is very powerful online. If a company does a great job of servicing its customers and providing them with the best possible service, these people will become evangelists, and they will help that company increase the size of its business. Turning customers into evangelists depends on creating an online service where it is easier to shop, learn more about the products, have a bigger selection, and buy at the lowest prices.

Amazon.com and bn.com each have unique advantages and disadvantages in this battle. Amazon.com clearly has a strong understanding of how to use the Internet to provide a superior customer experience. However, Amazon.com faces challenges in managing its 300 percent growth effectively. It remains to be seen whether Amazon.com has the capital, the management talent, the systems, the order fulfillment capability, and the marketing skill needed to continue this growth, even as it makes acquisitions and expands into new business lines. Bn.com is starting from a much smaller base, but it has the advantage of financial and promotional backing from Barnes & Noble and Bertelsmann. Of course, this parentage could also be a disadvantage if these bricks-and-mortar-based companies decide to limit bn.com's strategic flexibility in order to avoid cannibalizing their core business.

Principles of E-Commerce and Competitive Advantage

What general principles does this online book-selling case suggest for e-commerce and competitive advantage? To answer that, it is worth reflecting on the meaning of the oft-used concept of competitive advantage. Here I use the term to refer to a set of activities that the company performs, which enables that company to provide superior value to customers. Often, competitive advantage in an industry can be measured by the company's long-term return on capital relative to its competitors. Yet, for evaluating e-commerce, such a measure is generally useless since so few e-commerce companies have actually generated any profits.

In this case, it is perhaps more useful to focus on changes in relative market share among companies in an industry. By this measure, the online book-selling case is a useful model because Amazon.com's 313 percent annual growth suggests that if this rate is sustained, it will soon surpass Barnes & Noble and bn.com in terms of its relative market share. As we saw in the case, there were very clear differences between the way Amazon.com and Barnes & Noble conducted a variety of critical activities that determine the relative levels of customer satisfaction with the book-purchasing experience.

Thinking about the differences between new entrants and incumbents in the online book-selling industry suggests eight general principles for e-commerce and competitive advantage. In describing these principles, I will start by showing how they are derived from the case study, and conclude by drawing more general implications for senior executives seeking to use e-commerce for competitive advantage.

e   ***The Internet is the grain of sand, not the pearl.*** Oysters make pearls by forming calcium deposits around grains of sand that seep inside their shells. For Jeff Bezos, the grain of sand was the Internet's growth rate. Bezos conducted exhaustive industry analysis to figure out which product(s) would be best suited to selling on the Internet. His choice of books reflected his idea that competitive success in online book-selling would depend heavily on multiple sources of advantage, many of which were land-based, not virtual. The pearl was the cumulative impact of all these sources of advantage that enabled Amazon.com to grow at a 300 percent annual rate. Executives seeking competitive advantage from e-commerce need to think with a clean slate about how the Internet might transform their industry.

Competitive advantage in e-commerce begins with understanding the customer. It is both rare and effective for any company to focus all its capital and people on enhancing the customer's experience. A comparison of Amazon.com with bn.com indicates that consumer focus is not easy to replicate. For example, Amazon.com's site contains more useful customer information than bn's, such as book reviews, customer comments, author interviews, and recommendations. Concern about other details, such the appearance of CD jewel cases, reflect Amazon.com's focus on continuously improving the customer experience. Executives seeking advantage from e-commerce must think along similar lines about how their company might change its processes to serve customers more effectively.

Competitive advantage in e-commerce depends on gaining insight into how the company can use the Internet to take advantage of the forces that drive industry profit potential. Amazon.com realized that online book-selling could alter specific drivers of book-selling industry profit potential. For example, by gaining access to more than a million online book records, Amazon.com could affordably offer consumers access to many more titles—thereby enhancing the variety of selection. Similarly, because Amazon.com was online, it could remain open twenty-four hours a day, seven days a week—thereby increasing customer convenience. The cumulative effect of these capabilities was to enable Amazon.com to add large numbers of customers quickly, and subsequently build switching costs with them. This effect made it possible for

Amazon.com to keep its customers loyal—thereby generating repeat purchases. Executives seeking advantage from e-commerce should similarly consider how they can use the Internet to harness the forces of industry profit potential on their company's behalf.

e *Incumbents enjoy certain advantages when they attempt to engage in e-commerce.* Despite the advantages of being a new entrant into e-commerce, incumbents usually enjoy significant inherent advantages over new entrants. For example, in its response to Amazon.com, Barnes & Noble has been able to take advantage of its longstanding relationships with publishers. The competitive benefit of these relationships is that in many cases, Barnes & Noble can purchase large volumes of books directly from the publisher, thereby lowering its unit costs and enabling it to set lower prices than Amazon.com, where appropriate.

Executives seeking to exploit their own inherent sources of advantage should understand the requirements for competitive success in e-commerce, and compare their companies' capabilities with those of competitors. These executives should base their e-strategy on those capabilities that their company can perform better than new entrants and other competitors.

e *Incumbents must also overcome certain disadvantages if they wish to profit from e-commerce.* Incumbents must recognize and overcome their inherent disadvantages. For example, it took a full two years for Barnes & Noble to launch a Web site after Amazon.com began its online operations. It is common for incumbents to deny the significance of competition from the e-channel until the upstart competitors have made significant progress. Part of the slow response is due to hope that the upstart will fail. Part of the slow response is due to the reluctance to change fundamentally the company's business processes. For example, the emergence of online selling creates a new distribution channel that is perceived internally as creating a new competitor for the incumbent channels' commissions.

Unless senior management pushes hard to overcome internal resistance, e-commerce initiatives will fail. One possible solution is to set up the Internet channel as a separate legal entity that is managed as a separate business unit. Whether this works effectively for bn.com remains to be seen.

e **The Internet upstart must exploit its advantages and compensate for its disadvantages.** As with any competitive situation, it is essential for the Internet startup to have an objective understanding of its advantages and disadvantages. Amazon.com recognized its advantages in book-selling quite clearly. While it obviously had superior systems and customer service capabilities, it built an order fulfillment capability for the purpose of delivering customer orders quickly and accurately, as its Web site enabled customers to place orders.

With its entry into new products such as CDs, videos, auctions, and others, it remains to be seen whether Amazon.com will have the full range of capabilities needed to compete effectively in all these seemingly distinct markets. In particular, marketing and promotion is essential for competitive success in order to establish the company as the clear market leader. Over time, it will become more obvious whether Amazon.com can establish itself as such with regard to all these new products and services.

Executives seeking to defend themselves against such upstarts can benefit strategically from doing an objective analysis of the upstart's competitive strengths and weaknesses. As mentioned earlier, it makes sense to build the company's strategy around capabilities that matter to customers and good company performance.

e **Incumbents and upstarts must anticipate and respond effectively to new competitors.** While it is important to be aware of what competitors are doing, it is more important to focus on how customers perceive the relative value of competitors' products and services. A company should not feel compelled to replicate every strategic move of a competitor. In many cases, a competitor may be moving in a direction that does not create superior value for customers. In such cases, competitive mimicry could degrade the company's position in the eyes of customers, thereby leading to a loss of market share and the misallocation of corporate resources.

e ***On the Internet, no advantage is sustainable.*** As the online book-selling case suggests, no advantage in e-commerce is truly sustainable. New business strategies for creating superior customer value can emerge from incumbents and upstarts. It is often impossible to predict or foresee what the next greatest idea will be. This rapid pace of change puts a premium on management's ability to adapt. Executives seeking to use e-commerce to create competitive advantage should not embark down this path unless they truly believe that they are sufficiently adaptable to keep pace with the rapid changes in business models that characterize the world of e-commerce.

A Methodology for Using E-Commerce to Create Competitive Advantage

How can senior managers, including the CFO, harness e-commerce to create competitive advantage? Based on the experiences of successful e-commerce strategies and Peter S. Cohan & Associates' consulting experience, I have developed a methodology that companies can apply to the challenge of using e-commerce to create competitive advantage. This methodology has several benefits for senior executives:

- It forces senior executives to confront the fundamental strategic issues raised by the e-commerce technology. As a result, it is more likely that companies will be able to implement their strategies, and thereby achieve tangible performance improvements.
- It is based on rigorous analysis of customers, competitors, and the company's own capabilities. Therefore, there is much less of a chance that the company will be blindsided by unexpected threats or mismatches between its strategy and the needs of the marketplace.
- It provides a solid foundation for creative thinking about new strategies.

- It can be completed quickly enough so that the company can take advantage of the e-commerce opportunity without taking so long to implement the strategy that the company is likely to miss an opportunity.
- It recognizes that all advantages in Internet competition are provisional, and that the company must remain ever-vigilant about adapting to changing customer needs and competitor strategies.

Here is the nine-step methodology:

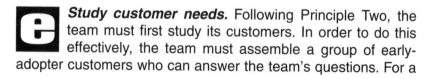 *Form an e-commerce strategy team.* Unlike some IT-related initiatives, e-commerce strategy depends on the support of operating and staff managers. Typically, an e-commerce strategy team can be either a corporate strategy initiative, driven by the CEO, or a business unit initiative that is led by the line manager responsible for the results of a specific business unit. As we saw with Cisco Systems, the idea for e-commerce may originate at a lower level in the organization. However, it cannot succeed unless a team is assembled, which includes the CEO and/or business unit manager, key functional managers, IT managers, and early-adopter customers.

Building an effective e-commerce strategy team depends on strong support from the CEO. With such support, the many obstacles that I alluded to earlier have a better chance of being overcome. The team should generally be led on a day-to-day basis by a management consultant who can provide the tools and the processes to help the team achieve its objectives. The team should also include a client project manager who is devoted full-time to seeing that the e-commerce strategy project succeeds. As with all such projects, the rest of the company will judge the importance of the project by the quality of the people involved and the impact that successful project completion has on their post-project careers.

Study customer needs. Following Principle Two, the team must first study its customers. In order to do this effectively, the team must assemble a group of early-adopter customers who can answer the team's questions. For a business-to-business product, for example, the team should get answers to questions such as:

- How much of the company's products have customers bought, and how has that purchase pattern changed over time?
- What process have the customers gone through to evaluate potential suppliers of the product?
- Who, within the customer organization, participated in the purchase process, and what were their respective levels of influence in the purchase process?
- What criteria were used to select the winning supplier, and what were the relative importance of these criteria?
- How did the various candidate vendors perform relative to these criteria?
- Why was the winning company selected?
- What are the unmet needs or sources of continuing dissatisfaction with the current product or service?
- How would the customer design the ideal online purchase process?

Using the results of this customer research, the company can begin to formulate ideas about specific opportunities for improving the customer experience.

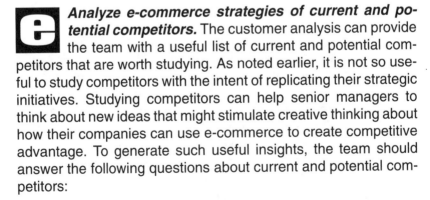 *Analyze e-commerce strategies of current and potential competitors.* The customer analysis can provide the team with a useful list of current and potential competitors that are worth studying. As noted earlier, it is not so useful to study competitors with the intent of replicating their strategic initiatives. Studying competitors can help senior managers to think about new ideas that might stimulate creative thinking about how their companies can use e-commerce to create competitive advantage. To generate such useful insights, the team should answer the following questions about current and potential competitors:

- Who are the customers that the competitor is targeting?
- What specific customer needs is the competitor attempting to serve?

- What capabilities does the competitor leverage to provide superior value to its target customers?
- Is the competitor using e-commerce as a means of enabling any of these capabilities?
- If so, how does e-commerce create advantage for the competitor?
- How is the competitor likely to use e-commerce in the future to extend its market position?
- What can the team learn from the competitor that could be useful in the formulation of the company's e-commerce strategy?

The team may find it particularly useful to map the insights generated from the analysis of the competitors' e-commerce strategies against the most critical unmet customer needs generated during the analysis here in step three. Such a mapping process may help the team discover potentially exploited opportunities for new and effective e-commerce strategies.

e *Identify capabilities needed to provide superior customer value.* In this stage, the team should synthesize the analysis of steps two and three. The synthesis draws information gathered in the previous steps, but sequences and analyzes the information in a new way. This synthesis should integrate the answers to the following questions:

- What are the ranked customer purchase criteria that customers use to determine who wins their business? How do customers evaluate potential suppliers, including the company, relative to these customer purchase criteria?
- Which company offers customers the best performance on each of these criteria?
- What capabilities do the winning companies have that enables them to win on these criteria?
- What is unique about the way the winning company manages and develops these capabilities in order to provide superior customer value?
- How would the company need to manage and develop these capabilities in order to provide customer value that

was measurably superior to the way the leading competitor performs them?

Based on this analysis, the team can develop a specific vision of the capabilities that it potentially needs to win with e-commerce.

e *Perform a strategic audit of capabilities needed to provide superior customer value.* This list of capabilities will provide managers with the basis for conducting a strategic audit. With the help of an outside party, the team should develop an assessment of how well it performs the capabilities needed to provide superior customer value. The strategic audit should include the following elements:

- A list of capabilities needed to use e-commerce to create competitive advantage.
- A detailed description of the ideal approach to performing each of these capabilities in order to win in the marketplace.
- A description of how the company currently performs each of these activities, if at all.
- A summary score that characterizes how well the company performs these activities relative to the ideal approach. The scores might range from 5 (far outperforms the ideal) to 1 (needs to improve dramatically in order to be competitive).

While these scores ultimately depend on the team's judgment, they should be based on as much objective data as the team can collect. These scores should provide the team with important insights about whether it is realistic for the company to use e-commerce for competitive advantage. In particular, this analysis should help identify key capabilities where the company will need to find partners if it is to compete effectively.

e *Envision e-commerce strategic options.* Steps two through five of the methodology involve collecting data and conducting analysis. This data and analysis provides the team with a foundation on which to develop creative ideas about how the company can use e-commerce to create competitive advantage. The team should brainstorm to develop a list of as many as five or ten strategic options for using e-commerce to create competitive advantage. These options might include using the Internet to sell products or services, purchase office supplies, provide customer service, or interact with employees. For each strategic option, the team should think through the following strategic choices:

- Name and brief description of the strategic option
- Specific performance targets that the strategic option is anticipated to achieve such as additional sales, cost reduction, improvement in customer satisfaction scores
- Target users
- Specific user needs that the strategy will target
- Level of customer satisfaction with meeting needs resulting from the strategy
- Specific capabilities needed to achieve these levels of customer satisfaction including Web site, back-end systems and processes, customer support, sales and marketing, order fulfillment, accounting and controls
- Specific partnerships, if any, needed to bolster the company's ability to perform critical capabilities
- Target competitors, reasons the strategic option will lead to superior performance relative to these competitors, and potential counter-strategies that these competitors might take
- Time to implement strategy and estimated budget and other resources required

e *Evaluate strategic options.* Once the team has envisioned a number of strategic options, it must shift back into an analytical mindset. The team must rank the strategic options, and pick the top two or three options based on criteria that it determine are most important to the company. Such criteria might be potential economic payoff, impact on customer satisfaction, impact on market share, or effect on productivity.

Select optimal strategy. Once the team has selected the top two or three strategic options, they should be evaluated in greater detail. The more detailed analysis might include an effort to develop a project plan for implementing the e-commerce strategy. This plan would be accompanied by a cash flow analysis that would include the cost of building the new strategy and the returns to the company associated with its implementation. Based on this cash flow analysis, the team could calculate the net-present-value of each option, and choose to implement the one with the highest net-present-value.

 Implement it. The team would then proceed to implement the selected strategy, a topic that I will examine in much greater detail in Part III of this book.

Conclusion

Despite the overwhelming volume of hype, the evidence on e-commerce and competitive advantage suggests that we are still discovering the extent and sustainability of the advantages that e-commerce can offer to companies. Clearly e-commerce creates a powerful, competitive dynamic between startups and incumbents. Depending on the industry, each participant in this dialectic brings certain advantages and disadvantages to the battle. If both groups of competitors focus on providing superior value to customers, then e-commerce will prove to be a tool that is valuable competitively. Executives can follow a rigorous process for developing e-commerce strategies that yield competitive advantage. Due to the rapid pace of change, all such advantages must realistically be seen as provisional.

Notes

1. Company 1998 Annual Reports.
2. Chip Bayers, "The Inner Bezos," *Wired,* March 1999 [http://www.wired.com/wired/archive/7.03/bezos.htm].
3. Karen Southwick, "Interview With Jeff Bezos of Amazon.com," *Upside,* September 30, 1996 [www.upside.com/texis/MVM/story?id=34712cl546].

4. Bayers, op. cit.
5. Kathleen Doler, "Filthy Rich," *Upside,* July 28, 1998 [http://www.upside.com/texis/MVM/story?id = 35bc9ca20].
6. Ibid.
7. Ibid.
8. Ibid.
9. Bayers, op. cit.
10. Warren Cohen, "Revenge of the Dinosaurs," *U.S. News & World Report,* April 12, 1999, p. 37.
11. Matthew Ragas, "What Makes an IPO Bestseller," *Red Herring,* August 26, 1998 [http://www.redherring.com/insider/1998/0826/books.html].
12. Ibid.
13. Steven Zeitchik, "Amazon.com to Open Its Fourth Distribution Center," *Publisher's Weekly,* April 19, 1999, p. 12.

PART II

Managing the Transition to E-Commerce

5

Getting Senior Management Online

How do you get senior executives enthusiastic about e-commerce? Many are not enthusiastic and will be out of their jobs before their lack of enthusiasm hurts their companies. Other executives are adopting a wait-and-see attitude. A small number have decided to experiment with e-commerce. Other senior executives have decided that e-commerce is the core to the future of their businesses. The short answer to the question about how to get senior executives enthusiastic about e-commerce is that it depends.

This chapter starts off by looking at some general statistics that gauge the trend in senior executive attitudes toward e-commerce. Next, the chapter examines a framework that executives can use to identify which of four types of organization they belong to with respect to the CEO's attitude toward e-commerce. Then, the chapter examines case studies of each of these types of organizations in order to explore the issues that face senior executives seeking to take advantage of e-commerce. The chapter concludes by outlining a process for getting the CEO engaged in building a new e-strategy that enables the company to maintain its competitive position against Internet-only competitors.

Senior Executive Attitudes toward E-Commerce

In general, senior executives are cautious about e-commerce in the short run but more optimistic about its potential to enhance the company's value over the longer run. According data from *Business Week* displayed in Figure 5-1, 75 percent of CEOs surveyed currently believe that e-commerce revenues are less than 5 percent of their companies' total business. However, five years from now, 20 percent of CEOs anticipate that more than 20 percent of their revenues will come from e-commerce.[1]

Even as significant growth in e-commerce is anticipated, there are important differences in the way that Internet and non-Internet CEOs perceive the economic benefits of e-commerce. According to *Business Week*, while CEOs from a wide variety of companies are becoming increasingly involved in online activities, as Figure 5-2 indicates, they approach these initiatives in different ways. Top executives from Internet-only companies tend to emphasize revenues and the number of cus-

Figure 5-1. Percentage of revenues from e-commerce anticipated by corporate CEOs (1999 and 2004).

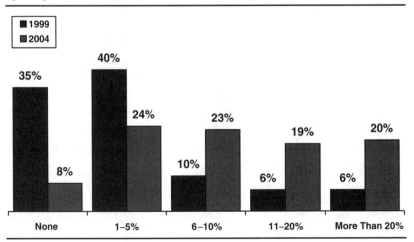

Figure 5-2. Online-only and traditional companies' perceived benefits of e-commerce.

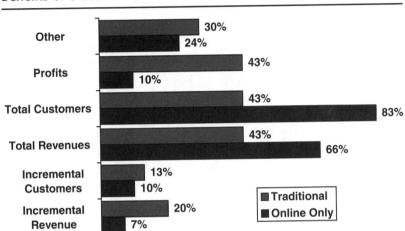

tomers. Traditional companies are more concerned with profits.[2]

In fact, it is this concern with achieving short-term payoff that may account for the strategic advantage that Internet-only companies are enjoying over their traditional counterparts—an advantage that is reflected in their higher market capitalizations as I noted in the book selling case in Chapter 4.

While executives are growing convinced of the importance of e-commerce, they have yet to take advantage of that perceived importance because they have difficulty quantifying a near-term payoff from e-commerce. According to *Information Week*, a study called *Competing in the Digital Age: Will the Internet Change Corporate Strategy?* produced by Booz-Allen & Hamilton and the Economist Intelligence Unit points out that 92 percent of the respondents in the study of 600 CEOs in twenty-four countries believe that the Internet will reshape the global marketplace by 2001.[3]

The study suggests that CEOs believe the Internet will change their corporate cultures, and help them improve tangible corporate performance. Eighty-five percent of the senior executives felt that the Internet was forcing change in their

corporate culture from hierarchical to collaborative. Sixty percent of the CEOs believed the Internet would help improve
customer satisfaction, reduce cost structures, globalize operations, foster innovation, and speed up time-to-market.

Due to the long payback period, CEOs were less likely to
act on these beliefs about the Internet's transforming potential.
For example, only 37 percent of the CEOs surveyed were from
companies that had already implemented an e-business plan.
Furthermore, while 60 percent intended to set up an "extranet" to do business with partners and customers, only 29 percent had actually done so. The reason for the implementation
gap is that 70 percent of those who are using the Internet said
that they did not expect to see a return on their investments
until 2001.[4]

One important element of the company's e-commerce
strategy is the role of the CEO. Simply put, the vast majority of
CEOs are Internet Luddites. According to a January 1999 survey of 800 CEOs in *Business Week,* fewer than 33 percent of
CEOs in the U.S. consider themselves Web-literate. Only 25
percent of the CEOs surveyed surf the Web regularly, and 69
percent describe their Internet sophistication as fair or poor.[5]

Framework for Assessing CEO Attitudes toward E-Commerce

The general lack of CEO sophistication toward the Internet actually masks some important differences among companies.
Research for this book suggests that CEO attitudes toward e-
commerce depend on two factors:

1. How much e-commerce can potentially change the
   structure of the industry or the company's relative position
2. How comfortable the CEO is with the Internet

Despite the hype, the Internet does not change everything. As
a practical matter, the Internet changes some industries more

than others. Most CEOs recognize that they must take a sober look at whether or not the Internet has the potential to be an opportunity or a threat to their competitive position and financial strength. In Chapter 4, we explored how CEOs can assess the Internet's potential for altering the company's competitive position. The actual strategic impact of the Internet is one important determinant of how the CEO should respond to the Internet.

In addition, it turns out to be quite important how comfortable the CEO is with the Internet. This comfort level is a function of several factors:

- Has the CEO personally gone online to send e-mail, buy books, track stocks, or do research?
- Does the CEO have a clear economic understanding of how the Internet can create competitive advantage for the company?
- Does the CEO trust either an internal executive or an outside partner who can help realize the economic potential of the Internet?

As Figure 5-3 indicates, the combination of these two factors—the strategic impact of e-commerce on the company and the CEO's level of comfort with the Internet—determine the CEO's attitude toward e-commerce.

Figure 5-3. Framework for assessing CEO's attitude toward e-commerce.

		High	Move Aggressively	Experiment
Strategic Impact of E-Commerce				
		Low	Be Creative	Ignore

	High	Low
	CEO Comfort with the Internet	

Here are the four possible scenarios:

- *High Strategic Impact/High CEO Comfort.* If the strategic impact of e-commerce on the company is high, and the CEO is very comfortable with the Internet, then the CEO is likely to move most aggressively to conceive and implement the use of the Internet to improve the company's competitive position and financial performance.
- *High Strategic Impact/Low CEO Comfort.* If the strategic impact of e-commerce on the company is high but the CEO is not comfortable with the Internet, then the CEO is likely to experiment with the Internet. This experimentation might take the form of setting up a separate subsidiary that does e-commerce or asking a small group within the IT department to do an e-commerce trial on a small scale.
- *Low Strategic Impact/High CEO Comfort.* If the strategic impact of e-commerce on the company is low but the CEO is very comfortable with the Internet, then the CEO is likely to try to conceive of a way that he or she can use the Internet to transform the industry. The danger of this approach is that the CEO ends up pushing a pet project that consumes resources, but does not have much of an impact on the company's competitive position. Of course, there is also a chance that the CEO's effort at creativity could yield an unexpected breakthrough.
- *Low Strategic Impact/Low CEO Comfort.* If the strategic impact of e-commerce on the company is low and the CEO is not comfortable with the Internet, then the CEO is likely to stay away from the Internet altogether. This posture could end up working effectively for CEOs in this category, unless it turns out that the Web does indeed transform everything.

Case Studies of CEO Attitudes toward E-Commerce

Using this framework, we will examine case studies of each of the four CEO attitudes toward e-commerce.

Moving Aggressively

There are many recent examples of companies whose executives became comfortable with the Internet and realized that the Internet had the potential to alter dramatically the company's competitive position.

We examine three very different examples. The Charles Schwab example shows how a forward-thinking company benefits from taking a short-term earnings hit in order to establish leadership in e-commerce because its CEO perceives the technology as so strategic. The Kosher Grocer example demonstrates how the owners of a tiny company can grab the advantages of e-commerce without using up too much capital. The CVS example shows how aggressive CEOs, who recognize the power of e-commerce to transform an industry, can form a strategic partnership that leverages the strengths of both companies.

Charles Schwab

With a market capitalization of $47 billion and a mere $3.2 billion in sales, discount broker and online trading house Charles Schwab in comparison dwarfs Merrill Lynch, which has a mere $27 billion market capitalization despite its $35 billion in sales. The stunning reality is that although Merrill is ten times larger than Schwab, the stock market assigns Merrill 57 percent of Schwab's stock market value. According to *Business Week*, Schwab's co-CEO David S. Pottruck believes it is impossible to lead a company if the CEO is not conversant and comfortable with Internet technology, and able to envision its opportunities.[6]

Pottruck knows firsthand how important Internet experience is to corporate leadership. In early 1998, Schwab decided to move its Internet business from a separate operation into the core of Schwab's financial-services strategy. Initially, this transition caused Schwab's stock and revenues to decline as it cut trading fees. The short-term pain led to long-term gain. In March 1999, 54 percent of Schwab's trades were done online—a key reason that Schwab is growing so fast. According to Pottruck, if senior management had not personally understood the Web and its potential impact on the brokerage industry, Schwab could have been left behind.[7]

Given the now obvious benefit to consumers of online trading, it is clear that the Internet has altered the structure of the brokerage industry. Merrill Lynch has spent years consumed by internal debates on what to do about the threat of the Internet to its full-service (and full-commissioned) brokers. The stock market has punished Merrill Lynch for this dawdling, assigning it a market capitalization to sales ratio of 0.78, one-nineteenth that of Schwab's 14.69 ratio. Schwab was willing to sacrifice in the short term in order to seize what its senior management perceived as an opportunity to be the leader in online brokerage. Schwab's strategic initiative has been amply rewarded.

Kosher Grocer, Inc.

Not all the CEOs who move aggressively on to the Web are heads of large, publicly traded companies. Some successful Web sellers have revenues less than $50 million. According to *Information Week*, Kosher Grocer, Inc., an online retailer whose only full-time employees are its two co-founders, is one such company. Kosher Grocer has hired an Intel/SAP joint venture, Pandesic, to host Kosher Grocer's entire computer system. This system does all Kosher Grocer's accounting. Working with Pandesic, customers pay an up-front fee of $25,000 to $100,000, then pay one percent to 4 percent of their e-commerce revenues to Pandesic. For that, Pandesic provides and hosts an e-commerce catalog and transaction-processing application based on Microsoft Site Server, as well as back-end fulfillment functions such as warehouse management, shipping, and real-time inventory updates, based on a dedicated R/3 application.[8]

Kosher Grocer's management realized that e-commerce could generate tremendous value for customers. According to Deborah Alexander, CEO and co-owner, Kosher Grocer had limited capital so structuring a deal in this way was an affordable way for the company to grow. Alexander replaced IBM's Net.Commerce with Pandesic in late 1997, primarily because Kosher Grocer did not want to invest in back-end systems. Alexander noted that in light of the rapid pace of technological change, it did not make sense for Kosher Grocer to put all its capital into the technology.[9]

Kosher Grocer is an example of a company that was clever enough to realize the benefits of e-commerce without sinking too much capital into the infrastructure needed to deploy it. Kosher Grocer was thus able to move aggressively despite its limited capital resources.

CVS

A third example of moving aggressively into e-commerce comes from the drug store industry. Here, the CEO of one of the leading land-based drugstore companies recognized that he needed to take advantage of the economic potential of the Internet to transform his $150 billion (U.S. sales) industry—$78 billion of which is in prescription drugs. According to *The Industry Standard*, in May 1999, CVS, a Rhode Island–based drug store chain purchased Seattle–based Soma.com in a $30 million, all-stock deal. This efficient transaction gave CVS, the largest drugstore chain, a head start on its rivals by enabling it to prepare for a summer 1999 launch of its e-commerce site. Soma gained access to a database of 55 million CVS customers and CVS's tie-ins with healthcare providers. In January 1999, Soma became the first online pharmacy to launch.[10]

CVS's CEO, Tom Ryan, saw the strategic importance of the Internet to the drug store industry, and he also felt personally comfortable with the Internet, so he moved aggressively. According to *The*

Wall Street Journal, buying Soma allowed CVS to open a full-service online pharmacy in the summer of 1999, instead of in November as previously planned. Ryan understood that a three-month acceleration in time-to-market was worth the $30 million investment. The benefit of opening the Web site earlier was particularly important in forming alliances with Internet portals that could funnel people to CVS's Web site. Ryan said that he planned to market the online service aggressively to add new customers and to increase the loyalty of existing ones.[11]

Ultimately, it was clear that CVS was paying for Soma people. According to *The Industry Standard*, Soma planned to operate as a separate subsidiary of CVS. The Soma executive core would continue to run the company out of its Seattle headquarters. Soma CEO Tom Piggott, a 30-year-old with a 75 percent stake in Soma, certainly believed that CVS was buying people. Piggott expected to report to CVS executive VP of Corporate Development Larry Zigarelli, one of the primary architects of the Soma acquisition.[12]

Clearly, CVS's CEO Tom Ryan saw the benefit of the deal to Soma as well. Soma and its peers, PlanetRx and Drugstore.com, lack access to the thousands of healthcare providers that cover customers' prescriptions. Since 75 percent of prescriptions filled are covered by some type of insurance plan, such access is crucial. Ryan estimated that Soma would get access to twice as many insurance plans after the deal was consummated.

Ryan also recognized that Soma.com would be able to expand its nonprescription business as well. From its inventory, CVS would add an additional 7,000 products and services to Soma including over-the-counter medication, CVS's private label pills, and vitamins. Through CVS, Soma would add a photo-finishing service for customers. Once the site went online, Ryan expected that Soma customers would be able to order from the site and have products either delivered to their homes or available for pickup at any one of the 4,100 CVS locations. Soma would also benefit from CVS's $200 million annual marketing budget. Initially, Ryan planned to include Soma's logo on CVS shopping bags, store circulars and mailings, and TV commercials.

The Soma deal gave CVS its first access to customers west of the Mississippi River. Ryan noted that the transaction enabled CVS to reach customers where it does not have stores, such as southern Florida or Arizona, where some CVS customers spend parts of their year.[13]

The CVS/Soma deal shows how important moving quickly can be in the e-commerce business. CVS's CEO recognized that the Internet could create many benefits for his company's customers, but that a mere three-month time-to-market advantage could be crucial to the success of CVS's e-commerce initiative. In light of the extraordinary prices paid for other health-related e-commerce companies—as we saw in Chapter 3 with WebMD—CVS's purchase of Soma as a means to gain that three-month time-to-market advantage may have been a bargain.

The "Experiment" Approach

Many companies are more prone to experiment with e-commerce because their CEOs are skeptical about the Internet. These CEOs are torn between hoping that the Internet hoopla will disappear and being afraid that the Internet is real, and that if they do not do something about it, they might lose their jobs. In some cases, CEOs may simply be uncertain about how best to take advantage of e-commerce, so they sponsor different kinds of e-commerce experiments, hoping to learn how to use e-commerce to enhance profits without undermining the company's accumulated advantages.

W. W. Grainger

One example of this approach comes from the industrial supply industry. According to *Information Week*, W. W. Grainger, a $4.1 billion industrial supplier based in Lincolnshire, Illinois, has been experimenting with e-commerce. Daniel Hamburger, President of Grainger Internet Commerce, notes that many companies are struggling with the issue of what to do about e-commerce. W. W. Grainger launched a commerce-enabled Web site in 1996, then created the separate online unit in 1997. In 1999, W. W. Grainger promoted Hamburger from Vice President to President, a move that emphasized the importance W. W. Grainger is placing on e-commerce.[14]

Having a senior executive in the right position on the organizational chart can make a substantial difference in how effective that person can be as an internal advocate for e-commerce. Without direct access to top executives, it is often too difficult for vice presidents of e-commerce to educate senior executives about the Internet and what they need to do in order to take advantage of it.

This executive power is particularly important because the Web cuts horizontally across traditional areas such as sales, marketing, and IT. As a result, many companies, including W. W. Grainger, have set up committees to coordinate their Web strategies. Hamburger notes that the Internet business cannot be run by committee. However, committees are required to get the Web site built. For example, Hamburger noted that W. W. Grainger has cross-functional project teams that carry out Internet projects.[15]

The W. W. Grainger example shows how companies can experiment with e-commerce productively. After Hamburger proved that his e-commerce unit was adding value to W. W. Grainger, he was promoted into an executive position. Despite the progress of the experiment, it remains clear that W. W. Grainger still views e-commerce as only a part of its business. While this approach may make good economic sense, W. W. Grainger may need to continue to evolve, depending on how much market share the company's e-commerce only competitors are able to take.

Chase Manhattan

The experiment approach is also found quite commonly in the banking industry. According to *Information Week*, Chase Manhattan has numerous e-commerce experiments underway with its corporate clients. Chase Manhattan is finding that the composition of the corporate groups that participate in these e-commerce experiments has broadened as executives realize how the Internet has affected every part of Chase Manhattan. Richard Erario, executive in charge of Chase Manhattan's Technology Greenhouse, a group that works with Chase Manhattan's corporate clients to develop new technologies, pointed out that in 1997, it was very difficult to assemble the people he needed to make e-commerce decisions at the bank.[16]

During 1998, Erario saw management control of a client's Web initiatives shift from marketing to IT (information technology) personnel. Now, as e-commerce expands, financial people increasingly become involved. When Erario goes to talk to organizations, he increasingly finds a wide variety of people involved, from Webmasters to CFOs. Erario notes that cross-functional groups are likely to have sounder e-commerce strategies, but they take longer to get work done. Erario has found that the challenge for Chase's clients is to build effective e-commerce steering committees, and coordinate information throughout their companies.[17]

The Chase Manhattan example demonstrates a real danger of the "experiment" approach to e-commerce. Companies can spend all their time worrying about who is responsible for what element of e-commerce, and ultimately never get anything meaningful accomplished. The result of all the dithering is that companies wait until a compelling external stimulus such as the loss of a major client or an unexpected plunge in revenue forces them to focus externally on improving their competitiveness. As Erario noted, the involvement of different functions in the e-commerce strategy can yield a more integrated result even as it slows down meaningful accomplishment. Ultimately, it is the commitment of the company's CEO to take advantage of e-commerce that makes the difference between dawdling and victory.

The "Be Creative" Approach

As I noted earlier, not all industries are equally good candidates for the adoption of e-commerce. In some cases, an industry that would appear to have very limited potential to be transformed by the Internet can benefit from a CEO who believes in the power of technology to transform even the most mundane business.

Cemex

An example of the power of the "Be Creative" approach comes from an unlikely location—the Mexican cement industry. The thought of cement makes people think of slow-moving ready-mix cement trucks. According to *Business Week*, Cemex, the third-largest cement producer in the world, uses high technology to help make it a low-cost producer. Since 1989, Cemex, led by CEO and technology evangelist Lorenzo Zambrano, has invested $200 million in computer systems that allow executives access to information on many business variables. The systems give executives information on inventory, delivery schedules, quality records, and oven temperatures at Cemex' operations in Spain, Venezuela, Colombia, Panama, the Philippines, Indonesia, or the U.S.[18]

Currently Cemex is using the Internet to link clients, suppliers, customs agents, and Cemex executives. In 1998, Cemex started using an Internet-based program for its customs brokers, which allows the agents and Cemex to share information on the status of arriving supplies, customs duties to be paid, and departing cement shipments. The system lets them anticipate costs and plan product shipments.

In June 1999, Cemex's twenty-five-person information technology department launched a broader, pilot program, which links clients, product distributors, and suppliers to Cemex. Distributors use the system to know the timing of shipments; Cemex will have access to information on a client's payment record and on the timeliness of deliveries.

Because timing is important in the cement business, the system's ability to provide clients with information on their shipment of packaged cement or ready-mix concrete is extremely valuable. In major Mexican cities, Cemex's ready-mix concrete trucks carry computers on board, and are tracked by global-positioning satellite systems. Clients can find out exactly where a delivery truck is stuck in traffic so they can plan their cement-pouring processes.

By early 2000, Cemex intends to introduce online sales to clients, probably starting with ready-mix concrete. Alejandro Garcia, Director of Informatics Planning at Cemex, notes that Cemex is moving toward electronic commerce, and wants to use the technology to bring benefits to clients.

To date, Cemex customers have been reluctant to use e-commerce. Gelacio Iniguez, Cemex's Director of Information Technology, noted that since security concerns have been resolved through the use of encryption technology. The main hurdle he faces is persuading customers to use online business. Iniguez notes that some companies want to move to the new technology quickly while others are not even close to being ready. In lesser-developed countries, Cemex will work with selected companies that are able to handle the new technology.

The Internet has already changed Cemex's business. In 1989, Cemex built an internal communications network. Due to the speed and cost-savings of Internet connections, Cemex distributes software applications and data to 8,300 PCs worldwide. That has increased the use of its communications network by executives and employees.

Cemex was one of the first multinational companies to use the

Web. In late 1995, Cemex created a corporate Web site. In addition to providing financial information about the company for analysts and investors, Cemex's Web site benefits clients by including a link to a catalog describing the different properties of cement and concrete for specialty uses.

Cemex's pilot program will streamline Cemex business activities using push technology, which that delivers information via the Internet to employees' computers. Cemex is developing programs that will give different business divisions access to their colleagues in related departments around the world. Division community members will have access to prices, business plans, news reports relevant to their business, and daily information on commodity prices that might affect their profitability.

Cemex's technology department looks for new uses of the technology. For example, it has introduced technology to keep expense accounts for Cemex executives. They can file the reports via the Internet to beat monthly accounting deadlines that might pass while they are away on a business trip.

Access to Cemex's internal network has made new acquisitions less difficult. Cemex's acquisition due diligence teams include an information technology expert, who provides access to Cemex's database regarding previous purchases. According to Homero Resendes, Manager of Cemex's Center for Business Practices, this access helps the due diligence team to know the total cost of ownership for Cemex.

The Cemex example demonstrates how the "Be Creative" strategy can help transform a company that may not be able to benefit as dramatically from e-commerce as other industries such as book selling. Because the CEO of Cemex is such a strong proponent of technology in general, and the Internet in particular, he has been able to find many ways to use the Internet to create many small advantages, the cumulative effect of which is to help Cemex to maintain its position as one of the leading cement companies in the world.

The "Ignore Approach"

There are many executives who have no interest in the Internet. But their lack of interest may not harm their companies because it is somewhat difficult to see how the Internet could alter the structure of the industry.

Astoria Financial

One example of a company with a CEO who had no interest in the Internet is Astoria Financial. According to *Business Week*, George L. Engelke, Jr., is the 60-year-old Chairman, President, and CEO of Astoria Financial Corp., a $20 billion thrift in Lake Success, New York. Engelke has no computer in his office, and does not plan on getting one. He says his work is unrelated to opening accounts or processing mortgages. Even voice mail, he says, is overrated, since it is far less customer-friendly than a real person. For tasks that require technical assistance, Engelke says he relies on his computer-trained staff or the use of a calculator he obtained fifteen years ago. In Engelke's view, the biggest role for an executive is to be a devil's advocate. Engelke notes that the PC does not have a "devil's advocacy key."[19]

Is Engelke simply too old to change his ways or does he understand intuitively that the Internet is not right for every industry and every company? Perhaps a little of both. Clearly he does not see the Internet as an important factor in changing the way the CEO performs his work. Whether the Internet could be used to change the structure of the mortgage banking industry may depend on how much market share the online mortgage processing companies end up taking over the next several years. It could be that by the time Engelke reaches retirement age, it will be time for Astoria Financial to adapt to e-mortgages or perish.

Engaging the CEO in E-Strategy

To engage the CEO in e-strategy, it matters which of the four types of organizations you belong to. In "Ignore" organizations, it is not likely that much progress will be made. In "Experiment" organizations, it is likely to be constructive to start off by educating senior executives on e-commerce. In "Be Creative" or "Move Aggressively" organizations (see Figure 5-3), it is more useful to spend time on the e-strategy formulation process.

Having said that, we will now examine a four-step process for getting the CEO engaged in setting the company's e-strategy:

Identify an Internet-only competitor that is growing rapidly in the company's market. While some CEOs may tend to dismiss the importance of small, new competitors as if they were gnats, other CEOs understand history and the potential for such small competitors to come out of nowhere and dominate an industry.

For example, Microsoft's Bill Gates realized, somewhat late, that Netscape's Web browser represented both a threat and an opportunity. Gates saw that if Netscape's browser went unchallenged from Microsoft, then people might stop purchasing Microsoft's cash cow, its Office software. Gates also wanted a piece of Netscape's extraordinarily high ratio of stock market capitalization to sales.

So, in 1995, Gates launched an aggressive effort to build a competing browser that would take away market share from Netscape. This battle culminated in America Online's takeover of Netscape in 1999 after Netscape was unable to survive Microsoft's assault.

Examples such as Microsoft's attack on Netscape are relatively rare. More frequently, executives in a traditional industry remain surprised by the success of their Internet-only competitors. If, however, the CEOs can recognize that these upstarts may prove dangerous to the company in the future, then the CEO should see that the upstart is worth studying now in order to open the company to a new way of thinking about how best to sustain its competitive position.

 Study the most dangerous Internet-only competitor's management and strategy. Once the CEO has decided to study its most dangerous Internet-only competitor, the company must decide what it needs to know and how it will get the information. In general, the company must obtain answers to the following questions about its Internet-only competitor:

- Which segment of the company's customers is the competitor targeting?
- Which customer needs does the competitor believe it can serve better than the company?
- What is the competitor's strategy for providing the company's customers with a superior value proposition?
- What advantages does the competitor have that would be difficult for the company to replicate?
- Where is the competitor vulnerable to the company's counterattack?

To answer these questions, the company must study the Internet-only competitor in some detail. This study could include reviewing the company's financial statements, if it is publicly traded, and studying the company's customers, strategies, management, and sources of advantage. While understanding each of these components of the competitor's strategy can be valuable, what is most useful for the company is to understand how the competitor is thinking about taking market share away from the company.

Set up teams to "war game" the company's competition with the Internet-only competitor. The best way to unlock the company's thinking about its competitive strategy is to set up two teams of business executives. One team plots the company's strategy against the Internet-only competitor. The other team plots the competitor's strategy against the company. This process is helped if a third party can model the market share and financial implications of various competitive strategy options developed by the two teams.

As the CEO observes the presentations of the two teams and the results of their strategies, it becomes increasingly clear that many of the company's assumptions about its competitive position may be less solid than had been assumed. While the insights from each company's "war gaming" session will be different, here are some possible insights that could unblock the CEO's thinking about the impact of the Internet-only competitor on the company:

- Customers perceive the competitor's value proposition to be so compelling that the revenue growth rate and market share of the Internet-only competitor could exceed that of the company in the next few years.
- The company's capital and management structure actually put the company at a competitive disadvantage because the perceived need to protect the existing structure makes it difficult for the company to cannibalize its existing businesses.
- The company's compensation system makes it very unlikely that it will be able to attract and retain the kinds of smart, aggressive, and technically savvy employees that dominate the employee population of the Internet-only competitor.
- Unless the company takes aggressive and relatively radical action, it will not be possible for the company to maintain its competitive position.

e ***Create a new e-strategy for the company based on the insights from the "war gaming" effort.*** If the war gaming effort generates these kinds of insights, the CEO will be faced with the need to develop an e-strategy. This e-strategy could lead the CEO to take initiatives such as the following:

- Create a separate unit, possibly with its own stock that can be used to compensate the unit's employees, which is dedicated to developing an e-strategy with the potential to cannibalize the company's existing business model.

- Hire a CEO for that unit who has prior experience starting and building a successful Internet startup.
- Give the new CEO the resources needed to hire a management team with depth, and the ability to develop and implement an e-strategy that blocks the growth of the Internet-only competitor.

Conclusion

Engaging senior management in e-strategy is absolutely crucial if a company is to use the Internet to improve its competitive position. The company's posture toward e-commerce will depend on the CEO's level of comfort with the Internet and e-commerce's potential to alter the company's competitive position. The evidence suggests a substantial gap between CEO's hopes for e-commerce and their actual implementation of e-commerce. Understanding the strategies of Internet-only competitors can unfreeze the CEOs thinking about how best to compete in e-commerce. This unfreezing can help the CEO to build a new e-strategy that may enhance the company's competitive position.

Notes

1. Geri Smith, "Concrete Benefits From a Plunge Into Cyberspace," *Business Week,* April 20, 1999 [http://www.businessweek.com/ebiz/index.-html].
2. Ibid.
3. Eileen Colkin and Clinton Wilder, "CEOs Recognize Internet's Impact, Study Says," *Information Week,* May 21, 1999 [http://www.informationweek.com/story/IWK1999052/].
4. Ibid.
5. Linda Himelstein, "Log On, Boss," *Business Week,* March 22, 1999 [http://www.businessweek.com/ebiz/index.html].
6. Ibid.
7. Ibid.
8. Clinton Wilder, "A Piece of the E-Sales Action—Pandesic's Much Maligned Model May Start paying Off for Its Parent Companies and Its

Startup," *Information Week,* March 29, 1999 [http://www.techweb.com/se/directlink.cgi?IWK1999032950037].

9. Ibid.

10. Bernhard Warner, "CVS Buys Soma.com in E-Commerce Play," *The Industry Standard,* May 18, 1999 [http://www.thestandard.net/articles/display/0,1449,4590,00.html?home.tf].

11. Laura Johannes, "CVS Agrees to Buy Soma.com for $30 Million in Stock Deal," *The Wall Street Journal,* May 18, 1999 [http://www.interactive.wsj.com/articles/SB926952602933006755.htm].

12. Warner, op. cit.

13. Ibid.

14. Gregory Dalton, "Web-Organized—The Net Is Changing Corporate Structures and Management," *Information Week,* January 25, 1999, p. 71.

15. Ibid.

16. Ibid.

17. Ibid.

18. Smith, op. cit.

19. Himelstein, op. cit.

6

Evaluating Potential Applications

There is no one best way to evaluate potential e-commerce applications. The research for this book suggests that the methods for evaluating e-commerce applications depend heavily on whether the company is trying to reinvent itself to maintain market leadership or seeking to avoid change by preserving its existing business methods. If the company is trying reinvent itself, it has different intellectual constraints than do companies trying to avoid change. One thing that emerges clearly from the research is that e-commerce is a force that cuts to the core of every company's business model. It is impossible for managers to consider potential e-commerce applications without examining how they create value for customers in a new light.

This chapter explores how companies evaluate potential e-commerce applications. Chapter 6 then organizes our thinking about this topic by discussing the different intellectual constraints faced by self-reinventors versus the change avoiders. The chapter then explores two cases that exemplify the different approaches to evaluating e-commerce applications: Citigroup, a self-reinventor, and Merrill Lynch, a change avoider. From these cases, I will describe specific principles for evaluating e-commerce applications. The chapter concludes by outlining a process for evaluating potential e-commerce applications that incorporates these principles.

E-Commerce, Self-Reinventors, and Change Avoiders

The means of evaluating e-commerce applications depends on whether a company is a self-reinventor or a change avoider. Change avoiders impose organizational constraints that limit their e-commerce options. Conversely, self-reinventors adapt to changing customer needs, thereby widening their latitude in evaluating e-commerce options. As a result, change avoiders and self-reinventors have different criteria for evaluating e-commerce applications.

How can you tell which type of company you belong to? Change avoiders have the following characteristics:

- They have become very successful using business models that are being attacked by e-commerce upstarts.
- They are being led by CEOs who are very concerned about defending these business models.
- Their CEOs have a financial incentive to preserve their companies' old business models.
- They are personally unfamiliar with information technology, and tend to delegate it to others.

Change avoiders tend to screen out many e-commerce options based on these organizational values. In particular, change avoiders will screen out e-commerce options with the following characteristics:

- They enable customers to obtain better service at a lower price.
- They lower the commissions of the traditional sales force.
- They result in the company incurring a temporary drop in sales and/or profits as the market adjusts to the new business model.
- They require a significant investment in new infrastructure with a payoff that is difficult to quantify.

Change avoiders do not screen out all e-commerce options, however. They tend to be dragged into e-commerce rather than recognizing it as a new opportunity. Change avoiders are more inclined to approve e-commerce applications with the following characteristics:

- They channel new customers into the traditional business model.
- They preserve the existing pricing structure and commission model.
- They reduce the cost of "back office" functions that the CEO views as nonstrategic.
- They provide short-term, quantifiable economic payoff.

Self-reinventors are less common and have very different characteristics, including:

- They firmly believe that it is better to attack their existing business model than to allow competitors to do so.
- They are led by CEOs who are very concerned about keeping competitors from gaining access to their customers.
- Their CEOs have a financial incentive to reinvent the company in order to sustain rapid profit growth.
- Their CEOs are personally open to learning more about e-commerce if that is what is necessary to maintain the strategic initiative in their industry.

While change avoiders screen out options based on their organizational values, self-reinventors tend to screen in many e-commerce options based on these organizational values. In particular, self-reinventors seek out e-commerce strategic options with the following characteristics:

- They have the potential to lead to massive increases in sales and market share.
- They are likely to tilt the basis of competition in favor of the company's competitive strengths.

- They may require a series of moderate investments in infrastructure that will be adjusted based on market reaction.
- They represent a series of bold, proactive initiatives rather than a tentative experiment.

In practice, many organizations display the characteristics of both change avoiders and self-reinventors. It is important for executives to realize that the way they will evaluate e-commerce options will depend on which of these two types their organization most closely resembles.

Case Studies

To demonstrate the importance of this distinction, let us examine the case of a self-reinventor, Citigroup, and a change avoider, Merrill Lynch.

Citigroup's e-Citi

While Citigroup was formed through the merger of Citicorp and Travelers, Citicorp has been known as a global leader throughout much of its history. Its recent global scale is impressive. According to *Information Week*, Citigroup had 1998 revenue of $76.43 billion and net income of $5.8 billion. Citigroup has 170,000 employees. It has 100 million consumer banking customers in five U.S. states and fifty-seven countries. It also has 1,700 corporate customers in 100 countries being serviced through 1,100 branches worldwide.[1]

The case of how Citigroup is building e-Citi illustrates the traits of a self-reinventor and the way these traits shape the self-reinventor's approach to evaluating e-commerce options. As we examine e-Citi, look for the organizational value that Citigroup places on market leadership and customer growth. This emphasis on growth gives e-Citi the freedom to explore a fundamental reinvention of what a bank means in the age of the Internet.

Citigroup is aggressively developing online banking. Despite the turmoil caused by the ongoing integration of Citicorp and Travelers, Citigroup's move into online banking is proceeding quickly. The reason for the rapid expansion is that Citigroup Co-Chairman John Reed remains a powerful executive to whom Senior Corporate Officer Ed Horowitz reports. And Reed is a big supporter of e-Citi.

The evidence of Citigroup's growth in online banking is impressive. According to *Information Week*, Citigroup has 300,000 U.S. customers banking on the Internet, and is adding 25,000 more each week. Horowitz says it costs Citigroup $450 a year to service a customer in branches, compared with less than $150 on the Internet. This dramatic cost difference is a just one compelling economic rationale for Citigroup's investment in e-commerce.

Citigroup's recent results reflect its broader objective of being the leader in online banking and e-commerce in the financial services industry. Citigroup also wants access to major Internet portals. However, its most ambitious goal is to expand its customer base from 100 million to 1 billion by 2012, Citigroup's 200th anniversary. While this goal is extremely ambitious, it suggests that Citigroup's tradition of market leadership is so important that it is willing to make big investments in e-commerce to preserve the value it places on leadership.

To achieve this ambitious goal, Citigroup is preparing an aggressive e-commerce strategy that involves all aspects of its organization. The e-Citi division Citigroup created in 1997 to lead its e-commerce effort is developing new products and services. e-Citi is exploring ways to make it easier for customers to interact with Citigroup. Furthermore, Citigroup's traditional IT organization is changing the infrastructure to support Citigroup's e-commerce initiatives.

While Citigroup will not eliminate branch banking, it perceives that the greatest potential for adding new customers and sustaining the loyalty of current customers will come from electronic banking and e-commerce. According to Horowitz, who is also the head of e-Citi, his group is initially building a broad electronic presence. Horowitz, who reports directly to Citigroup Co-Chairmen John Reed and Sanford Weill, is leading Citigroup's expansion plans. Horowitz came to Citigroup in 1997 after heading the interactive media division for Viacom.

Formed in 1997, e-Citi has 1,200 people, including managers, Web designers, and programmers, as well as marketing, distribution, advertising, sales, human resources, and financial personnel. As of May 1999, Citigroup had invested roughly $160 million in e-Citi. e-Citi is creating a company that performs all of Citigroup's business activities in a new way using Web technology.

e-Citi has accelerated the pace of introducing online products, services, and upgrades to quarterly "Web years." For example, e-Citi is introducing versions of the Direct Access online retail banking service with new features for savings and checking accounts, bill payment, stock trades, and credit card transactions each quarter. e-Citi plans to introduce banking, brokerage, and insurance products for the Web later in 1999. By August 1999, e-Citi plans to offer a Web-based financial and investment advisory service, Finance.com.

e-Citi's rapid pace of product introductions is motivated in part by the competitive strategies of Internet banking companies, such as Security First Network Bank and Scotiabank. However, Citigroup is studying the strategies of these competitors to ensure that e-Citi's strategy is competitively superior by tailoring Citigroup's financial services products to specific demographic groups. For example, e-Citi may create a cluster of services for married couples between 24 and 35. e-Citi is working on creating front ends for younger clients with MTV-type media qualities while maintaining Citigroup's basic account functionality.

To build relationships with more customers, and to tighten its hold over existing customers, Citigroup plans to take steps that more conservative companies would find very difficult to execute. For example, Citigroup plans to cross-sell its own banking, brokerage, and insurance services, a strategy that sounds simple in concept yet is difficult to execute because cross-selling requires more training, and demands that the cross-sellers have a financial incentive to cross-sell. Even more risky, Citigroup intends to offer products from other financial-services companies over the Web in an effort to gain customers by attracting them to Citigroup's site. The risk is that Citigroup could earn lower operating margins. These lower margins could be offset, however, by increased volume. Even as Citigroup seeks increased volume, it hopes to use Web technologies to personalize each customer's experience.

What is remarkable about the e-Citi initiative is that it is taking place at the same time as a number of other critical internal initiatives such as the effort to integrate the operations of Citibank and Travelers following their 1998 merger. Citibank and Travelers are consolidating call centers, back-office operations, and trading platforms. Citibank is adapting its IT infrastructure to support e-business, and the combined organization is dealing with year 2000 compliance activities.

e-Citi is introducing a range of services that reflect the value that Citigroup has placed on innovation and market leadership. These new services include Internet corporate banking services, Web-portal related personal finance services, electronic bill payment and presentment, an electronic wallet, and banking access via new distribution channels such as cellular phones and cable TV. Citigroup is also updating its network infrastructure and its customer service capabilities to support the addition of these news services and customers.

In May 1999, Citigroup introduced Internet corporate banking services, which it had been testing with twelve business customers. This business-to-business e-commerce system called Citibank Commerce was initially available in the Asia-Pacific region. Citibank Commerce lets users order products, monitor order status, and complete settlement and reconciliation processes. The software, which costs more than $10,000, uses smart cards, passwords, and digital certificates for security, and is tied in to the Citigroup network.

Preceding the introduction of Citibank Commerce, Citigroup

took a number of initiatives in 1998 to position itself to play a prominent role on the Web. In August 1998, Citigroup negotiated a deal with Netscape, which made Citigroup the "anchor tenant" on the Netcenter Personal Finance Channel and displayed Citigroup's brand on Netcenter's home page. The Personal Finance Channel provides financial advice, news, research reports, and interactive tools for investing and other transactions. Citigroup began offering online banking, insurance, and mortgage services on the site in the latter half of 1999.

The Netscape deal gives Citigroup a chance to attract customers from 150 countries at a much lower cost than if it had to open retail branches in all those areas. e-Citi believes that the portal is a global medium on which Citigroup can buy space and time to gain more reach into customer segments that were previously more expensive to reach. Citigroup hopes to acquire space on different types of portals focused on specific demographic groups.

In an earlier deal with Netscape, Citigroup licensed Netscape's CommerceXpert software. e-Citi is using the Netscape technology to build an electronic bill presentment and payment system. To support that effort, in September 1998, Citigroup took an equity interest in TransPoint, a bill payment service being developed by Microsoft and First Data. Citigroup began offering services through TransPoint in May 1999.

Horowitz expects electronic bill presentment will help attract customers to Citigroup's other online services. In his view, people who come to Citigroup's site will see "you have mail" and "you have bills," and that will provide a reason for customers to return to Citigroup's site each day.

e-Citi is also developing an electronic "wallet," a product that makes it convenient for users to buy goods and services on the Web by storing information that e-merchants commonly request during the transaction process. Users enter data, including name, billing and shipping addresses, and credit or debit card information, into the wallet. While Microsoft also plans to introduce an electronic wallet, Citigroup sees it as another way to attract customers. People who use the electronic wallet will be introduced to Citigroup's other services. Citigroup expected to introduce the wallet in some markets by the summer of 1999 and across the U.S. by September 1999.

e-Citi also wants to attract customers by making all electronic services available through an increasing number of distribution channels. Alan Young, a vice president of e-Citi responsible for access devices and distribution technologies, suggests that e-Citi wants to let people use any kind of device with a screen that can connect to a network to transact with Citigroup. Young wants customers to choose how they want to talk to Citigroup.

One example of a new distribution channel is the cellular phone. In 1999, Citigroup began a trial service in Singapore in partnership with carrier Mobile One, which lets users open accounts and transfer money by using cell phones equipped with screens. Citigroup plans to introduce cellular banking on a limited basis by the end of 1999. Before this system can work, however, Citigroup must complete its development of a Windows NT–based distribution architecture, initially in twenty-two countries, which will route customers to the appropriate systems. Citigroup is also creating an interface that will make it easy for customers to gain access to Citigroup's network, and is seeking out telecommunications partners to provide expertise and network facilities.

Citigroup is also developing a common networking platform among its banking, credit card, insurance, and brokerage services so that customers can switch among services while making cellular transactions. Ultimately, Young hopes to let people use their cell phones to do banking, sell stocks, and buy insurance. As long as customers can authenticate themselves, Citigroup will deliver information to them when they want it.

Citigroup is also experimenting with financial services delivered via digital cable TV using set-top boxes. Citigroup has begun discussions with cable operators to provide the service to subscribers. In December 1998, Citigroup signed a deal with TVN Entertainment, a provider of pay-per-view programming, to develop hardware and software for banking, brokerage, and insurance products.

Phase one of its project with TVN, in which the companies programmed retail banking functions onto a digital set-top box, was completed in early 1999 and is being tested by Citigroup internally. In the second phase, the companies will expand the technology to include other services. Citigroup expects to begin marketing it to cable operators worldwide in 2000. Citigroup also formed a partnership with WorldGate Communications, a provider of Internet TV over cable services. Citigroup will be the exclusive financial services provider for WorldGate's Internet/TV platform.

To support the increased number of customers that it hopes to add, Citigroup is enhancing its customer service centers. Citigroup will add automated call-routing technology, systems that give operators instant on-screen access to customer information, and multimedia systems that combine FAX, e-mail, and video.[2]

e-Citi is an example of how companies evaluate e-commerce when they are focused on wealth generation. e-Citi is working at a rapid pace, in Web years, reflecting its understanding of how fast change takes place in Internet business. Despite Citigroup's massive investment in branch banking, Citigroup is also investing in a wide array of different e-commerce initiatives that are designed to create more value for Citigroup's existing customers, and to add huge numbers of additional customers. The wide span of Citigroup's e-commerce initiatives reflects the top level push to reinvent Citigroup as a way to reconnect with its 200-year-old tradition of market leadership in the electronic age.

Merrill Lynch Direct Marketers

Few land-based companies are willing to invest as heavily in e-commerce as Citigroup. Change avoiders are more common than self-reinventors. The need to protect existing wealth and related ways of doing business is deeply ingrained in a company's thinking.

E-commerce will not change the way companies think about how to build their future. Rather, e-commerce exposes a new set of competitive vulnerabilities and strengths.

Merrill Lynch is a good example of this. Ever since brokerage commissions were deregulated in the 1970s, Merrill Lynch's business model has been under attack. The notion of the full-service broker who charges $400 to trade 500 shares of a $50 stock, and spends his or her days building up a client base is an idea that has not perished. Despite the advent of discount brokers, mutual funds, index funds, and online trading (Charles Schwab would charge $30 in for the same 500-share trade), Merrill Lynch's model has survived. In 1998, Merrill's 18,000 retail brokers helped generate $38 billion in revenues, $1.3 billion in net income, and $1.2 trillion in retail assets.

It is this notion of preserving the old way of doing things that seems to motivate Merrill Lynch's approach to evaluating e-commerce. This mentality is in stark contrast to the approach taken by Citigroup as well as Merrill's arch rival Charles Schwab. Schwab, as I noted in Chapter 5, was willing to risk cannibalizing its traditional approach to business in order to become a sizable player in the online brokerage business. The result, as I noted, is that Schwab's market capitalization is much higher than Merrill Lynch's despite Schwab's much smaller size.

In addition, rumors of Merrill's acquisition by Chase Manhattan are persistent. According to *Forbes*, Chase Manhattan's $74 billion market capitalization is more than double that of Merrill Lynch's. Chase is interested in Merrill for its equities business. Because Merrill Lynch employees own 30 percent of the company's stock, the Merrill employees would end up being major shareholders if the two companies were to combine. While a deal between the two was discussed in April 1998, the merger of Travelers and Citicorp pushed the two back together. One motivating factor was that the combined market capitalization of Travelers and Citigroup increased substantially after the deal was announced. The point is that despite surviving, Merrill Lynch's relative position has suffered so much that the company is clearly vulnerable to takeover. So the change avoider strategy can damage a company's long-term prospects.[3]

In the context of its eroding relative position, Merrill has taken measured steps in the direction of building an e-commerce strategy. For example, Merrill decided to make tentative steps in the direction of online trading because it did not want to lose customers to Schwab and E*Trade, who let consumers trade costs at less than a tenth of Merrill's commission rates. But Merrill's e-commerce strategy was a compromise between those at Merrill who rose through the ranks as full-service brokers and those who believed that Merrill could become a dinosaur if it did not create an online trading business. According to *Forbes*, Merrill Lynch Online is available to any client who wants it. By April 1999, 400,000 people had signed up. The service includes real-time audio and video to give clients news, portfolio tracking, research, and bill paying. However, except on a limited basis, clients must execute trades through their full-service brokers at high commissions.[4]

In April 1999, Merrill began letting some of its customers trade online. Specifically, 55,000 of Merrill's clients with at least $100,000 in one of two fee-based accounts were allowed to trade online through the company's "Asset Power" service. Asset Power customers can execute fifty-two trades a year for a fee of 2.25 percent, an effective commission rate of $43 per trade per $100,000 invested. A Merrill client who deposits $1 million pays 0.9 percent, or $94 per trade. This is three times what Schwab charges, and six times E*Trade's rate. In November 1998, Merrill also began giving away its research reports via the Web for anyone who would register. This tactic was intended to provide brokers with people to cold-call.[5]

Clearly, Merrill Lynch's retail e-commerce strategy is designed to create the perception that Merrill is adapting to change even as the details of the strategy are clearly intended to reinforce the continuation of the $375 million a day that Merrill's commissioned brokers bring into the company each day. Merrill wants to preserve wealth and the business approach that generated that wealth in the first place.

This desire to preserve what Merrill has achieved in the past is also reflected in its e-commerce strategy for corporate and institutional clients. For example, according to *Red Herring*, in May 1999, Merrill Lynch confirmed that it would launch a central online infrastructure targeted at its corporate and institutional clients, called Direct Markets. Merrill noted that Direct Markets would provide corporate and institutional clients with online research, analysis software, investment advice, underwriting, and trading.[6]

Merrill Lynch anticipated that the Internet could actually help to build switching costs between itself and its institutional clients. Unlike in the retail side of the business, where there was substantial competition from online brokers and discount brokers, the object of Direct Markets was to reduce the level of competition by using the Internet to make it harder for institutional and corporate clients to switch investment banks. With Direct Markets, Merrill Lynch intended to rebuild the network systems that institutional and corporate clients use to access Merrill Lynch's Corporate & Institutional Client Group (CICG) services. CICG services include buying and selling of securities, bonds, and options. Merrill's infrastructure would use a Web interface to create a common way for users to obtain security, help desk, training, and testing services. The goal of Direct Markets was to enable institutional customers to access their services through a single password.

Merrill Lynch's approach to evaluating its e-commerce activities is quite common one for companies that are change avoiders. Merrill was acutely aware of the competitive threat posed by online retail brokers who charged less than one-tenth of Merrill's commissions. Merrill weighed this competitive threat against the $375 million in customer assets being added each day through its 18,000 full-commissioned brokers. In theory, Merrill could have decided to follow the lead of Schwab, and risk lower revenues and profits by focusing exclusively on the online brokerage business while getting out of the retail brokerage business altogether. Instead Merrill Lynch decided to strike a compromise between building an online brokerage service that would compete with Schwab and E*Trade on the basis of price and service, and doing nothing at all with e-commerce. Merrill Lynch's compromise was to build an e-commerce site that would be designed to increase the volume of trading through its commissioned brokers.

Merrill Lynch applied the same logic to evaluating e-commerce options in its CICG. Here, Merrill Lynch recognized that despite the absence of price competition, the Internet could actually be used as a way of reducing competition by building switching costs with its corporate and institutional clients. These switching costs would take the form of an easier-to-use electronic interface between Merrill Lynch and its clients. This interface would make Merrill so easy to do business with that its competitors would have a more difficult time taking away Merrill's customers.

Whether Merrill's e-commerce strategy will help it survive as an independent company remains to be seen. The specter of being acquired by Chase Manhattan still looms. It is also possible that over the longer-term, Merrill Lynch's retail brokerage clients (who are of a generation that is not comfortable trading online) will die off while the younger generation goes online with the likes of Schwab or E*Trade.

Principles for Evaluating E-Commerce Applications

These cases suggest six principles for evaluating e-commerce options:

E-commerce strategy must be evaluated by senior management. E-commerce demands such fundamental reevaluation of how a company creates value for customers that it is impossible to delegate strategy evaluation below the senior executive level without threatening the company's long-term survival. In the case of Merrill Lynch, if the retail brokers had the power to decide what to do with e-commerce, Merrill might have done nothing at all. Similarly with Citigroup, the fact that Ed Horowitz reported to Citigroup Co-Chairmen Reed and Weill made it possible to approach the design and deployment of the e-Citi concept very broadly.

 E-commerce strategy evaluation demands an explicit statement of what matters most to the organization. E-commerce forces the company to be very clear about what it values. If the company does not have a rigorously articulated statement of values, then the debate over e-commerce will make it clear why it is so important to have such a statement. Simply put, if a company is more concerned about protecting what it has already created, then senior management should agree on that value as it begins to evaluate e-commerce options. Similarly, if the company is dedicated to long-term market leadership, and is willing to make short-term financial sacrifices to achieve such leadership, then senior management should agree on that value before evaluating e-commerce options. If the company is not clear about its values, then those values should be made clear before engaging in e-commerce evaluation.

The cases illustrated the importance of these values. For Merrill Lynch, it became clear that the company placed a huge value on preserving its retail brokerage network. This corporate value colored the subsequent evaluation of e-commerce projects. For Citigroup and Schwab, market leadership was clearly of paramount importance. Thus it was not as difficult for these companies to conceive and implement e-commerce options that demanded short-term investment to achieve longer-term market leadership.

 E-commerce strategy evaluation demands creative thinking that is tailored to the specific objectives of each company. As principle 2 suggests, the range of potential e-commerce options that a company is willing to consider is strongly shaped by its organizational values. The e-commerce strategy on which E*Trade depends for its existence is the kiss of death for Merrill Lynch. Merrill Lynch is thus unwilling even to discuss many e-commerce options that might make perfect sense to an outside observer. Thus the values of an organization provide clues about the constraints under which management will operate as it evaluates e-commerce options. These values also provide clues about what the organization perceives as its core competencies. If a company's self-assessment matches up with customers' perceptions, then these core competencies represent a solid basis upon which to evaluate e-commerce options.

In the case of Merrill Lynch, it may prove to be correct over the long term that its retail brokers represent an important source of advantage for the company. In this case, Merrill Lynch's retail strategy could have the intended effect of bolstering Merrill Lynch's market position. While Merrill's strategy certainly does not position Merrill to offer its customers lower commissions, it may ultimately succeed in funneling more business to its retail brokers. Therefore, Merrill Lynch's strategy is uniquely tailored to its specific objectives and values.

e ***E-commerce options must be evaluated in the context of customer value creation.*** If a company is evaluating e-commerce options in the absence of a deep understanding of customer needs, the company risks making e-commerce strategy choices that weaken its competitive position. There is a real danger that if a company does not use customer feedback as a central part of its e-commerce strategy evaluation, then it may choose e-commerce strategies that actually cost it some market share. This customer focus, or lack thereof, is so fundamental that its absence will be felt throughout the company's activities.

In the cases of Citigroup and Merrill Lynch, there is a danger that both companies' strategies are driven more by their business objectives than by the real needs and interests of specific target customers. Because Citigroup has articulated an awareness of the different needs of different demographic segments, it appears more likely that Citigroup is evaluating its e-commerce strategies in light of consumer needs. The ultimate test of both companies' e-commerce strategies is whether they ultimately produce competitively superior value for the specific market segments at which they are targeted.

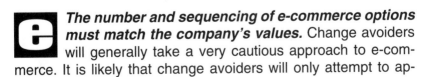 **E-commerce options must be understood in the context of current and potential competitors.** The strategies of current and potential competitors must be understood and incorporated into the process of evaluating e-commerce options. While companies must study competitors, competitors should not be the primary focus of e-commerce strategy evaluation. As principle 4 argues, superior customer value creation is the ultimate objective. In this context, the term *superior* refers to creating value for customers in a way that is better than the competition. So in evaluating e-commerce options, companies must understand in measurable terms how much value their e-commerce strategies will create for customers in the context of competitive products or services.

In this chapter's cases, competitors occupied different roles in helping Citigroup and Merrill Lynch evaluate their e-commerce strategies. For Citigroup, competitors seemed to spur on a more rapid pace of innovation. Still, Citigroup proceeded to gain an understanding of how its various e-commerce initiatives would help create superior value for customers. For example, Citigroup wanted to use the Web to appeal to the different information consumption styles of various demographic groups.

Merrill Lynch viewed competitors as dragging them into an arena that represented a real threat to its traditional way of creating value for customers. In fact, Merrill's retail e-commerce strategy provided customers with the same amount of investment-related information as competitors' Web sites while charging a far higher price than these competitors for trade execution. From a customer-value perspective, it is clear that Merrill Lynch's retail e-commerce strategy created more value for customers than before. However, it still offered customers less value for the money relative to Schwab's and E*Trade's e-commerce strategies.

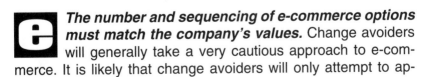 **The number and sequencing of e-commerce options must match the company's values.** Change avoiders will generally take a very cautious approach to e-commerce. It is likely that change avoiders will only attempt to ap-

prove and implement one e-commerce initiative at a time. Furthermore, the one option that the company decides to implement will be carefully conceived and executed so that if it fails, it can be eliminated without threatening the company's core sources of revenue and profit. For example, change avoiders think very carefully about what would happen if hackers attacked an e-commerce system, or what would happen if customers decided not to use the e-commerce system.

By contrast, self-reinventors will look at e-commerce as an opportunity to create a new economic order in which the self-reinventor enjoys market leadership. As a result, they will attack the new market with a series of related initiatives, all designed to achieve a common objective. Self-reinventors are willing to incur the risk that some of these e-commerce initiatives will fail. Unlike the change avoiders, self-reinventors will not look at these failures as an excuse to shut down the e-commerce system. Rather, self-reinventors will learn from the failure, and modify the system accordingly. Self-reinventors will continue to fix and experiment until they achieve success. In addition, self-reinventors are likely to pace the introduction of their strategies in "Web years," with an understanding that the pace of change and the need for innovation in the Internet business are much greater than in traditional businesses.

Methodology for Evaluating E-Commerce Applications

These principles provide a context for guiding financial executives and their senior management peers in the process of evaluating potential e-commerce applications. The proposed seven-step methodology for evaluating e-commerce applications provides the following benefits:

- *Is of a management consensus.* The process builds a consensus among senior managers regarding which e-commerce options should be pursued. Without such a consensus, it is not possible for companies to achieve meaningful results.

- *Is consistent with corporate values and mission.* By making corporate values explicit, companies can develop e-commerce options that are feasible within the confines of each company's culture. Although cultural factors can limit options, there is also a chance that cultural values will ensure that e-commerce options are based on competitive strengths.
- *Generates e-commerce options that provide superior customer value.* The process ensures that senior managers understand how the e-commerce options will meet customer needs in a competitively superior way. This benefit is achieved through customer interviews and competitor analysis.
- *Prioritizes e-commerce options based on explicit ranking criteria.* The process makes senior managers' e-commerce evaluation criteria explicit so that they can apply the criteria systematically to rank potential e-commerce options. This ranking process helps senior managers to choose which e-commerce applications to implement first.

Here is a seven-step methodology for evaluating e-commerce applications:

e **Engage senior management in the e-commerce evaluation process.** As I have noted in the methodologies outlined in previous chapters, building a senior management team is also essential for evaluating e-commerce strategy options. While it is often productive to generate e-commerce strategy options at levels below senior management (as we saw in the cases of Cisco Systems and GM), the process of evaluating the options must come from senior management consensus. Evaluation is a prelude to resource allocation, and senior management controls the resources. So in order to get to the step of actually doing something, senior management must be involved at the point of e-commerce evaluation. While the specific participants in the e-commerce evaluation team will vary by company, it is generally good to involve the CEO, CFO, CIO, and appropriate business unit managers in this evaluation process.

e ***Make corporate values explicit.*** Once the team is assembled, its first critical task is making corporate values explicit. While this may seem less than obvious, it is clear from the case studies that an explicit understanding of corporate values is an essential precondition to evaluating e-commerce options. Without a consensus on corporate values, it will ultimately be impossible for the company to agree on what e-commerce initiatives to implement. By corporate values, I mean here the enduring beliefs about the organization's fundamental purpose.

The case studies indicated that each company has different values. For Citigroup, the value was global market share leadership through corporate reinvention. For Merrill Lynch, the value was growing customer assets by strengthening the retail brokerage force. Their e-commerce evaluation criteria flowed from these values.

While corporate values flow from a process of self-evaluation that is unique to each company, here are some tests that management teams can apply to their statements of corporate value:

- Does the statement contain a broad list of corporate objectives?
- Does the statement describe how the company might achieve the objectives?
- Is the statement sufficiently general that it can be meaningful as technology and business models evolve over time?
- Does the statement motivate senior managers and their employees?

e ***Work with customers to identify ways to use e-commerce to create superior value for customers.*** Creating customer value depends on understanding the specific needs of customers who are the targets of the company's e-commerce initiatives. In addition to its values, the company should base the generation of potential e-commerce ideas on an understanding of unmet customer needs. Such unmet needs can provide the basis for e-commerce initiatives that competitors have not yet thought about. Furthermore, an understanding of customer needs might provide a useful filter for e-commerce ideas that have been generated in step 2. Simply put, if companies generate e-commerce ideas that are consistent with corporate values but do not meet customer needs, then those options should not be pursued. So understanding the needs of customers can be both a source of new e-commerce ideas and a way to filter out ideas that might otherwise be accepted.

While each company is likely to have a unique set of customers with unique needs, companies should make a list of these needs, and rank them based on their importance to their customers. Such needs might include:

- Lower prices
- Twenty-four-hour customer service
- Faster response time
- Wider product/service selection
- Customized products or services

e ***Study current and potential competitors' e-commerce strategies.*** As noted earlier in this chapter, competitors can be a useful source of ideas for potential e-commerce strategies. In the cases of Citigroup and Merrill Lynch, the strategies of new competitors have spurred the companies' e-commerce initiatives because they cost them market share. While Merrill Lynch decided to replicate part of its competitors' e-commerce strategy (e.g., the information), it neglected to match another part, the much lower commission rate. Citigroup used insights into its competitors to accelerate the pace at which it introduced e-commerce initiatives. Yet Citigroup appears determined to use technology to create superior value for the different segments of customers at which its e-commerce initiatives are targeted.

This step in the e-commerce evaluation process should result in a list of potential e-commerce strategies that are developed by following these analytical steps:

- Identify current and potential e-commerce competitors.
- Analyze competitors' e-commerce strategies by identify-

ing their business objectives, target-customer segments, target-customer needs, products and services to meet those needs, sources of competitive advantage, marketing strategies, operations infrastructure, and financial resources.

- Evaluate the strengths and weaknesses of these strategies in meeting the needs of the company's target customers.
- Use this analysis to envision new e-commerce options for the company.

e ***Develop potential e-commerce options consistent with values, customer needs, and competitive advantages.*** This stage integrates the lists of potential e-commerce options developed in steps 2, 3, and 4. The senior management team should place top priority on e-commerce options that reside at the intersection of the options from these stages. Simply put, this stage in the analysis will filter out all the potential e-commerce options that are not consistent with the company's values, and that do not create superior customer value. What is left is a list of potential e-commerce options to be ranked.

e ***Rank and weight e-commerce evaluation criteria.*** Assuming that Step Five results in a list of more e-commerce options than the company can implement, the next step is to develop a list of criteria for ranking these e-commerce options. While each company is likely to use different criteria, the senior management team should rank the criteria, and allocate 100 points among the criteria to quantify their relative importance. These potential e-commerce initiative evaluation criteria might include:

- Consistency with the company's values
- Ability to create superior customer value
- Cost to implement
- Time to implement
- Potential risk (e.g., risk of security breach, risk of system failure, risk of losing customers)

- Potential economic benefit (e.g., higher prices, increased volume, lower costs)
- Break-even point
- Net present value

 Prioritize potential e-commerce options based on weighted average scores. The final step in the process is to apply the weighted evaluation criteria to the e-commerce options under consideration. This process is accomplished by creating a table that lists each e-commerce option in the rows and each evaluation criterion in the columns. The senior management team ranks each option on each criterion on a scale from 1 = worst to n = best, where n equals the number of e-commerce options. Once this ranking has been completed, the team can calculate the weighted average score of each option by multiplying the weight for each criterion by the e-commerce options' score on each criterion. Then the e-commerce options can be ranked in descending order of their weighted average score.

Since these scores and weightings are based on subjective judgment, it is typical for teams to go through several iterations of this process before they are comfortable with the results. Once the ranking is complete, the teams can implement the e-commerce options in order of priority at a pace that is tailored to the resources that the company is making available for e-commerce, and the requirements of each project.

Conclusion

The way companies evaluate e-commerce options depends heavily on their corporate values. While these corporate values may inhibit the range of e-commerce options that the company may consider, these values must be made explicit. To the extent that e-commerce options provide superior customer value, they are more likely to enhance the company's competitive position and its shareholder value. Merrill Lynch and Citigroup took very different approaches to evaluating e-commerce options. While it is too early to reach conclusions about which approach will ultimately be more successful, it is likely that the winner will be the one that is able to deploy the e-commerce strategy that leads to the fastest earnings growth, not necessarily the biggest asset base.

Notes

1. Bob Violino, "Banking on E-Business—Citigroup Is Dramatically Expanding Its Internet Presence in an Effort to Approach Its Target of 1 Billion Customers," *Information Week,* May 3, 1999, p. 44.
2. Ibid.
3. Matthew Schifrin and Erika Brown "The Bull Has an Identity Crisis," *Forbes*, April 5, 1999, p. 111.
4. Ibid.
5. Ibid.
6. Scott Raynovich, "Merrill Shows Signs of Getting It," *Red Herring,* May 26, 1999 [http://www.redherring.com/insider/1999/0526/news-merrill.html].

7

Leading Change

E-commerce makes companies change in very fundamental ways. Is the change process spurred by e-commerce the same for all companies, or are there different change processes for companies in different situations? What are the compelling examples of these different change processes? Are there principles that can be derived from analyzing these cases that will help managers distinguish successful from unsuccessful change processes? What should managers do to help their companies make the changes necessary to reap the rewards of e-commerce?

Chapter 7 addresses these issues in sequence. First, the chapter describes four different kinds of change processes depending on the source of the e-commerce strategy and the extent to which that strategy alters the company's basic business model. Then the chapter examines cases from Microsoft, Merrill Lynch, and Provident American, which expose the anatomy of these change processes. The chapter then extracts principles for successful e-commerce–driven change management. It concludes by outlining a methodology that financial executives can use to help guide their organizations in a change process that will help them realize the expected returns from e-commerce.

Four Kinds of Change Processes

As I noted in Chapter 6, some organizations like to embrace change to maintain market leadership, and others like to resist change until their customers drag them into the "new world." Later in the chapter we will explore cases that illustrate how different companies approach change differently. For example, in the online brokerage business, Charles Schwab was much more willing to cannibalize itself while Merrill Lynch was dragged slowly into the field by defecting customers and their brokers. And Microsoft was quite willing to develop an electronic procurement system on its own initiative that would not only demonstrate a new product that its commercial customers might, but also save Microsoft quite a bit of money through purchasing efficiencies.

From looking at these and other cases, it becomes clear that different companies respond to change in different ways. In fact, the research for this book suggests that e-commerce initiatives induce different change processes depending on two factors:

1. *The source of the e-commerce strategy.* Is the e-commerce strategy coming from internal experimentation, or as a response to an external threat?
2. *The extent to which the e-commerce strategy alters the company's business model.* Does the e-commerce strategy complement the existing business model, or does it force the company into an entirely new way of doing business?

As Figure 7-1 indicates, there are four possible scenarios, each of which demands a different approach to managing change.

Executives must know which category their companies are in order to manage the change process appropriately. Following is a guide to each category.

Figure 7-1. Nature of change management process by source of e-commerce strategy and extent of business model change.

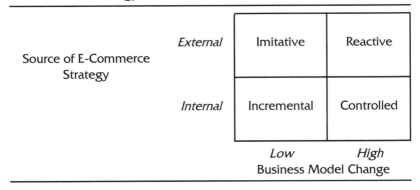

Incremental (Low Business Model Change/Internal Source of E-Commerce Strategy)

Companies in the Incremental category are making investments in e-commerce applications that are likely to lead to increased efficiency in the performance of an internal activity that does not have too much of an effect on the company's relationships with customers. To the extent that the source of the idea is an internal search for improved efficiency, it is likely that the process of implementing the e-commerce application will be incremental. The pace of the e-commerce implementation process will be set by an internal timetable instead of responding to an external threat that may be proceeding faster than the company might normally proceed. An example of this is a company that decides to use electronic catalogs to purchase office supplies. While the electronic procurement application increases efficiency, it is not likely to alter the company's competitive position in a dramatic fashion.

Imitative (Low Business Model Change/External Source of E-Commerce Strategy)

Companies in the Imitative category are making investments in e-commerce applications that are likely to lead to increased efficiency in the performance of an internal activity that does not have too much of an effect on the company's relationships with customers. Since the source of the idea is external, it is likely that a competitor is already further along in the implementation of the e-commerce application. As a result, the company may chose to rush the implementation in order not to fall behind the competitor. Even though the e-commerce initiative may not alter the company's position relative to customers, the company may perceive a need to keep pace by imitating the competitor's e-commerce application primarily as a matter of corporate pride. In these circumstances, there is a danger that the e-commerce application may not achieve the full benefit that might be achieved if the pace of the implementation were more deliberate.

Reactive (High *Business Model Change*/External *Source of E-Commerce Strategy)*

Companies in the Reactive category are making investments in e-commerce applications that are likely to change substantially the performance of an activity that has a significant impact on the company's relationships with customers. To the extent that the source of the idea is the success of an upstart competitor, it is likely that the process of implementing the e-commerce application will be reactive. The key qualitative differences between the reactive and the imitative change process are that the reactive process is much more intense, and the reactive process involves the resolution of very strategic business issues about which there may be serious internal disagreement. The pace of the reactive implementation process will be set by the way the tension is resolved between the company's desire to maintain the business model that led to its past success and the company's fear of losing further ground to the upstart competitor. An example of this is the case we saw in Chapter 6 on Merrill Lynch, and the challenge of online trading. We will explore the change process within Merrill Lynch later in this chapter as a means of exposing the anatomy of the reactive change process.

*Controlled (*High *Business Model Change/*Internal *Source of E-Commerce Strategy)*

Companies in the Controlled category are making investments in e-commerce applications that are likely to change substantially the performance of an activity that has a significant impact on the company's relationships with customers. Because the company directs this change process at its own initiative, the company is in control of the design of the e-commerce application and the pace of its implementation. The key qualitative differences between the controlled and the incremental change process are that the controlled process is much more complex, and it involves the resolution of very strategic business issues before the implementation process begins. The pace of the controlled implementation process will be set by the company working in collaboration with its customers to develop a Web-enabled business process that creates superior customer value. We will explore one example of an insurance firm, formerly called Provident American, which recognized that as an intermediary, it could be threatened in the future unless it developed an effective e-commerce strategy.

Cases

These different change models might appear abstract. To enliven them, we will explore several cases that exemplify three types of change processes:

1. Incremental: Microsoft E-Procurement
2. Reactive: Merrill Lynch
3. Controlled: HealthAxis.com

Incremental: Microsoft E-Procurement

An incremental change process happens when a company takes the initiative to change a back-office process in order to improve efficiency. The case of Microsoft's E-Procurement system, MS Market, illustrates the effectiveness of a change process that starts with clear business objectives, continues by selling senior management on the relatively risk-free path for achieving these objectives, and concludes with measurable cost savings.

Microsoft created the MS Market site to make its purchasing process more efficient, and to demonstrate the power of its technology. According to *Network World*, prior to the site, it used to take two weeks to turn a paper requisition into a purchase order. Microsoft's paper-based requisition process was slow and inefficient for employees and suppliers, and it was costly because it used an abundance of human resources.[1]

With MS Market, it now it takes less than three minutes to place an order and less than one minute for simple orders.

According to Clayton Fleming, Microsoft's former head of corporate services, MS Market had several objectives:

- Enable direct vendor relationships. For example, Microsoft uses MS Market to work directly with its PC vendor, Vanstar.
- Simplify what had been a complex and disorganized approval process.
- Streamline the process of purchasing high-volume, low-dollar items such as office supplies.
- Create a friendly user interface.

The results included the following:

- The time for an end-user to create a purchase order dropped from three minutes to one minute.
- The direct cost of processing a purchase order dropped from $12 per purchase order to $5 per purchase order.
- The number of purchase orders processed by a purchasing staff member increased from 20,000 purchase orders per year to 300,000 purchase orders per year. One reason for this in-

crease was that people who in the past had purchased items without creating purchase orders began to use the system.

- The number of people supporting the purchasing process in the U.S. decreased from nineteen to five.

Microsoft wanted to set up a tool that provided an easy-to-understand way for employees to purchase office supplies. Microsoft also wanted the site to include intellectual property that its buys, content for its external Web sites, and code that Microsoft incorporates into its own applications.

With MS Market, all of Microsoft's vendors, office suppliers, desktop computer makers, marketing people, and temporary agencies receive purchase orders through the site. Microsoft has sessions with vendors to make sure that Microsoft is getting detailed requests from them on how to make the site better for them. Microsoft wants to reduce its vendors' costs for using the system as well as its own.

MS Market is an online ordering system that works on Microsoft's intranet. It provides online forms for ordering office supplies, PCs, business cards, catering, or creating contracts to hire vendors. It also validates information such as pricing and availability. It ensures that each order is linked to the appropriate accounting code. It routes orders to managers for notification or approval.

In July 1996, Microsoft's corporate systems group implemented MS Market. It took three programmers four months to develop and release MS Market. A team of three developers, three testers, two program manager, and one product manager is responsible for taking user feedback and improving the site on a quarterly basis. Despite its usage in thirty-seven countries, there are only two people dedicated to supporting it.

Microsoft consumes $1 billion worth of goods and services over its MS Market site from nineteen countries running on a database server and Web server. The site processes 1,200 purchase orders daily; 6,000 to 7,000 requisitioning users within Microsoft have used the site within a six-month period.

Part of Microsoft's project is to benchmark usage and satisfaction at each release. There are three metrics that Microsoft looks at its releases on MS Market: velocity, end-user experience, and head-count reduction. Prior to the site, it used to take two weeks to turn a paper requisition into a purchase order, now it takes less than three minutes to place an order—less than one minute for simple ones. The head count of the individuals that support MS Market for the U.S. alone went from fourteen to two. These results were accomplished by shifting procurement activities from people in the procurement department to the MS Market user interface.

Microsoft will continue to improve its Market Site to achieve improvements in the specific measures outlined above: velocity, end-user experience, and head-count reduction.[2]

The MS Market example indicates the relative ease of "Webifying" a process when the source of the e-commerce application is internal, and the e-commerce application does not alter the company's business model in a fundamental way. Microsoft's competitive strategy did not change as a result of the MS Market system. Rather, the MS Market system served two purposes for Microsoft. It helped to streamline an inefficient internal process. And, more importantly, it helped demonstrate how companies can use Microsoft technology to cut costs. As a result, it was relatively easy for Fleming to get the limited internal resources needed to develop the MS Market system. As the system began to achieve tangible benefits on a local scale, it was rolled out worldwide.

Since Fleming succeeded in this role as a staff manager, the implication for financial executives is that the incremental change process can be achieved within the confines of a staff organization without going against the corporate grain (as we will see is an absolute necessity in the case of reactive change).

Reactive: Merrill Lynch

As I noted in Chapter 6, Merrill Lynch has been dragged reluctantly into the world of online trading. This dragging process culminated in Merrill Lynch's May 1999 announcement that it would offer its customers a way to trade online. Many of the details remain to be worked out. The process by which Merrill Lynch reversed its strategy toward online trading is an excellent example of how *not* to manage the change process induced by e-commerce. Nevertheless, Merrill Lynch's experience is typical of the reactive approach to change management that is likely to be most common in large organizations.

At the core of the change process was conflict at many levels within Merrill Lynch. There was conflict between the defenders of the brokers and their commissions and proponents of online investing. There was conflict between Merrill brokers who were concerned about losing customers to online brokers and Merrill brokers who were concerned about losing commissions. There was even conflict among Merrill executives between those who favored setting up a separate online unit to compete with the brokers and those who favored keeping the online unit under the same executive. In fact, according to *The Industry Standard*, in June 1998, that same executive, Merrill Lynch Vice Chairman John "Launny" Steffens, warned that the rise of Internet-based stock trading was a serious threat to Americans' financial lives. By May 1999, it became clear that Steffens and his colleagues in Merrill Lynch management had decided that the Internet represented a serious threat to the financial health of *Merrill Lynch*.[3]

This realization culminated in the announcement of plans for Merrill Lynch Direct, a Web-based trading service that charges $29.95 a trade. Threatened by the fear of losing large numbers of customers to E-Trade, Schwab, Ameritrade, and other online trading companies, Merrill capitulated to the power of the Internet.

The shift was spurred by two Merrill executives: Maddy Weinstein, Senior VP and director of Merrill's business innovation group, and Bob Brewster, VP and Director of Merrill Lynch Direct. Weinstein, who sets strategy for Merrill's retail-brokerage operation, and trains its financial consultants, hired Brewster in the Summer of

1998, about the same time Steffens made his public comments about the dangers of Internet trading.

The inspiration for the online venture, according to Weinstein, came in part from Charles Schwab. As I noted in Chapter 5, Schwab successfully changed its strategy, steering toward the Web customers who had been using local offices and telephone call centers to make trades. Schwab demonstrated to the brokerage industry that a shift to Web-based trading made economic sense.

Weinstein thought that if Schwab could make online trading work, then Merrill ought to be able to do it as well, despite Merrill's different business model. David Pottruck of Schwab responded to Merrill's announcement of Merrill Lynch Direct by pointing out that Merrill was doing in 1999 what Schwab had done in 1995. Pottruck pointed out that Merrill was Schwab 1.0, the multi-tiered pricing structure, which Schwab abandoned in January 1998 in favor of a $29.95 flat fee.

As I noted in Chapter 5, Schwab restructured its business model in part because its customers were confused. Schwab management decided to simplify its pricing structure. The result was that Pottruck worried about Schwab's choice to forgo profits and a climbing stock price for an indefinite period of time.

After a six-month struggle with Wall Street, however, Schwab won with the help of a bull market that attracted first-time investors to the Web. In June 1999, Merrill's executive team entered the difficult phase of convincing investors that it is in Merrill's best interest to sacrifice short-term commissions in order to maintain customer relationships in the long run.

For Merrill, the most delicate issue remains the reaction of its 14,800 brokers. A key influence on Merrill executives' decision to offer online trading was the loss of Merrill brokers' big accounts to online brokers. And it was Merrill's brokers who began asking about how Merrill planned to use the Internet to keep any more big customers from jumping to online trading. Merrill brokers came to

Weinstein and asked whether Merrill had a specific plan for online financial trading and at what price the service would be offered.

While Merrill tried to create the impression that all members of top management were supportive of Merrill's plans for online trading, the reality is that Merrill executives, including Steffens, had previously downplayed customer demand for trading via the Web. Merrill executives also insisted that Merrill would never compete directly with discount firms. Furthermore, Steffens had insisted that a bull market makes anyone look like a financial genius conducting their own trades. When the market drops, Steffens argued, people would return to the safety of broker-assisted trading. In effect, this posturing masks a more complex reality. According to the *The Wall Street Journal*, internal debate within Merrill Lynch lasted for months before top executives agreed they would incorporate the Internet into their business, and developed their strategy. Only after proponents suggested starting a separate online unit—which would have competed from within against Merrill's stockbrokers—did internal critics of online service drop their opposition to online trading through Merrill itself.[4]

By capitulating to the Internet, Merrill's brokers are expected to pay a personal price. An internal Merrill Lynch study suggests that brokers who are paid chiefly in commissions might see their incomes decline by 18 percent initially. To offset this loss, Merrill is considering issuing its stock to brokers who lose the most business from investors who switch to the Merrill Lynch Direct accounts.

Merrill Lynch executives had to bind up cultural and business divisions in order to make the shift to online trading. Many Merrill executives only recently became comfortable with the Internet. The 60-year-old Merrill Lynch CEO, David Komansky, for example, finally realized that the Federal Express packages frequently arriving at his home were from his adult children's Internet shopping expeditions. Komansky was surprised to find that his daughters could actually buy their mother flowers online. After Launny Steffens, who is

57, publicly attacked Internet trading in 1998, his son Drew, a Merrill stockbroker in North Carolina, called to ask his father to "get his act together."

Ironically, Launny Steffens is leading the Internet initiative. For a time, Steffens's resistance to the Internet approach appeared as though it would prevail at Merrill. As I noted in Chapter 5, Merrill introduced online trading earlier in 1999 to 55,000 customers in two types of accounts requiring at least $100,000 in assets (one percent of its 5 million brokerage customers).

The gradual approach had isolated Steffens. Herbert Allison, Merrill's President, began suggesting in executive meetings that Merrill should embrace the Internet more quickly. Within the Merrill power structure, Allison, 55, was regarded as a person who was interested in the Internet.

At several points, Allison and others raised the issue of whether Merrill should create an online unit outside of Mr. Steffens's retail brokerage group. The suggestion caused an intense exchange. Some Merrill executives questioned the commitment of Steffens and the rest of his group to make an Internet strategy work. Steffens responded that a separate Internet unit was unacceptable. The strategy, he insisted, must be under his control. Ultimately, both he and Mr. Allison agreed that putting the Internet strategy under Steffens was the most appropriate decision.

As I noted earlier, Merrill's reluctance to embrace online trading had cost Merrill Lynch clients. Steffens began receiving about ten e-mail messages a day from concerned brokers. One afternoon in January 1999, Steffens received a call from Donna Di Ianni, a New Jersey broker, who said three of her best clients had taken money out of Merrill to open accounts at online companies. Soon, another leading Merrill broker complained that he had just had a similar experience.

Steffens and his top advisers began visiting clients and leaders in the technology business. A client from Austin, Texas (who had a twenty-year relationship with Merrill Lynch) told Steffens that he used a separate, online account for his frequent trades. Among the stocks he traded in that account: Merrill Lynch.

The experience humbled Steffens. Steffens is a fierce competitor. However, in the early part of 1999, he became increasingly concerned about his business legacy.

Tired of epitomizing Merrill's problems in online investing, Steffens began to develop a new online strategy for Merrill Lynch. One choice facing Merrill was whether to target Schwab and its prices; to set prices lower and compete with deep-discount firms; or to price its online service higher than Schwab's. Merrill rejected the third option after executives concluded that any prices higher than Schwab's would be interpreted as reflecting a lack of commitment to online investing.

Slowly, Merrill began to assemble the pieces of its online strategy. In February 1999, Merrill decided to buy the online trading technology unit of D. E. Shaw & Co. for $25 million. While Komansky was uncertain whether the acquisition was significant enough to even mention to his board, Merrill's stock price increased four dollars per share after the announcement.

In March 1999, Steffens made an eight-hour presentation to Merrill's executive committee, providing the outlines of a new Internet strategy. The committee approved the proposal to make discount online trading a core business, but for more than two months, the plan remained secret. When Steffens was asked about online trading at a Spring 1999 conference, he restricted himself to saying that Schwab had won round one, but that the battle for online business was not over. Merrill gave several large accounts early warning of the change. Steffens, for example, convinced the investor in Austin to switch his Internet trading back to Merrill by offering a service similar to the Merrill Lynch Direct account that had been announced in May.[5]

Merrill Lynch's experience in coping with the business issues that e-commerce presents was as messy and awkward as it is likely to be common. The majority of large companies is likely to be forced by competitors to change their approaches to business. Merrill's experience exemplifies the internal struggle that accompanies the reactive approach to change. As we will see later in this chapter, there is a better way. However, that better way depends heavily on educating the CEO early on so that he or she can lead the process with a clear focus on the ultimate business objectives.

Controlled: HealthAxis.com

The Controlled approach to change is based on the notion that it is better to take charge of the cannibalization process than to let competitors do it for you. Companies that take the Controlled approach to managing e-commerce–induced change are able to size up the key trends likely to drive the future of their businesses, and convert themselves into online businesses before upstart competitors force them to by taking away their customers.

One compelling example of this controlled change process is that of a 110-year-old insurance firm that reshaped itself into an e-commerce company. According to *Business Week*, Provident American Life & Health Insurance eliminated its -bricks-and-mortar operations, and remade itself into an online-only businesses. Michael Ashker, CEO of HealthAxis.com, the online insurance agency once known as Provident American, recognized that his company faced competitive pressures and limited resources. Ashker was convinced that Provident American had no choice between the bricks-and-mortar and online. Ashker was convinced that bricks-and-mortar represented the past, and that online was the future.[6]

In the 1970s, Provident American Chief Executive Al Clemens helped raise awareness of this medical insurer. By using popular television celebrities such as Michael Landon and Burl Ives to sell policies directly to consumers, he bypassed insurance agents. This approach was considered a revolutionary idea at the time. Now, Clemens, 61 (and owner of a third of the company's stock), is eager to revolutionize insurance distribution again. Intrigued by the potential of e-commerce, he pushed Provident American in the spring of 1998 to establish a small, experimental online subsidiary called HealthAxis.com.

The experiment paid off for Provident American. Within months of establishing the subsidiary, HealthAxis.com, Chief Executive Ashker presented Clemens with a business plan that would change Provident American from a one-product underwriter into the first full-service online insurance agency in the U.S. Ashker signed an exclusive, three-year online-distribution arrangement with America Online. This agreement convinced Clemens and the Provident board that the rest of Provident American should go online. At the end of 1998, after negotiating additional marketing partnerships with Lycos and other Internet portals, Provident American sold its traditional underwriting business, and cut its relationships with 20,000 insurance agents.

In early 1999, Provident American was reborn as HealthAxis.com in Norristown, Pennsylvania. With Clemens as chairman, HealthAxis.com sells policies issued by major carriers as well as information about insurance and rate comparisons across the industry.

HealthAxis.com realized that it needed to become an online business or it would lose significant market share. Ashker noted that Provident had been a small firm, overshadowed by Aetna and Prudential. Ashker recognized that Provident had one intangible, but valuable asset: information. He also recognized that unlike the book and record industries, Provident lacked packaging and shipping costs. Instead, Provident had middlemen in an industry with inefficient distribution.

Ashker recognized that cutting out the middleman would allow HealthAxis.com to sell insurance at prices 15 percent lower than it had been selling offline. Furthermore, being the first online insurance agency in the U.S. gave HealthAxis.com an opportunity to dominate its industry, at least on the Internet. As Ashker pointed out, there was not a first-mover advantage in 1999 in writing insurance, however, there is one in distributing insurance over the Internet.

Wall Street responded favorably. As Provident American, the company's stock had an all-time high of $14 per share. As Health Axis.com, it traded at about $27 in June 1999.[7]

The transformation of Provident American into HealthAxis.com epitomizes the concept of controlled e-commerce–induced change management. The company recognized that it needed to shape its future, or its competitors would take away their business. By seizing the initiative in a very tradition-bound industry, the company was able to grab a lead in the online distribution of insurance. While the story does not yet have a clear happy ending (Provident American is unprofitable) it *does* demonstrate the power of a forward-thinking leader to create a company's future.

Principles of Managing E-Commerce–Induced Change

What general principles can we extract from these cases that could be useful for managers? Here are five.

e *If senior management understands the Internet's potential impact on the business, proceed to principle 3, otherwise educate senior management.* Until senior management understands how the Internet can transform the company's business, there is no benefit in attempting to change the organization to accommodate e-commerce. E-commerce can have too much of an impact on the business, even if the company chooses to use the Internet for "back-office" activities, to keep senior management at arms length from the process. As we saw in the case of Merrill Lynch, a fundamental reason that some companies struggle with their e-commerce strategies is that key executives are not comfortable with the Internet, and even less comfortable admitting their ignorance about it. This fear leads to avoidance and delay. Only when the Internet starts taking their customers are executives forced to face the financial consequences of their fear of the unknown.

 Senior management should receive education that is tailored to their specific needs. Most senior managers are reluctant to admit weakness in a public forum. Nevertheless, senior managers cannot understand the impact of the Internet on their business unless they are willing to seek out that understanding from a forum that is specifically tailored to senior managers' needs. Often this education will involve getting senior managers online to conduct such basic activities as e-mail, checking stock prices, and researching competitors. From there, senior managers can begin to appreciate the power of the Internet, and will then be driven to learn about how the Web can transform business models and create competitive advantage.

In the case of Merrill Lynch, senior executives were dragged into understanding the importance of the Internet from their children. By contrast, in the case of Provident American, the company's chairman recognized that the Internet had the same transforming power in the 1990s as direct response TV had in the 1970s. The key idea is that education process must match the learning style of the senior executives.

 Senior management must develop a vision for how e-commerce will change the business. Getting senior management comfortable with the Internet is clearly a significant requirement for managing the change process. The quality of the company's ultimate e-commerce business operation depends in part on the quality of the vision that drives it. In the case of Merrill Lynch, that vision was driven by Launny Steffens when he decided he wanted to leave a legacy of success in online trading. Steffens got input from customers and brokers, as well as his staff, to develop a strategy that he hoped would optimize the company's results. Steffens also obtained the advice and consent of Merrill's executive committee. The point is that the vision must be clear and must be developed in collaboration with those who will implement that vision.

The company should implement the vision as a series of experiments. While leaders must develop a clear vision for how the e-commerce application will work, the pursuit of that vision must be experimental. The idea is to think through the key issues ahead of time, and then put a best guess online as quickly as possible. Once the first version is online, it is possible to collect feedback, and modify the site so that it responds effectively to changing market requirements. Provident American started off with a prototype and expanded it accordingly. Microsoft took a similar approach with MS Market. The key notion is to implement quickly (and reasonably cheaply), and then modify aggressively based on market feedback.

The company must communicate the vision to employees and customers. It is not sufficient for managers to conceptualize an e-commerce strategy, and build a system. Employees and customers must participate. E-commerce changes the nature of the employees' work. Managers must explain the vision and objectives of the e-commerce initiative to employees. Management must let employees work with a prototype of the e-commerce system, and help to participate in defining how their jobs will be different as a result of the e-commerce initiative.

One key difference is that Web applications, particularly when they involve transactions with customers, generate rapid and voluminous e-mail feedback. This e-mail must be answered by employees. So employees must redesign their jobs so that they can answer the e-mail, and work with others in the organization who are responsible for changing the system to adapt to customer needs.

Similarly, management must explain the e-commerce initiative to customers—enlisting their support and their willingness to deliver feedback, and to demand an effective response to that feedback.

A Methodology for Managing E-Commerce Change

What can financial managers do to help lead change in their organizations? The E-Commerce Change Management Process detailed below offers financial managers the following benefits:

- *Consensus.* The E-Commerce Change Management Process gets the right people involved in the process at an early enough stage so that a consensus is built. This consensus creates the necessary conditions for their contribution to the design and implementation of the e-commerce initiative.
- *Action.* The E-Commerce Change Management Process creates the conditions that will lead to rapid and tightly directed action. It ensures that participants understand the need for moving quickly to implement the e-commerce initiative.
- *Results.* The E-Commerce Change Management Process sets tangible measures, and then expects e-commerce initiative participants to work effectively to achieve those results.
- *Learning.* The E-Commerce Change Management Process creates the conditions under which the organization will need to take inputs from customers and the marketplace, and use these inputs to spur adaptation. The result is that the company modifies its e-commerce business process so that it provides ever-improving customer value.

Here are the five steps of the E-Commerce Change Management Process:

 Get senior management on board. While ideas for e-commerce initiatives can profitably originate below the senior management level of the organization, the E-

Commerce Change Management Process cannot begin until senior management understands, accepts, and supports the e-commerce initiative. This may create a delicate situation in which lower-level managers are responsible for educating senior executives. It may be necessary to work with outsiders who can educate senior management without creating the awkwardness that might ensue if lower-level managers did the education. If senior management is already onboard, then proceed to step 2.

Identify the type of change. As I noted early in this chapter, there are four types of e-commerce change-management processes depending on the source of the e-commerce initiative and the extent to which the e-commerce initiative changes the company's business model. The second step in the E-Commerce Change Management Process is to apply the tests detailed earlier in this chapter to identify which type of change most closely matches the company's.

Devise a change process specifically tailored to the type of change. The change process will vary depending on the type of change. However, for each type of change, there will be common elements. For example, each type of change involves building a cross-functional team, developing a vision of the outcome, setting specific objectives, and implementing rapidly.

But there are also important differences by type of change including:

- _Incremental._ When managing an incremental change process, financial executives can take a leadership role. Financial executive may be in a position, for example, to drive the process of building an electronic procurement process. The team in such an incremental change process would include procurement, IT, finance, and key suppliers. The objective would be to drive down the cost of purchased items, and to streamline processing costs. Employees would be involved in testing the system, and would receive significant education. Senior management would be advised, but would not necessarily need to drive the process. Customers might not be interested at all.

- *Imitative.* The imitative change process would be quite similar to the incremental one. The big difference would be that while the idea for creating the new process would come from the outside, it would need to find an internal process leader. Once that internal process leader was found (again it could be a key financial executive) the change process would proceed in a fashion similar to the imitative process.
- *Reactive.* The challenge with the reactive process would be managing the internal debate between proponents of preserving the existing model and the advocates of the new e-commerce–driven business model. The reactive process works most effectively if the CEO takes the lead in mediating the conflict. Unfortunately, in many organizations, the CEO does not want to get in the middle of the battle, and would prefer to let the different factions resolve the conflict themselves. If the CEO does take charge, the process can proceed quite similarly to the controlled approach to change.
- *Controlled.* The controlled approach to is the most rational and systematic. Here, the most senior executive recognizes the need for change, and then drives that change in a well-researched and systematic fashion. Such controlled change works most effectively if the senior executive has clear control of the company, as we saw in the Provident American case. Here, senior management can work effectively to design an e-commerce process that creates superior value for customers. The design is based on an understanding of customer needs, involves the right functions within the company, is implemented in a series of experiments, and evolves in response to feedback.

Implement quickly. Once the vision is developed, it is essential to implement quickly. Though the implementation is quick, it must also be of high quality. Because the Internet changes so rapidly, it is more important to put the new system online even if it is not perfect. The system should be designed so that it is relatively easy to modify based on feedback.

e **Get feedback and modify.** The company will need to seek out feedback, often via e-mail and conversations with customers and employees. There needs to be a process in place for capturing the feedback and acting on it rapidly. Internet customers will not tolerate long delays in feedback cycles. Internet customers are also very blunt about what they do not like. Therefore, the ability to capture and respond to feedback will determine the ongoing success or failure of the company's e-commerce initiative.

Conclusion

E-commerce makes companies change in very fundamental ways. There are different change processes for different kinds of e-commerce situations, depending on the source of the e-commerce initiative and the extent to which that initiative alters the company's fundamental business model. While Microsoft's MS Market and Provident American's transformation into HealthAxis.com were cases that proceeded in a relatively systematic fashion, Merrill Lynch's approach to online trading was tumultuous and remains a work-in-progress. It is critical for senior management to be educated in the power of e-commerce, and to recognize its experimental nature. Managers can lead e-commerce effectively by following the E-Commerce Change Management Process, which embodies such principles.

Notes

1. Mark Gibbs, "The Big Piggy Goes to MS Market," *Network World,* February 22, 1999, p. 64.
2. Ibid.
3. Megan Barnett and Bernhard Warner, "Merrill Lynch Faces a 'Schwabized' Market," *The Industry Standard,* June 4, 1999 [http://www.the standard.net/articles/display10,1449,4834,00.html?home.tf].
4. Rebecca Buckman and Charles Gasparino, "Facing Internet Threat, Merrill Plans to Offer Trading Online for Low Fees," *The Wall Street Journal,*

June 1, 1999 [http://www.interactive.wsj.com/articles/SB928191612437 564613.htm].

5. Ibid.
6. Marcia Stepanek, "Closed, Gone to the Net," *Business Week,* June 2, 1999 [http://www.businessweek.com/ebiz/index.html].
7. Ibid.

8

Sustaining Change

The best way to sustain change is to create a culture that rewards change. As technology has taken a bigger share of the economy, the companies that manage technology effectively are also good at managing the change that technology induces. The capital markets have rewarded companies that manage technology-induced change effectively. And the companies that share these capital market rewards with their employees do the best job of sustaining change. Whether the technology in question is product technology, information technology in general, or e-commerce in particular, the skills required to sustain change are similar.

Chapter 8 explores the management techniques that work most effectively for sustaining change induced by technology by presenting two brief cases from Digital Equipment Corporation (DEC) and Microsoft. The chapter then uses these brief cases to develop principles for sustaining change and principles for inhibiting it. It continues by presenting the case of Hewlett-Packard (HP) and the InkJet printer market to illustrate how a large, successful company like HP can adapt—going from being a change inhibitor to a change sustainer. Chapter 8 concludes by presenting the implications for managers seeking to sustain the change induced by e-commerce.

Management Techniques for Sustaining Change

There are very few organizations that manage change effectively. It is much more common to find organizations that become successful, and then find that their success leads to failure. Examples of this phenomenon are so common that it forms the basis of the ancient Greek myth of Icarus. Icarus wanted to fly. He was told that he could do so by creating wings out of bird feathers and wax. He was warned that his wings would work fine as long as he did not fly too close to the sun. Sure enough, Icarus's wings worked well. Unfortunately, Icarus was not satisfied with keeping the proper distance from the sun. He needed to fly higher. The result was that he ended up flying too close to the sun. The wax melted, his wings fell apart, and Icarus plummeted to his death in the Aegean Sea.

DEC

So what does this have to do with managing change? Consider the example of DEC. DEC was started by an MIT graduate named Ken Olson in an old mill in Massachusetts. It grew to more than 100,000 employees during the 1970s because its minicomputers offered customers an attractive alternative to IBM's mainframes. In the 1980s, companies such as IBM, Apple, and Compaq began selling personal computers (PCs). Olson's response to the PC was to comment that there was no compelling reason people would buy one. Despite Olson's comment, the PC market exploded. Olson tried four separate times to market a PC, but failed. In the late 1980s, Olson was ousted by his board as DEC imploded. Ultimately DEC sold out to the world's largest PC maker, Compaq, in 1998.

What does DEC have to do with Icarus? Just as Icarus thought he could outsmart the heat of the sun, Olson thought he could evade the forces of change enabled by inexorable improvements in the price/performance ratio of information technologies. The irony for Olson was that in the transition from mainframes to minicomputers, Olson was the beneficiary of these improvements. However, in the transition from minicomputers to PCs, Olson could not adapt. Olson perceived that DEC's survival was threatened by a technology that he had not developed himself. Furthermore, DEC's business model depended on the continued preeminence of the minicomputer. DEC was unable to change its business model to incorporate the PC.

Microsoft

Not all companies fall victim to the DEC disease. Consider the case of Microsoft. Since its founding in 1975, Microsoft had done well selling office software for PCs. In 1995, a company called Netscape went public, and quickly generated a huge market capitalization. Netscape produced a piece of software that gave people access to a part of the Internet called the World Wide Web. The software, called a Web browser, was developed at the University of Illinois. In its short existence, Netscape had succeeded at becoming the dominant Web browser. While Netscape's market dominance had not escaped Microsoft's attention, it was not until Netscape's initial public offering that Bill Gates decided that Microsoft needed to siphon off Netscape's stock market value.

Bill Gates realized that Web browsers in particular, and the Internet more broadly, represented a huge threat to Microsoft's PC-centric business model. Gates reasoned that if people could access all the information they needed from the Internet, then they might not need to buy so much PC software.

As soon as Gates had finished the global introduction of the Windows 95 operating system, he told hundreds of programmers to drop what they were doing, and go to work on developing a Web browser to compete with Netscape's. After introducing three versions of Microsoft's Internet Explorer in quick succession, Netscape's market share began tumbling. Microsoft's fourth version was so good that many considered it better than Netscape's browser.

As the quality of Microsoft's product rose, so did its Web browser market share. Microsoft did not use quality alone as a competitive weapon. While Netscape's browser price was "almost free," Microsoft's price was "completely free." Netscape matched Microsoft's price. By dropping its price, Netscape was able to defend its market share. However, the battle with Microsoft contributed to Netscape's loss of independence. In 1999, Netscape was purchased by America Online. Microsoft won the battle against Netscape in Web browsers as it had previously won the battle with Lotus Development in spreadsheets. The difference with Netscape, however, was that Microsoft was able to adapt to a technology with the potential to alter fundamentally its way of making money.

Principles for Sustaining Change

The following stories suggest managerial principles for sustaining change. Here we explore the principles of how to sustain change, as exemplified by Microsoft; and how to inhibit change, as exemplified by DEC. Obviously managers should promote the former and root out the latter. As I noted earlier, very few organizations are actually good at adapting to change. Therefore, managers can also use these principles as diagnostic tests. If an organization adheres to change-inhibiting principles, then e-commerce–induced change will be difficult to sustain. If an organization is one of the few that sustains change effectively, then these principles for sustaining change will work effectively to sustain e-commerce induced change.

The small number of companies that are good at sustaining change seem to follow six managerial principles that enable them to sustain change effectively. These principles are technology independent. Therefore, they work effectively for e-commerce–induced change as much as for other technologies. The principles are:

e ***Develop new services and products in close con-
junction with customers.*** Companies that are good at
sustaining change do not develop new products in the
isolation of the research lab. Rather, they work closely with their
most innovative customers in developing new products and services. This working relationship binds together the work of internal functional disciplines such as engineering, marketing, sales,
manufacturing, and finance, as well as the specifically articulated
unmet needs of customers. Companies that sustain change effectively are good at producing new product or service prototypes very quickly. These companies give the prototypes to
customers, and adapt them in response to their customers' feedback. By working collaboratively with customers, these companies are pulled into the future in a way that the market rewards.
By working through internal teams, these companies solve problems more quickly and get products to market faster.

This principle applies directly to the development of e-commerce. Companies must work closely with customers when they
develop e-commerce business models. The customer-related
work includes getting feedback on Web site prototypes, and responding effectively to customer e-mail. The Web creates much
more customer feedback along with the expectation that the
company will respond to this feedback quickly and effectively.

e ***Go outside for new technologies and products if the
customer demands them.*** Sometimes companies that
are good at sustaining change find that they cannot develop with sufficient speed the products or services that customers need. As a result, these companies are willing to make
acquisitions or find partners who can get them the technologies
that customers need. The objective is to keep competitors away
from companies' customers. Microsoft did this when it decided it
needed a graphics presentation package, ultimately acquiring
the company whose technology formed the basis of its Power-
Point presentation package.

The implications for sustaining e-commerce–induced
change is that managers must decide whether they can hire e-
commerce experts, and train them fast enough to help build and
support their e-commerce efforts. If not, managers must be will-

ing to look outside for those skills. In many organizations, this means hiring Web consultants. In some organizations, it might even mean acquiring a Web consulting firm in order to have access to the talent needed to build and support its e-commerce initiatives on an ongoing basis.

e **Win the war for talent.** As I noted in Chapter 1, the most valuable companies, such as Microsoft, have very few tangible assets in relation to their stock market capitalization. The most valuable companies—and those who are most effective at sustaining change—have a plethora of intangible assets. Among these intangible assets, the most valuable are their talented and properly motivated employees. In order for companies to sustain change, they must have very smart people who can anticipate change and react to it effectively—ahead of competitors. The way to do this is to win the war for talent.

Winning the war for talent is a complex challenge. The short answer is to create an environment that attracts the smartest people. This sort of environment is one that gives people a feeling that their work is meaningful to many people. Smart people want to make a difference in the world. In addition, smart people want to work in an environment where other smart people are working. Last, but not least, smart people want a chance to be compensated very well in proportion to their accomplishments.

For companies trying to sustain e-commerce–induced change, the implications of this principle are clear. Companies must rethink whether or not their entire human resources strategy is appropriate for winning the war for talent. Over the long run, sustaining change will determine whether or not a company can prosper in the world of Internet business. Companies that are geared to win the war for talent will be well positioned to lead their industries because they will employ and motivate the most talented people.

e **Engage in objective self-criticism.** Companies that sustain change effectively are sometimes afraid of becoming arrogant and self-satisfied. Often they are led by individuals who worked at companies like DEC and Wang— companies that failed because they thought that customers would buy whatever new inventions they could dream up. The experience of watching an organization fail because its executives could not take criticism left an indelible impression.

Hence, the few companies that do sustain change in their organizations encourage fact-based self-criticism. This criticism can be quite brutal. For example, at Microsoft, project managers will write 100-page memos criticizing everything that went wrong during a software-development project. These memos are distributed to everyone on the project team and to Bill Gates.

Self-criticism at Microsoft has led to improvements in its product development process. These improvements include increasing the number of people who test software during its development, and an increased rigor in the quality assurance process. In addition, Microsoft has become much more rigorous in using customer input into its product-development process. Such input includes having developers listen to customer service calls, using customer wish lists, and watching customers use it's the company's products in a usability lab before the products are released.

Companies that are good at sustaining e-commerce–induced change encourage fact-based self-criticism. These companies' cultures are able to manage the process of self-criticism so that people are able to attack business processes without alienating the people who perform the processes. By creating an intellectual separation between these two, these companies can make the process improvements that are the essence of sustaining e-commerce–induced change effectively.

e *Tie employee compensation to improvements in customer satisfaction and shareholder value.* Part of winning the war for talent is creating a compensation system that rewards improvements in customer satisfaction and increases in share price. Cisco Systems has created such a system. Cisco gives all its employees stock options. Cisco also conducts quarterly customer satisfaction surveys. These surveys are administered by independent firms. If Cisco's customer satisfaction survey results improve, employees receive substantial bonuses. If the scores do not improve, they do not receive the bonuses.

While this is an extremely simple idea, only a small number of companies actually use such compensation systems. But these systems reward sustained change. These systems encourage company employees to devise new ways to make customers even more satisfied.

These systems also encourage Cisco employees to be frugal. They also make it acceptable to pay substantial sales commissions for salespeople who can bring in $50 million orders. These commissions are seen as a small investment in sustaining Cisco's sales-and-profit growth. Why? Because the sales-and-profit growth drives up the price of Cisco stock, which increases the personal wealth of all Cisco employees.

As we saw earlier, Cisco is one of the few companies that is good at sustaining e-commerce–induced change. Cisco has adapted its Web site to the point where it claims to have added half a billion dollars to its profits as a result of its site. Part of Cisco's success in e-commerce is its culture of innovation, an important part of which is the way it compensates its people. Companies that follow Cisco's approach to compensation are more likely to be good at sustaining e-commerce–induced change.

Principles for Inhibiting Change

Most companies are not so good at sustaining change. In fact, while most companies would never admit it, they are eager to inhibit change. While this resistance to change certainly applies to e-commerce–induced change, most companies would be happier if they could switch off the new technologies, new competitors, and new customer needs that cause their executives to lose sleep. In fact, this desire to inhibit change is so common that we can identify a set of five principles that these change inhibitors follow to keep change from happening. While companies would not admit to following these principles because they consciously want to inhibit change, many organizations will recognize these principles as real. Here they are:

e ***Put the outcasts on change projects.*** Few executive enjoy taking the criticism associated with being out of step with their times. As e-commerce has become the mantra in business over the last couple of years, it is quite difficult for an executive to go to the board of directors and answer "nothing" in response to the question "What is the company doing about the Internet?" While the number of executives who are willing to be out of step is quite small, many more executives are willing to keep one foot in the nonInternet camp and one foot in the "let's try the Internet" camp.

One way to do this is to deputize an executive who is somewhat of an outcast and an annoyance to others on the top management team. If the CEO can deputize such an individual to lead the charge toward e-commerce, and then the deputized executive is not successful, the CEO can report back to the board that he tried e-commerce but it just does not apply to the company.

e ***Let the opponents of change secretly undermine its success.*** To inhibit change, it is useful for senior executives to allow the opponents of change to undermine it in secret. Since the senior executive may have deputized a relatively unpopular executive to lead the e-commerce initiative, it follows that other executives who are not directly involved in that change initiative will be more popular. Therefore, these opponents of the e-commerce initiative may be in an excellent position to support the initiative in public while secretly plotting for the change initiative to fail. While the CEO will not publicly support these enemies of change, he or she will do nothing to stop them either.

e ***Give change projects insufficient resources.*** Another useful way for executives to undermine change initiatives such as e-commerce is to deny them the full resources that they need in order to succeed. Senior executives might deny these projects outside consulting assistance, adequate staff, or the senior executive support needed to generate enthusiasm and cooperation from the rest of the organization. In many cases, the motivation of senior management may be the desire to use the e-commerce project to flush out certain unwanted executives, or simply to place the blame for a likely failure on another executive in the interest of self-preservation.

e *Promote those who resist change and fire those who lead the failed change initiatives.* As a result of these tactics to inhibit change, such e-commerce initiatives often fail to achieve the desired benefits. When the failure takes place, the CEO can then suggest that the e-commerce project leader leave the company, and then promote those who resisted the initiative. The message that this outcome sends to the rest of the organization is that when future change initiatives arise, only the foolish will participate. Long-term survivors will distance themselves from such projects.

e *Delay change until the company starts to lose major customers.* Of course, there are situations in which the best efforts of senior management to stall the advent of a new technology are not practical. Stalling is least successful when it results in the loss of important customers. Such losses cannot always be solved by firing "incompetent" subordinates—particularly if the departing customers make it clear that they departed due to the company's unwillingness to adapt to their needs. Then and only then will the change inhibitor begin to take the change seriously. This is the situation we observed in Chapter 7 with Merrill Lynch.

And when this capitulation to e-commerce finally comes, the "smart" players will often recognize that their resistance to change could cost them their jobs. So they reverse their positions, and take the lead on e-commerce so that they can keep their jobs. Once they decide to lead the change initiative, such companies can often proceed rationally, although they will be inhibited by their commitment to the past that held them back to begin with.

HP InkJet Printers

Hewlett-Packard (HP) was founded in the 1950s, and today is one of the leading high-technology companies in the world. Despite its prominence, HP has clearly suffered since the death of its founder

David Packard. Given its recent difficulties, it is not clear whether HP's management principles have failed, whether current HP management is simply not adhering to its principles, or whether current HP management has failed to adapt these principles to the current state of its business. Nevertheless, because it is such a large company, it is worth pointing out that earlier in this decade, HP was able to show real signs of successful adaptation as it used a chance discovery in the research lab of a division that was about to be closed down to create what became a $6 billion business. Before we examine this case, it is worthwhile noting that HP has certain organizational characteristics that have enabled it to adapt effectively to change. HP believes in the importance of the individual. This belief causes HP to spin off new divisions when they reach about 1,000 employees. The reason for creating the new divisions is to provide opportunities for talented individuals to hone their management skills by turning the new divisions into successful businesses. Each division is forced to generate sufficient profit to earn research dollars from the corporate treasury. If a division does not generate sufficient profit, it is closed down.

This sense of individual responsibility plays an important role in the case of HP in the ink-jet printer business. This was the key factor that enabled HP to capitalize on its internally developed ink-jet technology to take PC printer market leadership from Epson, the dominant dot matrix printer vendor. According to *The Wall Street Journal*, between 1988 and 1995, overall ink-jet unit volume rose from zero to almost 8 million units, while dot matrix unit volume dropped from 6 million to 3 million units.[1]

An HP engineer discovered ink-jet printing in a converted janitor's closet in the company's Vancouver office. In 1979, an HP scientist noticed drops of liquid splattered over his lab bench. He had been charging a thin metal film with electricity, and when the metal grew hot, liquid trapped underneath began to boil and spurted out. This discovery evolved into the "thermal" ink-jet. HP's executive in charge, Richard Hackborn, recognized that ink-jet technology had several advantages over laser printers for the mass market: It was less expensive, more easily adaptable for color printing, and had not been perfected by competitors.

HP's first ink-jet printer, introduced in 1984, was not a success. It required special paper, and it printed only 96 dots per inch (compared to 600 dots per inch in 1995). While Epson, a vendor of dot matrix printers, thought that HP's first product was an embarrassment, HP saw the ink-jet technology as the basis for satisfying a mass market that would demand higher-quality printouts of text, graphics, and photographs. Hackborn chose to "learn from the Japanese" by investing heavily in its low-cost ink-jet technology, building it into a family of products that could fill retail shelves.

Canon, which had patented early ink-jet designs and then shared them with HP, chose a complex implementation that would take many years to develop. Epson's U.S. executives tried unsuccessfully to convince its Japanese headquarters that Epson should introduce a high-quality printer to meet the demands of low-budget U.S. PC users. Because of Epson's large dot matrix revenue base, profits, and technological history, Epson declined to develop its expensive ink-jet technology variant.

Meanwhile, HP engineers filed several patents on its own ink-jet technology, and began a process of continual improvement to solve the ink-jet's problems. HP developed print heads that could generate 300 dots per inch, and made inks that would stay liquid in the cartridge, but dry instantly on plain paper.

In 1988, HP introduced the Deskjet, the first version of the plain-paper copier that ultimately took share from the Japanese products. Although HP had no ink-jet rivals at the time, the product was not meeting its sales goals in 1989. The ink-jet was competing with HP's more costly laser printers. Ink-jet sales were too low to support its high research and manufacturing costs. Due to HP's policy of requiring its divisions to be financially self-supporting, the ink-jet division needed new markets to avert a financial crisis.

In the autumn of 1989, a group of engineers and managers held a two-day retreat at Mount Hood in Oregon. While reviewing market share charts, HP realized that it had been targeting the wrong enemy. Instead of positioning the ink-jet as a low-cost alternative to HP's laser printers, the managers decided to attack the Japanese-dominated dot matrix market. Dot matrix had poor print quality and color. Furthermore, Epson, the dot matrix leader, had no competitive ink-jet, and was distracted by an expensive and failing effort to sell a PC.

HP attacked Epson beginning with an in-depth analysis of its market share, marketing strategies, public financial data, loyal customers, and top managers. In addition, HP engineers reverse-engineered Epson printers to search for design and manufacturing ideas. HP's analysis of Epson generated useful insights. HP discovered that Epson marketers convinced stores to put printers in the most prominent locations. HP also learned that Epson used price cuts to defend itself from challengers. HP found out that consumers liked Epson reliability. Finally, HP found out that Epson printers were designed to be easy to manufacture.

HP responded by demanding that stores put its printers next to Epson's. HP also tripled its warranty. And HP redesigned its printers for ease of manufacturing. In its competitor analysis, HP had also learned that Epson could create a very broad product line by making slight variations in the same basic platform. HP, on the other hand, had a history of creating an entirely new platform for each new product version.

Engineers were very upset at the suggestion to make minor modifications to the existing platform. They reluctantly agreed, however, only after the product manager forced engineers to conduct a telephone poll of customers that showed that customers wanted to buy a product that was a slight variation of HP's existing platform. By remaining with this platform, HP was able to introduce a product to market far earlier than its competitors for the now rapidly growing color printer market.

When Tandy opened its stores in 1991, it told suppliers to make ink-jets available to meet what it anticipated to be very strong demand. Only HP had product available. When Japanese printer makers that had been investing in ink-jet research tried to enter the market, they found that HP had locked up many important patents. Citizens Watch Company, for example, found that HP had fifty patents covering how ink travels through the cartridge head. At Nippon Electric Company (NEC), years went by during which it was unable to replicate HP's technology, enabling HP to gain an even greater lead over its competitors.

By the time Canon introduced the first credible competition, HP had already sold millions of its printers, and had thousands of outlets for its replacement cartridges. HP used its experience to make continuous improvements in manufacturing. As a result, by 1994, the Deskjet cost half its 1988 level in inflation-adjusted dollars.

When Canon was about to introduce a color ink-jet printer in 1993, HP cut the price of its own version before Canon reached the market. The black and white printer, priced at $995 in 1988, listed for $365 in 1994. When NEC tried to introduce an inexpensive monochrome ink-jet printer, HP launched an improved color version, and cut the price of its best-selling black-and-white model by 40 percent over six months.

HP's willingness to compete with its prior versions enabled it to grow revenues, and to dominate increasingly value-conscious segments of its market while blocking the entry of new competitors. Between 1984 and 1994, for example, HP's share of the U.S. printer market grew from two to 55 percent.[2]

What does this case have to do with sustaining change induced by e-commerce? HP's experience with ink-jet printers illustrates that power of the company's attitude toward growth and innovation. HP's culture encouraged the Vancouver division to make a last-ditch attempt to save itself by commercializing its ink-jet discoveries. Companies seeking to sustain change would be more effective if they shared HP's cultural attributes. HP's culture also encouraged its people to learn how to compete in a retail business, something that HP had never done before. The result was that HP engineers began talking to customers, and adapting to their needs. In addition, HP learned how to compete successfully in retail electronics. HP's ability to learn new skills is essential for companies seeking to sustain change induced by e-commerce. Finally, HP built into its product-development process the notion that it was better for the company to make its existing products obsolete than to let competitors do it. This ability to take the initiative in providing customers with ever-increasing value was crucial to its ability to keep competitors at bay. HP's notion of cannibalization is essential for succeeding in e-commerce. As we saw in the case of Merrill Lynch, the inability to cannibalize is a critical impediment to success in e-commerce. This inability creates opportunities for competitors who are not bogged down by the legacy of a land-based approach to business.

Methodology for Sustaining Change

What can senior management do to create an organization that sustains change? As I have emphasized, managers can create an organization that rewards change. This kind of organization will be able to sustain the change induced by e-commerce as well as it can sustain the change induced by other technologies. Here are five steps that managers can take to sustain change:

Get the CEO on board. As we saw in Chapter 7, the initial precondition for sustaining change is getting the CEO to believe that the benefits of change exceed its costs. In many organizations, the CEO does not believe it is worthwhile to encourage change and innovation. Without such support, the environment in which managers attempt to build e-commerce will be toxic. Changing the CEO's mind about the importance of adapting to change is an undertaking that may be very difficult to achieve. One way to do this is to use an outside consultant whom the CEO respects to make the case for change. If the consultant is successful, the entire organization benefits. If the consultant fails, it is the consultant, not an internal person, who takes the hit.

On the other hand, if the CEO has an indomitable will to win, then the CEO will recognize that winning depends on adapting to changing customer needs, new technologies, and upstart competitors. Under such circumstances, the CEO will be open to creating an organization that is effective at sustaining change.

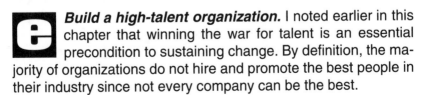 ***Build a "Create the Future" culture.*** A critical step for sustaining change is to create a culture that values creating the future. This kind of culture is precisely what the most talented people yearn to be part of. Creating such a culture will help sustain the change induced by e-commerce. Creating such a culture also makes it much easier to attract and motivate the very best people.

What is a "Create the Future" culture? Such a culture celebrates the company's ability to bring to market new products and services that create value for the company's customers as their needs change. Such a culture motivates the entire organization to create products and services that win in the marketplace, and make a difference in many people's lives. Achieving this is important to talented people who want to believe that the work they do has meaning. One benefit of such a culture is that if employees believe that their work has meaning, they will be happy to devote their waking hours to doing that work.

How can a company build such a culture? This is a big part of the CEO's job. The CEO can create such a culture by telling employees stories that communicate how important creating the future is to the company's business. These stories should be simple, direct, compelling, and real. The CEO should also promote people who exemplify the values in these stories, and punish those who do not. Over time, the consistent communication of the value of creating the future coupled with actions that clearly reinforce these values will result in a "Creating the Future" culture. Such a culture will be well positioned to help the company sustain change.

Build a high-talent organization. I noted earlier in this chapter that winning the war for talent is an essential precondition to sustaining change. By definition, the majority of organizations do not hire and promote the best people in their industry since not every company can be the best.

If an company decides to build a high-talent organization, there are several things to do. First, define in specific terms what the most talented people can do. Make the definition of the best people quite explicit. Second, do market research. Find high-talent people, and ask them what they would like in their ideal work environment. Third, change the organization so that it matches the most important characteristics of a high-talent organization. Fourth, develop and execute recruiting strategies that lead to the hiring of the most-talented people.

Obviously, doing these things requires significant investment in money and time. It may also involve the pain of replacing senior people who are not the best people in the industry. Furthermore, creating a high-talent organization has implications that go well beyond the requirements of sustaining the change induced by e-commerce. Creating such an organization will also produce benefits that will make the organization open to change from technologies that emerge for many years into the future. This is precisely why creating a high-talent organization is so important for *sustaining* change.

e *Communicate the company's commitment to change.* People at all levels of an organization fear change. The best way to combat that fear is extensive communication. Managers must speak with the organization, and make the case for why change is important. Managers must also listen to people in the organization, and understand their fears about change. Communication must be very frequent and as open as possible if the change is to be sustained. As managers consider the costs and benefits of change, they should be careful not to underestimate the time commitment that they will need to make in this communication process.

e *Make customers the magnetic North Pole.* A key notion that we saw in the cases on Microsoft, Cisco, and HP was that working collaboratively with customers is the most important driver of success. To sustain change, companies must watch how customers spend their money, and make sure that they offer the services and products to garner the lion's share of that money. Simply put, if a company wants to sustain change, it must view customers as the magnetic North Pole of the company. As we saw in the Cisco example, one way to do this is to measure customer satisfaction independently, and to tie bonus payments to improvement in the customer satisfaction score.

An ancillary benefit of the focus on customer satisfaction is that people across departments have a clear financial incentive to work together to make customers more satisfied. The greater the importance of customer satisfaction to the employees' compensation, the more likely they will be delighted to place their primary loyalty to helping the company—not their particular department—do a better job of creating value for the customer. Consequently, the company will find itself changing in a way that sustains market leadership.

Conclusion

Entire books have been written about how organizations can sustain change. Here we have examined the principles that distinguish companies that *sustain* change from those that *inhibit* change. Ultimately, the organizational capabilities that enable companies to sustain change in a more general sense will be essential for enabling companies to build on the victories, and learn from the failures that are associated with e-commerce.

Most critically, organizations that sustain change are led by CEOs who are convinced that the benefits of change outweigh its costs. These CEOs create cultures that value-create the future, win the war for talent, communicate the importance of change in an ongoing dialogue with employees, and create compensation systems that pay for change that creates ever-higher levels of customer value.

Notes

1. S. Yoder, "How H-P Used Tactics of the Japanese to Beat Them at Their Game," *The Wall Street Journal,* September 8, 1994, pp. A1, A9.
2. Ibid.

PART III

Building the E-Commerce Infrastructure

9

Designing the Architecture

What do senior managers need to understand about the architecture of an e-commerce system? In this chapter we will explore this question in detail. The answer, we will discover, is that senior management's role in crafting the e-commerce architecture depends to a large extent on how dependent the business will be on the effective operation of the e-commerce–enabling technology.

If the business is not heavily dependent on e-commerce, then senior management must be aware of the e-commerce architecture only to the extent that its failure to operate will potentially anger a relatively small number of customers. If the business depends on the e-commerce architecture for its continued survival, then senior management must be actively involved in setting the vision for e-commerce, establishing performance standards for the system, and ensuring that the organization has the resources it needs to satisfy those standards as demand on the system grows.

This chapter explores these issues based on the assumption that many readers may be starting to employ e-commerce, and are looking to become more dependent on e-commerce in the future, depending on their levels of success with their initial efforts. Based on this assumption, the chapter will move along this spectrum of e-commerce involvement, showing the role of senior management in each case. Figure 9-1 depicts the spectrum of e-commerce architectures.

Companies start off trying to learn about e-commerce often by putting brochures online with an Internet Service Pro-

Figure 9-1. Spectrum of e-commerce architectures.

Experiment	Back-Office Re-Architecting	Front-Office Re-Architecting
Online Store	Electronic Procurement	Online Trading

vider (ISP). As companies find that they are gaining significant value from the e-commerce architecture, they may choose a more ambitious application such as electronic procurement. Electronic procurement involves a significant amount of re-architecting of technology and changing of internal business processes. In general, such changes do not put customer relationships at risk. The ultimate level of re-architecting takes place when the company decides that it must take advantage of the power of the Web to transform the customer's experience with the company.

Chapter 9 will first define what is meant by e-commerce architecture. Then it will describe how companies can partner with ISPs to experiment with e-commerce in a way that does not put their entire businesses at risk while also enabling the businesses to learn. The chapter will continue by exploring how Eastman Chemical and Weyerhaeuser established e-commerce architectures for their electronic procurement systems. The chapter will continue by describing two e-commerce architectures, one from Charles Schwab and the other from eBay, to demonstrate effective and ineffective handling of e-commerce architecture. Next, Chapter 9 will develop six principles for designing e-commerce architectures. The chapter will conclude with a methodology that senior managers can use to design effective e-commerce architectures.

E-Commerce Architecture Defined

The notion of the "e-commerce architecture" must be defined if we are to use it effectively throughout this chapter. The e-commerce architecture refers to both a *business process* and its *enabling technology*. As I have stressed throughout this book, e-commerce has the potential to change the company's competitive strategy. The implementation of this new competitive strategy depends on a new way of conducting business. The new way of conducting business happens, in part, because of changes in peoples' jobs. The new way of conducting business also depends on new information technology. As we will see, the role of senior management is to decide who will provide this technology (e.g., an outside company or the company's own information technology department) and the performance standards to which this technology must adhere.

As we will see later in this chapter, these performance standards are measured in terms of many factors. Such standards include:

- How many users the system can support
- How smoothly the system can adapt to rapid demand growth
- The extent of system uptime
- The level of system security
- The speed of system response
- The level of customer service
- The system's cost to build and maintain

Experiment: Partnering with ISPs

As I noted above, there is a spectrum of e-commerce architectures. On one end of the spectrum is a company that is just beginning to experiment with e-commerce. Companies in this category are reluctant to bet their entire businesses on successful e-commerce implementation. Instead, these companies are interested in experimenting with e-commerce in a way that can enable them to learn without risking the business. If the e-commerce implementation does not succeed, a company would want an efficient way to cut its losses.

For companies in this position, an ideal e-commerce architecture is to outsource the operation of the e-commerce system to an ISP. This outsourcing strategy puts the burden on the company to design its e-commerce application. However, the ISP actually assumes the risk of building and maintaining the technology that enables the application. A company pays a monthly fee to the ISP. The company can generally terminate its involvement with the ISP without too much notice if the e-commerce application does not succeed. On the other hand, if the e-commerce application is successful, the company can take its e-commerce application in-house if the company decides it needs greater control.

One example of experimenting with e-commerce is to set up an online store with an ISP. According to *Windows Magazine*, online stores can display products, hold sales and offer special deals, take orders from customers, process credit card transactions, calculate applicable taxes on purchases, and process shipping. Software manages the product catalog and transactions, and uses a Web software language called Hyper-Text Markup Language (HTML) to make the online stores operate. Companies can operate such online stores at affordable prices and with just a small amount of technological skill.[1]

Working with an ISP is one of the best ways to build an e-commerce architecture that includes the following key elements:

- *Design.* Companies need to make design decisions regarding the look and feel of the online store. ISPs provide design templates that simplify this design process.

- *Catalog.* Companies need to build and maintain online product catalogs. The ISPs offer catalogs that enable companies to display images of their products. The catalogs also organize products by categories and subcategories, and include names, descriptions, Stock Keeping Unit (SKU) numbers, and prices.

- *Shopping Carts.* Online shopping carts allow online customers to click on buttons to add items to their carts. When they have completed the process of loading their shopping carts, the cart system allows them to proceed to checkout, where the final elements of the transaction are handled.

• *Credit Card Payments.* Consumers have grown more comfortable with the security measures that e-commerce sites have taken to protect against theft. ISPs let companies process credit card transactions using the security features in Web browsers and a variety of encryption methods. To accept credit card payments over the Web, companies must have a merchant account, which allows merchants to accept and process credit card transactions. Many ISPs have partnerships to help Web vendors obtain merchant accounts at better rates. Many ISPs also handle credit card authorizations online.

• *Security.* To make online shopping sites secure, companies need encryption. One standard option is to offer security via a Secure Sockets Layer (SSL) certificate and connection. This ensures that passwords and credit card numbers are encrypted during transmission. To ensure that the site is legitimate, and that the visitor is connecting to an authentic site, an independent certificate authority issues the security certificates. This authority verifies the ownership and identity of the site for which the company is purchasing a certificate. The company's name is then encrypted into the certificate that is issued.

• *Shipping and Taxes.* Sites must calculate shipping and tax costs once an order has been placed. ISPs offer a variety of options, such as calculating the rate by number of items or weight, and shipping methods (such as Federal Express, UPS Ground, and one- and two-day air). Taxes can be calculated or turned on only for states that require taxes. Items can also be marked as taxable or nontaxable.

• *Customer Tracking.* Companies also need software that provides clear reports regarding who visits the site, where the visitors come from, what pages they visit, and what products they purchase.

• *Merchandising.* Online stores need to feature sales and items of special interest. More sophisticated applications allow online stores to create cross promotions and special deals for certain customers.

One example of an ISP that provides this service is Atlanta-based MindSpring. MindSpring hosts online stores for prices that begin at about $50 per month for up to 50 products. The monthly e-commerce fee increases as the number of products increases. The e-commerce fees are in addition to monthly hosting fees, which range from about $50 to $100.[2]

As the MindSpring example demonstrates, companies can experiment with online stores for a very modest amount of money. These experiments are quite useful for companies that are eager to learn and afraid to risk their reputations by shifting their entire operations online. If the volume of e-commerce business becomes so significant that it is no longer cost-effective to host the site on an ISP, the site can be shifted to an internally managed operation.

Back-Office E-Architecting: Weyerhaeuser and Eastman Chemical

For experimenting with e-commerce, working with an ISP is an excellent solution. Many companies are beginning to move beyond the experimentation phase to e-architecting a "back-office" process. These companies are not yet willing to e-architect a process that will alter their competitive positioning. However, they are eager to achieve what they perceive as tangible economic benefits from altering internal processes that do not have such a direct impact on their relationships with customers.

One example of such a back-office process is the procurement of office supplies. While this process sounds mundane, it can be a source of significant economic benefits for large companies. As I noted earlier, for example, GE spends $5 billion on office supplies. Electronic procurement is anticipated to save GE $1 billion. The savings come from consolidating the purchases of GE's business units into one high-volume corporate purchase with a preferred supplier. The electronic procurement systems' ease of use increases the number of employees who purchase from the electronic catalog.

When a company installs an electronic procurement system, it must develop a new e-commerce architecture. This new architecture involves the aforementioned changes in the way the company does purchasing. It also involves new computer systems. According to *Purchasing*, Weyerhaeuser and Eastman Chemical have learned both of these lessons as they have been installing an electronic procurement system.

Weyerhaeuser

For pulp and paper manufacturer Weyerhaeuser, the process change began with a strategic assessment and reevaluation of its procurement function in 1995. Scott Walker, Weyerhaeuser's director of finances and business processes for procurement and supply management, pointed out that the company's purchasing had always been fragmented and decentralized. Weyerhaeuser needed to analyze the magnitude of its purchasing costs and its base of suppliers. Then Weyerhaeuser conceptualized a new procurement process that was more automated and consistent.[3]

By 1998, Weyerhaeuser had consolidated most of its office supply spending, and was selecting an electronic catalog and requisition tool for 18,000 employees across the company by the end of 1999. In the first phase of the project, Weyerhaeuser employees will have controlled access to preferred suppliers' catalogs on its intranet. Ultimately, Weyerhaeuser intended to connect its electronic procurement system to its Enterprise Resource Planning (ERP) system, and to increase the extent to which Weyerhaueser's supplier interactions are conducted online.

Eastman Chemical

Similarly, buyers at Eastman Chemical Company intended to use e-commerce to accelerate cycle times and consolidate fragmented spending. Eddie Page, Eastman Chemical's purchasing manager, realized after two years that Web technology could help his company achieve these business objectives.

Eastman created a team to evaluate electronic procurement options. The team consisted of buyers, IT staff, and consultants. This team conducted a two-month analysis of Eastman's procurement patterns. The team discovered that one-time spot purchases with purchasing cards prevented Eastman purchasers from consolidating their purchases and negotiating volume discounts with suppliers.

After evaluating five major electronic procurement providers, Eastman chose Commerce One's Commerce Chain Solution. In a pilot launched in late 1998, Eastman employees buy office and lab supplies at negotiated prices through key suppliers' catalogs on Eastman's intranet. The system skips invoicing, receiving, stocking, and issuing. Instead, the system delivers the goods directly to the employee.

E-Commerce Architecture Performance Criteria

The e-commerce architecture for back-office applications such as electronic procurement must satisfy six performance criteria:

- *Cost-Effectiveness.* Electronic procurement applications like the ones being installed at Weyerhaeuser and Eastman Chemical can cost millions of dollars. Commerce One estimates that the return on investment can reach 500 percent. Scott Walker noted that Weyerhaeuser saved 3 to 5 percent on its acquisition costs alone. As I noted earlier, GE estimates that it will save $1 billion through its electronic procurement system.

- *Integratability.* E-commerce systems are so expensive themselves that companies are unwilling to invest in them if they also demand the reconfiguration of existing ERP or account management systems. Therefore, buyers of electronic procurement systems want them to work in seamless fashion with their existing ERPs or account management systems.

Scott Walker noted that Weyerhaeuser's IT resources were scarce with a high priority on dealing with Y2K remediation. Therefore, Walker placed a strong emphasis on the need for its electronic procurement system to fit Weyerhaeuser's technology and complement its ERP system. Eddie Page noted that Eastman Chemical chose Commerce One's Commerce Chain Solution largely because it was compatible with Eastman's ERP system and its client/server operating system software.

● *Scalability.* E-commerce systems must be able to adapt effectively to changes in the volumes and natures of their users. In the case of electronic procurement systems, the number of employees, products, and suppliers that places demands on the system are likely to grow over time. At the pilot stage, most companies start with a few types of indirect production materials, key test facilities, and some preferred suppliers. But as the program evolves, it must be able to accommodate a new supplier's catalog or 10,000 new concurrent users, for instance. For example, while Eddie Page noted that Eastman Chemical was starting with office and lab supplies, in the future Eastman hoped to use its system to purchase hand tools, janitorial and welding supplies, and consumable items. Eastman also plans for routine commodities to be available through their intranet, as well as Request for Proposal (RFP) and supplier-selection capabilities.

● *Ease of End-Use.* If an e-commerce system is difficult to use, a company will not achieve the desired business benefits. For example, according to Eddie Page, Eastman Chemical's on-line buying system has on-screen "wizards" that guide users to place an order with three mouse clicks: Enter desired product, select from qualified suppliers, and place the order.

● *Supplier Participation.* Similarly, suppliers must also find systems easy for achieving the benefits of e-commerce. For example, Eastman's key suppliers receive orders electronically into their sales systems, saving them time spent on the phone, and saving money from lower inventories sustained by predictable purchase patterns. Furthermore, Eastman suppliers can modify their catalog content quickly through their Web browsers. Suppliers are also important to Weyerhaeuser's e-commerce strategy. Scott Walker noted that it is just as expensive for a supplier to process a sales order as it is for Weyerhaeuser to place a purchase order. Walker's efforts to reduce its suppliers' costs benefited Weyerhaeuser as well.

• *Ease of Maintenance.* Once an e-commerce system is installed and working, maintaining its content and functionality should not be too costly. In-house IT departments should be able to handle routine network maintenance, buyers and/or suppliers should be able to manage catalog content through a Web-based interface, and purchasing departments should be able to modify end-user buying rules.[4]

As companies begin to integrate e-commerce into their back-office operations, senior management's responsibility for its architecture becomes more complex. Senior management must take action to set specific performance standards for the e-commerce architecture's cost, economic return, and value to the company's employees and suppliers. The cases of Weyerhaeuser and Eastman Chemical provide a useful basis on which to develop and implement such standards.

Front-Office E-Architecting: Charles Schwab and eBay

While designing the architecture for a back-office system is more complex than the experimentation I described earlier in the chapter, "front-office" e-architecting is the most complex of all. Here, the company's competitive strategy is placed at risk. All the strategizing described earlier in this book must be accomplished before management can consider the front-office e-commerce architecture.

Because the front-office e-commerce architecture touches the customer, the role of the CEO becomes paramount in distinguishing effective and ineffective front-office e-architecting. Simply put, if the CEO pushes the organization to set and achieve high standards, the company can make great strides in enhancing its competitive position. If the company's CEO does not take such an active role, the erosion of performance standards can significantly damage the company's position. The case of Schwab exemplifies the former condition. The case of eBay typifies the latter one.

Charles Schwab

Tracing the development of Charles Schwab's e-commerce architecture provides one of the best available examples of how senior management can drive success in e-commerce. As I noted earlier, Schwab took a short-term risk when it invested in online trading. The risk has clearly paid off for Schwab. One of the reasons is that Schwab's CEO took such an aggressive role in setting high-performance standards for the e-commerce architecture, and made certain that the Schwab organization met those standards. According to *Internet Week*, Schwab's success is due to swift business decisions by top management, technical solutions by an IT team that agrees with management's vision, and the budget and time required to get the job done.[5]

By 2000, Schwab expects 80 to 90 percent of trades to occur online at a rate of 4 million transactions an hour. Schwab's hopes for meeting this level of demand began in October 1995. James Chong, then Vice President of Transaction Processing Architecture, and his five programmers had just completed the prototype of a Web front-end for Schwab's back-end trading system. Other than Schwab, rivals such as Lombard Securities and E*Trade were starting to offer trading on the Web, but at the time it was not clear whether such services would become popular. Chong knew that Schwab Chairman Chuck Schwab was tracking competitors' Web strategies. However, Schwab had not yet asked Chong to develop an online trading system.

Chong was most focused on building software that would link the Schwab's back-end host trading system with specific financial services software, such as equity trading. This linking software, called "middleware," ultimately became a key part of Schwab's Web-trading architecture.

That October, Chong offered an impromptu demonstration of the middleware, named Sentry, to Schwab's Chief Information Officer (CIO) and Executive Vice President Dawn Lepore. Lepore brought along David Pottruck, Schwab President and co-CEO; Chuck Schwab; Roger Neaves, Vice President of Infrastructure; and Ken Richmond, the Project Manager of the Sentry product.

Schwab's executive team was pleasantly surprised by the demonstration. According to Chong, Chuck Schwab was surprised that Chong's team had created a browser front-end. Chong also noted that Chuck Schwab became very animated after he placed and completed a trade for 100 shares of Schwab in a test account from the browser.

The executive team stayed at Chong's computer laboratory for an hour while Chuck Schwab asked detailed questions regarding the viability and security of Web-based trading. The discussion continued with Pottruck saying that the security risk was not necessarily from outside hackers, but from people slipping through the firewalls, and accidentally damaging the integrity of databases.

Once Charles Schwab saw that secure Web trading could become a reality, the company moved quickly. On October. 7, 1995, four people met at the first brainstorming session to evaluate the Web development. The party included Vincent Phillips, Vice President of Web Systems; James Chong, now Vice President and Chief Architect of the IT Group; Ken Richmond, Project Director of Sentry Middleware; and Cynthia Alley, Director of Electronic Brokerage Product Development.

The group decided that its members lacked the resources to conduct an internal Web development project itself. As a result, the group decided to outsource the task, and immediately issue an RFP. On November 7, 1995, the RFP went out.

In late November of that same year, Schwab recruited a senior executive who was familiar with Web business. This new executive, Gideon Sasson, had been Vice President of Information Services at

IBM, and was responsible for IBM's proposed Web business and e-mail services. Sasson was hired as Schwab's Executive Vice President of Electronic Brokerage in the last week of November 1995—before such a business existed.

Soon after Sasson began work at Schwab, he received a call from Chuck Schwab. Mr. Schwab announced from an off-site meeting at the Clairmont Hotel that Web trading was an important strategy for Schwab, and that he wanted to launch Web trading in sixty days—on Valentine's Day. The Schwab team managed to convince Chuck Schwab that it would take another thirty days to deliver a Web trading system.

The project was called "Cupid" for the original Valentine's Day launch. In the meantime, the RFPs from IBM, MCI, Sun Microsystems, and three smaller vendors came back. Most required nine to twelve months, and cost more than $2 million. Schwab did not have the time. As a result, the company decided to build the system internally. The team succeeded in building the system in three months for a cost of less than $1 million as opposed to the nine to twelve months and the $2 million that outsourcers had asked.

But then, Schwab had much greater-than-expected demand. Schwab originally expected to have 10,000 customers using its Web-trading service by the end of 1996. That number was reached by the end of May 1996.

This rapid growth forced Schwab's systems staff to add servers, on a daily basis at times, going from three in April 1996 to fifty in May 1998. Adding forty-seven Web servers required expansion to the network infrastructure. For example, Roger Wong, Schwab's Technical Director of Communications Services, noted that Schwab went from two Cisco 7500 routers to eight 7500 routers between April 1996 and May 1998.

By May 1998, Schwab's global network used 550 Cisco routers and several unspecified Catalyst 5500 switches. Metropolitan ATM high-speed communications services linked Schwab's most important urban regional offices. Schwab's network also included network management software from IBM's Tivoli Systems unit and Hewlett-Packard's OpenView.

In April 1996, Sasson needed to craft another makeshift solution to the unexpectedly high level of demand for its online trading service. In particular, Sasson needed to install security software, called digital certificates, on eight Web servers. The digital certificate vendor, VeriSign, said they needed forty-eight hours to accomplish this. Sasson could not wait that long, so he phoned VeriSign's President and CEO directly. By exercising Sasson's influence as a large VeriSign customer, Schwab had its digital certificates installed within hours.

In the first week of May 1996, volume grew more, and Schwab was forced to turn away customers. Sasson again used his connections, and approached IBM, which was supplying the server hardware. IBM had a new server called the SP/2 AIX, which allowed new processors be added. Quickly, sixteen SP/2 servers were installed at Schwab, increasing system capacity there.

Simultaneously, Schwab developers began updating their legacy systems to Java technology, which would allow for the addition of more compelling customer interfaces. The Java program also would allow for new services, such as Asset Allocation, which would walk customers through more investment choices. Service launched in August 1997, and by May 1998, Schwab had 200 Java developments in progress.

In a year, the number of active online accounts doubled from 617,000 in December 1996 to 1.2 million, while associated assets increased from $42 billion to $80 billion.[6]

Schwab, however, suffered setbacks due to the failure of its systems to cope with the tremendous increase in trading volume. According to *Information Week*, in early 1999, Schwab's trading system failed twice due to problems with its mainframe computers. Despite the problems, Schwab persisted with its mainframe-based e-commerce architecture. In fact, in the second quarter of 1999, Schwab began a migration from batch processing to real-time processing of trades on its mainframe computers. Schwab also planned to completely redesign its Web site, and to add new services and technology for active traders. By May 1999, Schwab added two mainframes to the three IBM and three Hitachi mainframes in its primary data center. It also increased the scale of its Web system from eighty-eight IBM RS/6000 Web servers to 154.[7]

Despite these efforts, in the first half of 1999, Schwab continued to struggle to keep up with demand. According to the *San Jose Mercury News*, Schwab spent 15 to 17 percent of its annual revenue on information technology, amounting to $400 million in 1998. Of Schwab's 6 million customers, 2.7 million were using the online trading service. According to Fred Matteson, Chief Technologist at Schwab, between March 1998 and June 1999, the number of users signed on to Schwab's system at the time the market opens had grown from 3,000 to 30,000.[8]

Matteson noted that as the number of online investors increased, so did their expectations of quality. By June 1999, customers expected Schwab's online system to work 100 percent of the time. As a result, Schwab has had to change its ideas about how to build computer systems. By June 1999, most of Schwab's Web applications ran on Sun servers. But the crucial, time-sensitive trading system ran on seven mainframes and three backup mainframes in two locations in Phoenix. In early June 1999, Schwab, working with IBM, launched a plan to add thirty-two new mainframes, if needed, in a configuration in which they all would act as one computer. If one went down, another would instantly take over, so that the user would detect no downtime.[9]

While Schwab continues to invest in order to keep up with its growing demand for online trading, other companies are not so aggressive.

eBay

eBay is a leading online auction site that has grown very rapidly since its initial public offering in October 1998. eBay's popularity has caused tremendous strains on its systems capabilities. The repeated problems have also strained eBay's customer relations, leading an increasing number of customers to defect to competing services.

Despite these problems, eBay still enjoys the advantages of market leadership. As the largest online auction site, sellers are drawn to eBay because the large number of users increases the size of the potential market for items being auctioned. The more sellers that are attracted to the site, the wider the selection that potential auction bidders can anticipate. This wider selection in turn attracts more bidders, which then attracts more sellers. This network effect causes significant growth in demand for eBay's service.

The increase in demand places a real premium on eBay's ability to keep up. According to the *San Jose Mercury News*, in June 1999, eBay failed to keep up with this demand. For some eBay customers, the twenty-two-hour June 1999 outage was the straw that broke the camel's back. While eBay assured its customers that is was doing everything possible to make sure the nearly day-long outage did not recur, John Horner, was one customer who did not believe eBay's claim.[10]

For the eighteen months that Horner, an investor and consultant, had been buying and selling items on eBay, he had seen the Web site go down more times than he could remember. Horner noted that after every episode, eBay offered customers the same response. Horner recounted how eBay sent out messages to their customers saying, "Thanks for your forbearance. We have everything under control now." Horner did *not* believe that eBay had things under control, and *did* believe that the episodes would certainly recur.

When eBay crashed, users complained via e-mails and postings that eBay's management does not understand technology. In fact, with the exception of President and Chief Executive Meg Whitman, most eBay senior managers have technical backgrounds.

eBay hosts auctions for 2 million items on a single, powerful server from Sun Microsystems, and had promised to add more engineers, review its software and hardware, and speed up its plans for redundancy.

As Anil Gadre, Vice President and General Manager of Sun's Solaris software group noted, it is very easy to get caught up just keeping up with the growth. Gadre points out that companies must pay attention to infrastructure because the expectation level of the community grows and changes. Since consumers expect that a phone dial tone works even when there is a hurricane, they are beginning to have the same expectation for the Web.

One of the disadvantages of the Web as a business medium is that there usually is not a human buffer between the customer and a difficult piece of equipment. Since there is no service representative to offer an explanation, when there is a problem, customers stay away.

While eBay claimed that customers had returned after the June problem was fixed, customers complained that they could not access their personal pages, and that the volume of bidding was low. The number of items up for auction the Monday morning after the crash had declined 18 percent from the 2.2 million recorded before the system went down the previous Thursday. Over the subsequent weekend, traffic at other online auction sites rose.

One of the reasons for eBay's low post-crash volume was customer defections. An example of such defections is Russ Morris. Morris, who ran the Knife Hut, had been selling knives and other goods on both eBay and at Amazon.com's new auction site. After the twenty-two-hour shutdown in June 1999, he said he would give eBay one last chance to keep his business. Morris noted that Amazon had never let him down. As a result, Morris decided that if eBay could not solve its operational problems, he planned to move all his business to Amazon.

During the weekend after the crash, eBay changed its policy on extending auctions during outages. Previously, eBay had extended the time only for those auctions that were scheduled to end during the period when the site was down. After the crash, eBay changed its policy so that if an outage lasted more than two hours, all auctions under way would automatically be extended for twenty-four hours.

According to Internet audience measurement numbers from Nielsen/NetRatings, Yahoo's auction site benefited significantly from eBay's outage. Yahoo quickly began a campaign of radio ads highlighting the fact that its auction site was operating.

The traffic for auctions at Yahoo.com rose from about 62,000 visitors on the Thursday of the crash to 105,000 on Friday, and 135,000 on the Saturday after the crash, according to Nielsen/NetRatings. At Amazon.com's auction site, meanwhile, that number went from 86,000 on the Thursday of the crash to 41,000 Friday, then increased to 132,000 on the Saturday after the crash.

According to Allen Weiner, a NetRatings analyst, the number of visitors to the eBay site remained far higher—852,000 on the Saturday after the crash, for example—but the amount of time they spent online and the number of pages they viewed dropped sharply.

While eBay did not have a backup system, it claimed to be working on building one so that a second system could take over if the primary server failed. The server that eBay uses is powerful and reliable—Sun's Enterprise 10000 machine. As eBay's June crash illustrated, no server can operate at 100 percent uptime.

By contrast, Amazon has redundancy for its entire site, not only for auctions. Amazon strives for 100 percent availability. While Amazon has invested millions of dollars to increase the availability and reliability of its systems, it cannot control these complex systems well enough to guarantee that there will not be a site outage.

To put the situation into perspective, auction customers do not evaluate online auction sites based on reliability alone. For example, Louise Evans, an eBay customer for almost a year, said she had looked at Amazon's and Yahoo's auctions, but was not happy with these sites. Evans found that Amazon's site was difficult to use and Yahoo did not have a wide selection. On the other hand, Evans noted, eBay was much easier for computer novices like her to use.[11]

As the eBay situation indicates, a successful front-end Web business creates such huge growth in demand that it is very difficult to keep up. The question for managers is whether they can anticipate such demand increases, and build the capacity needed to minimize service disruptions. If the e-commerce architectures are sufficiently responsive, the opportunities for competitors to pounce on the service disruptions of market leaders will be diminished. If the e-commerce architectures cannot adapt with sufficient speed, new competitors may be able to disrupt the growth of market leaders.

Principles of E-Commerce Architecture

What principles emerge from these cases that managers can apply to the design of e-commerce architectures? Here are six:

Senior management must set the vision. As we saw in the case of Schwab, Chuck Schwab was monitoring his competitors, and realized that his company needed to compete in the online trading market. Chuck Schwab's realization created the context in which the company's technology developers would operate. Without Chuck Schwab's support, it would not have been possible for the company to develop and improve its online trading infrastructure.

The company should match the architecture to the extent to which it embraces e-commerce. As I emphasized earlier in this chapter, it is essential for senior management to recognize where the company stands in the spectrum of e-commerce architectures. Senior management must match the company's e-commerce architecture with the company's place in that spectrum. If the company is just starting out utilizing the Internet, it may make more sense to outsource the operation of the e-commerce application. As the company moves toward making e-commerce a more strategic part of its competitive strategy, the company may want to take full responsibility for the e-commerce infrastructure.

e *Senior management must establish performance standards.* While the role of senior management is not to pick the hardware and software that enables the e-commerce system, senior management must set specific performance standards. As we saw in the cases of Schwab, Weyerhaeuser, and Eastman Chemical, the ambitious targets for return on investment, system uptime, security, and many other attributes were set by senior management. These standards must be based on the company's intent to provide superior customer value.

e *Senior management must drive the company's compliance with the performance standards.* Senior management must assure that the company continues to adapt its e-commerce architecture to ever higher-performance standards. Senior management must keep track of what competitors are offering, and how customer expectations are changing. Senior management must assure that the e-commerce architecture evolves to keep the company in the vanguard of the industry in meeting these evolving performance standards.

e *Companies must build e-commerce capacity to anticipate rapid demand growth.* As we saw in the cases of Schwab and eBay, e-commerce success can lead to failure if the company's e-commerce capacity is not sufficiently robust to satisfy rapidly growing demand. The implications are that companies must monitor e-commerce demand constantly so that it can make realistic forecasts of future demand, and design their e-commerce architectures to keep ahead of that demand. Given the very high stock market capitalizations of many e-commerce companies, there should not be significant capital barriers to building that capacity.

e *Companies must respond decisively to network interruptions.* As we saw in the cases of Schwab and eBay, it is almost inevitable that companies will experience network interruptions. When these interruptions happen, senior management must step in to cover reasonable losses that customers experience as a result of the interruptions. While senior management may bemoan the short-term losses associated with this insurance, a greater danger would befall the company if it did not cover customer losses somehow. Over the longer run, if a company does not take responsibility for its failures, it loses customer loyalty. This loss of loyalty creates a vicious cycle that can cause a leading company to lose its market position to other companies that are willing to invest in sustaining customer loyalty by taking responsibility for such interruptions.

Methodology for Effective E-Commerce Architectural Design

How can managers build effective e-commerce architectures? Here is my recommended approach, based on the aforementioned principles:

 Set the vision. The e-commerce architecture is a by-product of the company's strategy. I have developed a process in Chapter 4 for how senior managers can develop such strategies. Senior management must ground the strategy in a detailed understanding of customer needs and competitor strategies to meet those needs. Only through such grounding can the subsequent stages in the e-commerce architectural design process be carried out effectively.

 Build the team. Once the vision for e-commerce has been established, senior management must decide who will be responsible for carrying out that vision. For example, senior management should decide who within the IT department will drive the details of the e-commerce architectural design process. Senior management must also decide which business unit executives and staff executives should participate. Finally, senior management should decide which early-adopter customers should participate in the development of the e-commerce architecture.

 Choose the level of integration. Senior management must next match the level of integration to the vision for e-commerce. As I noted before, senior management should decide whether or not to outsource the design and/or operation of the e-commerce architecture. These decisions should be resolved based on considerations of cost, time-to-market, and the ability to control the outcome of the process.

e *Set performance standards.* Senior management must then set the performance standards for the e-commerce architecture. As I noted earlier, these standards should pertain to factors such as the return on investment in the e-commerce system, the level of system uptime, the number of users it can support, the speed of system response, the system ease of use, and its cost to build and maintain. These standards should be set based on strategic variables such as a detailed understanding of customer needs and competitor performance levels.

e *Monitor compliance with standards.* Senior management must set the performance standards and make sure that the company delivers. Senior management should set tight deadlines for the design and implementation of the e-commerce architecture. These deadlines should be based on an understanding of the pace of competitor strategies as well as the internal capabilities of the company. Given the very rapid rate of change in Internet business, senior managers may be willing to pay heavily to achieve rapid e-commerce development.

e *Adapt to change.* Once the system is built, senior management must monitor how the system is used. This monitoring should include a detailed understanding of how many users there are, how quickly the system responds to user requests, how effectively the company responds to customer questions, and how well the company adheres to its uptime standards. This monitoring process should enable the company to anticipate the need to add to system capacity and to alter the system's functions and appearance. This step is really an ongoing process that will force senior management to invest in adapting the company's e-commerce architecture to changing customer expectations.

Conclusion

E-commerce forces senior managers to develop a vision, and then get involved in the implementation of that vision. For many managers, this involvement could require developing a level of understanding of Web technology that they have never had before. The key responsibility of senior management in designing the e-commerce architecture is translating the vision for e-commerce into specific system performance measurements. IT management must propose technical solutions that meet these performance standards, and explain to senior management how these architectural decisions will influence the performance measures. Ultimately, senior management monitors how well the e-commerce architecture is keeping up with evolving customer demands and increase capacity to anticipate those changes.

Notes

1. Lynn Ginsburg, "Open for E-Business—Ready to Join the E-Commerce Revolution? We'll Tell You How to Get Your Store Up and Running," *Windows Magazine*, June 15, 1999 [http://www.techweb.com/se/direct-link.cgi?WIN1999061550011].
2. Ibid.
3. Mark Vigoroso, "Success Depends on Much More Than Supplier Pick," *Purchasing*, November 19, 1998 p. 46.
4. Ibid.
5. Saroja Girishankar, "E-Commerce Architecture: Schwab Makes the Trade," *Internet Week*, May 25, 1998 [http://www.internetwk.com/trends/052598.htm].
6. Ibid.
7. Gregory Dalton, "Setbacks Won't Stop Schwab's E-Commerce Plan," *Information Week*, March 8, 1999 [http://www.informationweek.com/story/IWK1999030850004].
8. Monua Janah, "Embarrassing Sights for E-Commerce," *San Jose Mercury News*, June 19, 1999 [http://www.sjmercury.com/svtech/news/indepth/docs/ebay062099.htm].
9. Ibid.
10. Ibid.
11. Ibid.

10

Evaluating Suppliers

I n Chapter 9, we saw the important role that senior executives play in setting the performance standards to which e-commerce architectures must adhere. In Chapter 10, we will examine how senior executives must develop and administer a process for selecting e-commerce technology vendors whose products help a company adhere to these performance standards.

To make the transition from defining standards to picking products that meet these standards, senior executives must address important issues. Who should participate on the team that evaluates e-commerce technology suppliers? How can a Request for Proposal (RFP) be developed that captures the objectives of the project precisely, yet does not overly constrain the creativity of potential suppliers? How can a company identify the best potential vendors to receive the RFP? How can a company define specific evaluation criteria that reflect the project performance characteristics, and yet can be measured with sufficient precision to provide useful insights for managerial decision making? How can a company collect objective data on the evaluation criteria, and use this data to select the winning suppliers?

To help managers address these issues, Chapter 10 will present two case studies of e-commerce supplier evaluation. The first case study will focus on the evaluation of five e-commerce application software packages. This case study will help managers gain insights into the specific characteristics of an effective e-commerce software evaluation process. The second case study will illustrate the process that the Defense Advanced Research Projects Agency (DARPA) used to evaluate suppliers of Virtual Private Networks (VPNs) for its intranet. This case will help demonstrate the complexities of evaluating the purchase of network services. Following each case, the chapter develops a set of lessons on how best to conduct e-commerce vendor evaluation. Chapter 10 concludes by presenting a methodology that senior managers can use to help build and administer a process for evaluating e-commerce suppliers.

Cases

To understand how managers can establish an effective process for evaluating e-commerce technology suppliers, it is most useful to examine specific cases. As we will see, there are common elements of the evaluation processes across the specific technologies being purchased. These common elements include establishing a clear set of project objectives, translating these objectives into evaluation criteria, finding potential suppliers who are good candidates to meet the objectives, collecting and weighing data to evaluate suppliers, and picking the winner.

Despite these common elements, every case has its unique characteristics. The process for evaluating e-commerce application software clearly differs from the process of evaluating VPN suppliers. Furthermore, each organization may pursue a different process due to specific characteristics of that organization. In reviewing these cases, it is useful to recognize ways that these examples can be modified to fit the specific needs of each organization and each technology being evaluated.

E-Commerce Applications Software Evaluation

The process of evaluating software for e-commerce is relatively straightforward. According to *PC Week*, a leading computer industry publication, five e-commerce application products demonstrated different strengths and weaknesses in creating and maintaining e-commerce storefronts. Much of the evaluation in this case was performed by *PC Week Labs* analysts and *PC Week* consultant Bruce Brorson. The analysis was based on how well each product met the online commerce needs of Firetec Apparatus Brokers, a company in Tunbridge, Vermont, which provided the business problem for the product comparison, as well as the data to test the systems.[1]

Although this case describes how an independent media outlet (rather than a corporation) evaluated e-commerce software, the approach described here is a useful model for how corporate managers can approach the process. Five vendors of e-commerce site-building applications participated in the product evaluation. Each e-commerce vendor formed a partnership with a Web-site developer to deliver a working solution.

E-Commerce Application Vendors

The names of most of the companies here are not familiar to most general managers. This lack of familiarity is quite common in e-commerce vendor evaluation. An important role for the company's IT department is to keep abreast of these unfamiliar vendors to determine which are likely to offer viable solutions and survive. Here is the list of the five e-commerce application software providers and the Internet Service Providers (ISPs) with which they partnered:

- Intershop Communications teamed Intershop 3 with host partner e-Media.
- iCat teamed its Electronic Commerce Suite 3.0 with E-Commerce Corporation, a developer of e-commerce sites.
- Inex paired Commerce Court Pro 3.0 with Microsoft's Site Server 3.0 and host provider United Interactive Technologies.
- The Internet Factory paired Merchant Builder 3.0 with provider Wave Communications.

- Viaweb served as its own host of Viaweb 4.1 (which was acquired by Yahoo in June 1998).

Summary Evaluation of E-Commerce Application Vendors

Before examining the details of the evaluation process, I will summarize the results of the evaluation. The summary of the results illustrates the complexities of determining the appropriate evaluation criteria and the challenges of measuring how well each vendor meets these criteria. Each solution that *PC Week* examined exhibited different strengths. Viaweb and Merchant Builder were strong in site-building and design, for example, and Intershop was skillful at integrating the front-end Web-ordering systems with the back-end fulfillment and delivery systems. Intershop 3, released in April 1998, was judged to have excellent catalog-building and data-handling capabilities such as membership tracking.

PC Week judged Intershop 3 as the best of the group because it was seen as making it easy to manage a Web site, and easy to track customer activity. *PC Week* also judged that Intershop 3 was easy to customize to meet virtually any customer need. Intershop 3 was assessed as weak in site design and layout. Therefore companies implementing Intershop 3 would need an experienced Web-site designer in order to use the product effectively.

Like Intershop, iCat's Electronic Commerce Suite 3.0, which was introduced in April 1997, was deemed strong on the back-end and weak on the front-end. However, iCat's weaknesses were much more pronounced. *PC Week* found that the iCat Electronic Commerce Suite did not provide help in setting up the layout of a site. These problems were also found in using iCat's product to build catalogs. While Intershop required hiring a site authoring expert, iCat's suite required an experienced database developer. The strength of the iCat Electronic Commerce Suite was its ability to handle sales and incentive pricing better than the other products examined. The iCat product also had useful and unique features, including the ability to save seasonal catalog information.

Inex's Commerce Court Pro 3.0, which was introduced in April 1998, and is used as a front-end to Microsoft's Site Server 3.0, allows users to build and manage a site offline, and then synchronize changes to the host server. *PC Week* judged that Commerce Court Pro's integration with Microsoft's Site Server allowed Web sites built with the Inex package to be integrated into a company's back-end systems. Despite this strength, *PC Week* determined that Commerce Court Pro's interface suffered from poor design decisions. For example, when the *PC Week* judges built a site using the package, items had to have the same property fields across the site. There was no way to set up specific properties by category, a requirement for a site such as Firetec, which sells a wide variety of items.

The Internet Factory's Merchant Builder 3.0, which shipped in May 1998, was judged to have a good interface that simplified editing a live site and making updates. Merchant Builder also had some strong back-end capabilities, such as order-tracking and customer membership, as well as capable management features. *PC Week* judged that Merchant Builder 3.0 seemed incomplete, and, using it, the judges found it too easy to make major mistakes, such as accidentally copying an empty prototype site over a fully built live site. *PC Week* determined that the Merchant Builder 3.0 needed time to mature.

In *PC Week's* view, companies whose e-commerce sites are online catalogs would find Viaweb 4.1 a useful product. With Viaweb, *PC Week* judges were able to create a working storefront in less than an hour. *PC Week* also determined that Viaweb was capable of handling very large catalogs. *PC Week* was also able to adapt some of Viaweb 4.1's features to tasks for which they were not intended. However, *PC Week* found that Viaweb 4.1 was the most difficult to extend to other applications of the products tested. In addition, while the rest of the products allow businesses to choose the best Internet service provider, Viaweb was the only host for its software.

While these products' performance attributes are important to evaluate, their cost is also a crucial decision criterion. In this case, the ability of all the e-commerce applications to handle high traffic loads depended heavily on the arrangement made with the host provider. Although prices varied, a medium-size e-commerce site expected to pay between $300 and $500 a month for a hosted commerce site. Also, depending on software requirements and any fees to design firms or consultants, startup costs could range from $1,000 to $10,000 for a medium-size site.

E-Commerce Application Evaluation Criteria

PC Week evaluated each of the products based on five criteria:

1. *Site layout and design* is the ability of the product to allow users to manage the look and feel of a site, as well as any site-building aids.
2. *Catalog-building and database integration* is the ease with which the product allows users to add product information and images, and set up payment, shipping and tax information, as well as database synchronization.
3. *Advanced e-commerce features* is the product's inclusion of advanced features such as membership tracking, specialized pricing and volume discounts, and the product's ability to handle unique requests such as auctions and bidding models.
4. *Site management and reporting* is the ease with which the product allows the user to administer and update the site on a regular basis, and view and process orders, customer information, and other statistics.
5. *Extensibility* is the potential of the product to grow along with customer needs, including security and pricing.

Site Layout and Design

Site layout and design capability was an important factor in evaluating the e-commerce applications. While a company building an e-commerce site is not seeking a design tool, the company does need a site-building application that at least provides a basic site layout. The descriptions of the judges' evaluation of the products' site layout and design provide good examples of how companies should assess an e-commerce vendors' ability to meet their needs within each attribute.

PC Week judges found that Viaweb and Merchant Builder were most effective at configuring the look and feel of the test Firetec sites. Both products were deemed to have well-configured, browser-based interfaces. The judges did find Viaweb's setup wizard annoying, however, since they were forced to go through the wizard step by step. Fortunately, the judges only had to stay in the wizard for the initial phase of design. And, once out of it, they experienced additional freedom that improved site design.

Viaweb let the judges choose from a simple, regular or advanced editing interface. The judges used the advanced interface, which gave them control over the site's look and feel. The judges also found that Viaweb did a very good job of handling images.

The judges conducted similar evaluations of site layout and design for the other products.

Catalog Building and Database Integration

It is important that a company's e-commerce site look good. However, the main function of the e-commerce site is to sell products. *PC Week* determined that all the products considered in its e-commerce application evaluation process did a good job of allowing the judges to create categories and add products (although in iCat's Electronic Commerce Suite, the judges found it too easy to accidentally delete something).

All the products also allowed the judges to manage and configure key elements, such as payment methods, tax rates, and shipping costs. However, Merchant Builder was less flexible than the rest. For example, the judges made a mistake in setting up tax options for Firetec's home state of Vermont, and Merchant Builder forced the judges to rebuild the tax entries for every state.

Firetec uses FileMaker Pro for its product database, a format none of the products could import directly. However, all the products accepted comma-separated text, so the judges exported the database to the appropriate format. All the products except Intershop 3 required the judges to edit the file before they could import it into the Filemaker Pro database.

With Intershop 3, the judges were able to upload the file easily. Once they had uploaded the file, they were presented with an interface that made it easy to map the database fields to property fields within the online store.

Advanced E-Commerce Features

The judges attempted to implement several advanced features that they built with each product into the Firetec sites. They wanted to allow customers to register on the site and receive some personalization, to implement sales pricing, and to configure a way for customers to bid on the price of fire apparatus.

Viaweb was the only product that allowed the judges to implement the bidding model. The bidding model on Viaweb was actually built using a feature intended for another purpose. Viaweb has a feature that lets customers include a message for inscription on an item, such as jewelry. The judges adapted this item and called it the "Make a Bid" field. By setting the actual product price to zero, the judges made it possible for customers to enter a bid and for their information to appear in the order forms.

Viaweb did not, however, have any membership features, and was unable to implement any of the judges' remaining requirements.

In the judge's view, the Intershop, Electronic Commerce Suite, and Merchant Builder each handled registration and membership requirements well, providing customer-tracking for site managers, and giving customers a more personal experience.

The judges determined that Merchant Builder had good order-tracking and mail notification for customers, and a feature that informed registered customers how much money they had spent at the site. However, the judges encountered some inconsistencies with these features, which displayed incorrect amounts at times. Both Intershop and iCat performed well with sales pricing, and iCat's product had more sales options than the other products.

One of the judges' test sales involved giving customers a free pair of boots if they bought five pair. iCat's Electronic Commerce Suite was the only one that handled this by default, although the judges concluded that most of the other products could probably have accomplished this task with customized computer programming. Electronic Commerce Suite also enabled the judges to offer a related product if a requested one was not available.

With Inex's Commerce Court Pro, the judges were unable to set up a registration point, although the package could provide membership features to visitors to the site who placed an order. Commerce Court Pro did not support most of the judges' advanced feature requirements. However, the judges found that most of the advanced feature requirements could be created using a combination of Active Server Pages and Site Server features.

Management and Reporting Features

All the products the judges tested provided good order-tracking tools that allowed them to view items purchased. However, differences among the products became more pronounced when more in-depth analysis was required.

The judges concluded that the reporting and statistical analysis tools in Intershop were among the best, providing much detail when analyzing site activity. They decided that Viaweb also had good reporting tools that were useful for marketing departments and executives, although the tools were not as customizable as the judges wanted. Although not as good as Intershop's and Viaweb's, the judges concluded that the reporting tools in the iCat, Inex, and Internet Factory products were all very capable.[2]

E-Commerce Application Vendor Decision Matrix

The analysis of each vendor is summarized in Table 10-1. As the analysis indicates, the PC Week judges attempted to convert their experiences with each product on each evaluation criterion into a grade from A (excellent) to D (poor). From this table, it appears that Intershop is the clear winner based on its performance on most of the evaluation criteria. Intershop is not the strongest on site layout. However, the *PC Week* judges determined that this weakness could be addressed by hiring a staff person with expertise in site layout.

Table 10-1. Summary analysis of e-commerce application software.

	iCat	Inex	Intershop	Internet Factory	Viaweb
Site Layout	D	B	C	B	B
Catalog Building	B	C	B	C	C
Advanced E-Commerce Features	B	B	B	C	C
Site Management	B	C	A	B	B
Extensibility	B	B	A	C	C
Hosting Fee	$350/mo.	$50/mo.	$350/mo.	$200/mo.	$100/mo.
Software Price	$1,495–$3,500	$995	$995	No software	No software

Case Lessons

This case illustrates several important lessons. First, it is important to have a clear understanding of the business problem that the e-commerce site is being designed to solve. The business problem helps the company develop the evaluation criteria that will be used to assess potential vendors. Second, it is crucial to generate a list of potential vendors that is sufficiently rich and includes good vendors who may not be well-established, as well as more established vendors that may not be as good. Third, it is important to develop independent tests that a company can use to assess objectively how well each potential supplier performs on each of the evaluation criteria. Fourth, it is crucial to summarize the results of the testing in a way that managers can use to evaluate the different suppliers. Finally, management must weigh the relative importance of the evaluation criteria so that the selection of the winning supplier is based on that supplier's relative performance on the most crucial evaluation criteria.

DARPA's VPN

The previous case on e-commerce application software vendors was relatively simple in that it involved the evaluation of software. Even this case was somewhat complicated, however, by the introduction of ISP partners for each application software vendor. In the case of DARPA's VPN evaluation, however, the level of complexity is much greater because VPN is a much more complex technology. VPNs are basically private Internets that organizations typically rent from third-party providers. The benefit of VPNs is that they have many of the ease-of-communication benefits of the Internet without the perceived security weaknesses. For a government agency with the strategic importance of DARPA, such security considerations are quite important.

DARPA's adoption of VPN technology is both an important acknowledgment of the technology's high level of security, and an excellent example of how managers can design and administer a process for evaluating vendors of such a complex Internet technology. According to *PC Week*, DARPA funds and conducts research for national security. Since security is a high priority, DARPA's June 1999 RFP for outsourcing a VPN should cause IT managers who had been undecided on VPN's safety to reconsider them.[3]

DARPA knows the Internet and defensive measures well. DARPA's best-known developments include the ARPAnet (the predecessor of the Internet) and the technology behind the Stealth bomber and fighter. DARPA sought a VPN solution that would provide access to the Internet and DARPA's internal network without compromising its security. DARPA wanted to provide its users with continuous connectivity without acting as its own ISP.

DARPA's RFP was issued in April 1999. In May 1999, a team at DARPA's Arlington, Virginia, headquarters conducted a detailed evaluation of the proposals that met DARPA's stringent evaluation criteria. This included corporate uptime, integration, and security requirements.

VPN Vendors

Six proposals were evaluated in the final stage of DARPA's process:

1. Computer Generated Solutions (CGS)
2. Information Access Technologies (IAT)
3. International Systems Marketing (ISM)
4. Network Access Solutions (NAS)
5. Sprint
6. V-One

DARPA Requirements

Although DARPA's security standards were high, its requirements were simple. DARPA wanted to provide the same connection experience to each of its employees, regardless of location. This general objective translated into three more specific attributes that DARPA's management sought in its VPN:

1. DARPA employees needed to obtain transparent access to all its internal network services whether the employee was located at DARPA headquarters or connecting remotely.
2. DARPA needed a solution that would be equally effective regardless of the way employees obtained access to the system. The intention was for users able to access the network via a dial-up modem or via higher-speed service such as Digital Subscriber Line (DSL).
3. DARPA wanted to maintain management control of the VPN while outsourcing the VPN connection network.

The DARPA RFP

Consistent with these requirements, DARPA created and issued an RFP. The RFP was developed both to define DARPA's needs internally, and to solicit proposals from VPN suppliers. DARPA's RFP consisted of six key elements:

1. *Use off-the-shelf technology.* DARPA wished to use current industry infrastructure, support services, and commercial off-the-shelf technologies to satisfy its requirement. Particularly where security is concerned, it is important for organizations to use industry-standard technologies, which have been peer reviewed and tested.

2. *Separate VPN traffic.* DARPA's RFP specified the separation of VPN traffic from its then current Internet service and internal traffic. As DARPA's Stealth technology demonstrated, this practice was an effective way to protect sensitive information, and to ensure reliability. Since VPNs were based on new technology that may not have integrated effectively with traditional networks, it made sense for DARPA to separate VPN and traditional Internet access.

3. *Maintain administrative control.* DARPA wanted to maintain administrative control of all systems that were attached to its inter-

nal network. DARPA concluded that control of the VPN should not be outsourced because it would have been too time-consuming for DARPA to conduct a full security audit of an ISP or VPN provider.

4. *Offer scalability.* DARPA required a VPN that could grow in the future to accommodate an increase in the number of simultaneous active connections and off-site users. In addition, DARPA required a VPN that could implement new technologies as they become available. Since VPNs were changing rapidly, DARPA was eager to avoid using outdated technology. DARPA's requirement of a VPN—adaptable to new technologies and scalable to accommodate increases in users and bandwidth—was broadly applicable to other large organizations.

5. *Deliver 24/7 customer service.* DARPA needed a VPN to provide technical service to users twenty-four hours a day, seven days a week to resolve end-users' dial-in and contact problems. DARPA also required its users to have the ability to place their own service orders to resolve remote access problems. DARPA's help desk requirement was another that is a significant concern for most organizations. Organizations seeking a VPN need to outsource technical support to enable their internal help desks to handle only problems pertinent to them.

6. *Deploy rapidly.* DARPA required its VPN provider to implement the VPN for twenty employees within 120 days after contract award, and to provide full implementation to 150 employees within the first year of the contract. DARPA's rapid deployment requirement was another generally applicable one. Organizations that outsource an important part of their operation must provide specific performance targets for implementation.

VPN Vendor Evaluation Criteria

Each vendor's proposal consisted of a method of Internet access, a dial-up and a DSL means of access, a VPN concentrator, client software, and, in some cases, firewalls. In order to evaluate the six proposals, DARPA translated the RFP requirements described above into the following specific criteria:

• *Client configuration and security* is the ability to customize clients and lock security options. This was particularly important to DARPA because it would determine the level of network security that each VPN would be expected to support.

• *VPN and network integration* is the ease with which the VPN can be integrated into an existing network infrastructure, and the ability of VPN tools to work within a network. This was important to DARPA because the easier the network integration, the more satisfied the end-users of the system would be.

• *ISP services* include the connection speeds offered, breadth of ISP network, and Internet services such as Web publishing. DARPA felt that ISP services were important because these services would enable more end-users to be able to gain high-speed access to DARPA's network from more remote locations.

• *Reporting and management* is the ability to administer and monitor the VPN, and process user accounts. Reporting and management was important to DARPA because it would help its network managers to match the resources of the network to the changing levels of demand. Furthermore, with effective reporting and management, DARPA's network managers would be able to monitor the changing users of the system, thereby decreasing the likelihood of unauthorized access to the system by a former DARPA employee.

• *Help desk integration* is how well the ISP and integrator support services work with the internal help desk, as well as training issues. DARPA viewed this as important because its network managers realized that user satisfaction with the system would depend on the quality and responsiveness of the network help desk personnel, as well as the quality of the user-training for the VPN.

• *Extensibility* is the ability of the package to grow with customer needs. DARPA's network managers used extensibility to evaluate vendors because DARPA anticipated that its users' needs would change once they began to use the VPN. They also thought that the network managers would be judged, in part, on how well they would be able to adapt the network to these changing needs.

Assessment of VPN Vendors

DARPA assessed how well each of the VPN suppliers met these criteria, and reached the following summarized conclusions about each:

- *CGS.* CGS's proposed VPN package provided a fully outsourced VPN. However, this high level of service sacrificed some security.
- *IAT.* With the combination of the Nortel Contivity Extranet Switch and Internet access from PSINet, IAT provided a VPN that balanced service and security.
- *ISM.* ISM's VPN proposal offered high redundancy and security. This solution appeared to be well suited for mission-critical VPNs such as DARPA's proposed VPN.
- *NAS.* NAS's proposed use of a hardware-based VPN offered superior ease-of-use and excellent performance. A specific technology used in the NAS package (Ravlin devices) had the potential to integrate effectively into any network providing good VPN integration.
- *Sprint.* Sprint's high level of integration in its VPN proposal helped Sprint guarantee 100 percent uptime at a relatively high price.
- *V-One.* By combining technologies such as session-level proxies and Internet Protocol Security (IPSec) in the same end-user machine or client, V-One offered a flexible VPN package. This proposal was best suited to organizations with unique requirements for session-level communication.

Table 10-2 summarizes how each of the proposals met DARPA's evaluation criteria.

Table 10-2. Summary analysis of DARPA's VPN proposals.

	CGS	IAT	ISM	NAS	Sprint	V-One
Client Configuration & Security	C	B	C	B	C	A
VPN and Network Integration	C	A	B	A	C	B
ISP Services	B	B	B	C	A	C
Reporting and Management	C	A	B	A	B	B
Help Desk Integration	B	C	C	B	A	A
Extensibility	B	B	B	B	B	B

Case Lessons

In July 1999, the DARPA case was a work in progress. A clear challenge remained for management: how to pick the winning supplier. As Table 10-2 suggests, there are two or three suppliers who seemed to be in the running to win the DARPA contract. DARPA's choice depended heavily on its relative weighting of the VPN evaluation criteria. For example, if client configuration and security was the most important criterion, V-One would win. If reporting and management is most important, there would be a toss-up between IAT and NAS. This case is particularly useful then for demonstrating the importance of ranking evaluation criteria to the selection of the winning e-commerce supplier.

The DARPA case also offers other important lessons. DARPA did an excellent job of developing requirements and reflecting these requirements in its RFP. The RFP fit well with DARPA's mission and with the specific goals for the VPN. DARPA translated its requirements into a set of evaluation criteria that was measurable and comprehensive. DARPA collected a group of VPN suppliers that included a mix of well-known and lesser-known vendors. Each vendor produced a credible proposal, although a few emerged as superior. DARPA also conducted a fact-based evaluation of each supplier to reach conclusions about how well each vendor met its evaluation criteria.

Methodology for Evaluating E-Commerce Suppliers

The two cases suggest a nine-step methodology for the effective evaluation of e-commerce suppliers. The proposed methodology offers managers the following benefits:

- Creates continuity between the design and implementation of the e-commerce initiative by keeping many of the same individuals involved in the evaluation process.
- Links business objectives with the criteria used to evaluate potential e-commerce vendors.
- Creates a means by which objective analysis can be conducted on each potential e-commerce supplier.
- Uses this data in combination with a company's business objectives to select the winning supplier.

This methodology is intended to be useful for the evaluation of different e-commerce–related technologies including software, hardware, network services, and consulting services. Here are the nine steps of the e-commerce vendor-evaluation methodology:

e *Create an interdisciplinary team for evaluating e-commerce suppliers.* Managers should create a team for evaluating e-commerce suppliers that includes general managers, information technology staff, financial staff, and others who have been involved in the e-commerce strategy–development process. By creating continuity among team members, a company will have a greater chance of actually realizing the vision for e-commerce.

e *Agree on the specific business objectives that the e-commerce technology is intended to meet.* The team should develop measurable business objectives that the e-commerce technology is intended to meet. These objectives should be measured in terms that customers will consider important such as system uptime, ease-of-use, and speed-of-response. Without such measures, there is a danger that the e-commerce technology will not succeed from a business perspective, even though it may work in a technical sense.

e *Translate the business objectives into an RFP.* The team should create an RFP that describes the most important things that management wants the e-commerce system to do for the business. These requirements should be sufficiently general so that the team is able to measure how well each potential supplier will perform on each requirement. The requirements should also be developed in order not to constrain the creativity of the suppliers when they develop proposals.

e *Identify between five and ten potential vendors who are expected to respond effectively to the RFP.* The team should develop a list of potential suppliers that is balanced between well-known vendors who may be venturing into an area of new technology, as well as lesser-known startups that may specialize in the new-technology area. The sources of potential suppliers could include trade publications, consultants, competing companies' suppliers, and investment analysts.

e *Develop specific criteria for evaluating these suppliers.* The team must next translate the specific business objectives into a set of evaluation criteria that the team can use to evaluate these potential suppliers. The evaluation criteria should be testable, and should apply to each potential vendor.

e *Create tests to assess how well each supplier meets these evaluation criteria.* The team should next develop specific ways of testing how well each potential vendor meets the evaluation criteria. Frequently, external consultants can provide useful assistance in designing and executing these tests as long as the consultants have the appropriate experience, and are free of any conflicts of interest in the evaluation process. The key outcome of this step is to design and execute the tests in a rigorous way for each potential supplier.

 Score each supplier on the evaluation criteria. The team must create decision matrixes, such as the ones in the case studies, which array the vendors against the evaluation criteria and grade each supplier on each criterion. The scoring will be based on a subjective evaluation of the test results developed in the previous item in this list, concerning the creation of tests to assess how well each supplier meets evaluation criteria.

 Rank the evaluation criteria in terms of their relative importance to meeting the e-commerce project objectives. Once the data is arrayed in the decision matrix, the team must agree on the relative importance of the evaluation criteria. One way of quantifying this consensus is to allocate 100 points among the evaluation criteria, giving the most points to the most important criterion. Once the criteria are weighted, it is possible to convert the scores into numbers (e.g., an "A" might be scored as a 5, a "B" as a 4, and so on). Then the team could multiply the weights for each evaluation criterion by each vendor's score. The result of this process would be a weighted average score for each vendor.

 Choose the winning supplier based with the highest weighted average score. The team could then rank the suppliers in descending order of the weighted average score. The winning supplier would be at the top of the list.

Conclusion

Senior management has an important role to play in designing and administering the process of evaluating e-commerce suppliers. It is essential for senior management to preserve the continuity of team members between the e-commerce strategy–development and its implementation. Managers must also articulate the specific business objectives that the e-commerce application is designed to meet, and translate these objectives into criteria that the team can use to evaluate potential E-commerce suppliers. Ultimately, the winning supplier will emerge from a process that maps the relative importance of the evaluation criteria to the relative performance of the suppliers on each criterion.

Notes

1. Jim Rapoza, "Shoot-Out Puts E-Com Apps to Test," *PC Week,* June 12, 1998 [http://www.zdnet.com/products/stories/reviews/0,4161,324870,00. html].
2. Ibid.
3. Pankaj Chowdhry, "VPNs Get Security Clearance," *PC Week,* June 20, 1999 [http://www.zdnet.com/products/stories/reviews/0,4161,406918,00. html].

11

Negotiating the Deals

Negotiating the purchase of the products and services needed to build an e-commerce system is a crucial test of management's ability to translate its vision for e-commerce into reality. Management must anticipate and plan for many risks in order to make the negotiation process successful. What does the outcome of a successful negotiation process look like? What risks must this negotiation process anticipate? How can managers plan for these risks? What is the best process for managers to conduct a successful purchase negotiation?

Chapter 11 addresses these issues. It begins by outlining the vision for a successful purchase negotiation outcome. The chapter continues by outlining the risks that managers must anticipate and overcome in order to achieve this vision. Chapter 11 presents four mini-cases of successful and less-than-successful contract negotiations (Horizon Healthcare, Children's Hospital of Los Angeles, Whirlpool, and Toronto Hospital), to illustrate these concepts in greater detail. It concludes by outlining a methodology that managers can follow to translate their vision for e-commerce into a successful purchase-negotiation process.

Successful E-Commerce Purchase Negotiation Outcome

At the beginning of the e-commerce purchase-negotiation process, managers will find it helpful to communicate to participants what success looks like. By communicating this vision for the successful outcome of the process—and repeating this vision throughout the process—managers can increase the likelihood that this vision will actually happen.

The vision for a successful e-commerce purchase negotiation consists of many elements. These range from the obvious decisions about which companies will supply the system components to the more difficult issues of identifying risks and performance standards, and articulating procedures for who is accountable for addressing the outcome of "risk events" or deviation from standard performance levels.

In light of this complexity, a successful e-commerce contract negotiation yields the following outcomes:

• *Clear Understanding of the E-Commerce System Architecture.* A company and its vendors should all share a common understanding of what its e-commerce system architecture will look like. This architecture will include network equipment and/or network services, servers, databases, middleware, Web "front-end" software, and a variety of other technical components. Articulating the e-commerce system architecture is crucial for successful negotiations because only if a company and its suppliers are aiming in the same direction can the negotiation process hope to succeed.

• *Specific Understanding of How the System Components Will Work Together.* While knowing the system components is important, so is understanding how these components will work together. For example, if a vendor of database software cannot build an interface with the Web browser that is used to place an order, then the entire purpose of the e-commerce system will be defeated. As a result, it is important for a company and its vendors to know how all the pieces of the system will work together. Without such a clear understanding, there is a danger that the company will contract with suppliers whose products and services work effectively in isolation, but not in concert. By forging a clear image of how the system components will work together, the outcome of the negotiation is more likely to be mutually beneficial for the company and its vendors.

- *Choice of the "Best" Vendors to Supply the System Components.* While it is obvious that one of the outcomes of the negotiation process should be a list of winning vendors, it is less obvious what the specific criteria are that managers should use to pick the winning vendors. In some cases, for example, the vendor willing to sell at the lowest price would be the winner. In other cases, the vendor who can solve a particularly challenging technical problem most effectively would emerge victorious. Decisions about how the best vendors are defined make an important difference in the choice of vendor.

- *Details of Vendor Costs and Implementation Deadlines.* Managers need an understanding of how much the company will need to pay vendors, and the specific conditions that the vendors must satisfy in order to receive payment. For example, managers should have a clear understanding of whether paying a particular vendor is contingent on completing work by a particular day. The successful e-commerce contract negotiation process would produce the information needed to develop a comprehensive schedule of costs and implementation deadlines.

- *Specific Articulation of Risks, and Who Must Address Them.* As noted earlier, the e-commerce development process is fraught with risk. Management must anticipate these risks in its contracts with suppliers. In addition to itemizing the risks, management must work with the vendors to assign clear responsibility for addressing the risks. Examples of risks that should be included in the contracts are the risk of missing an installation deadline, a technical failure due to poor product design or manufacture, lost business due to a product breakdown, and the failure of the product to perform to specifications. An effective e-commerce contract negotiation process should anticipate these risks, and specify who is responsible for addressing them.

• *Linking Vendor Compensation to Explicit Performance Standards.* In cases where a company outsources the provision of a service for its e-commerce system, such as network services or customer service, management must define very specific performance standards. These performance standards must be measurable, and should be linked to vendor payment. If a vendor meets the performance standards—such as network uptime, number of rings before answering a telephone, etc.— then the vendor should receive timely payment for its services. If the vendor does not meet the performance standards, the contract should trigger a process that could result in the vendor bringing its performance up to standards or being subject to termination. However such contracts are structured, they should incorporate specific performance criteria, and link vendor compensation to actual performance compared to standards.

E-Commerce Purchase Negotiation Risks and Ways to Address Them

In the real world, such idealized outcomes do not simply happen—they must be managed into existence. To achieve successful e-commerce contract negotiations, it helps to think about all the things that could go wrong, what actions will be taken, and who is responsible for taking these actions. While I alluded above to the value of articulating and addressing these risks, I will now discuss ways to achieve this.

To identify potential risks in the e-commerce contract negotiation process, managers may want to consider asking themselves and their vendors a number of probing questions about the e-commerce architecture. These questions might pertain to how the e-commerce architecture will be built, and what could go wrong during its construction and subsequent maintenance.

For example, managers might consider the following questions:

- What are the different e-commerce architecture options and examples of how they have worked in the past?
- What specific measures are most effective in measuring the types of e-commerce architectures being proposed?
- Is the time line for the e-commerce architecture reasonable?
- Does the e-commerce vendor have a bias toward one type of technology or vendor?
- What provisions will be made to update technologies during the life of the contract?
- What are the industry-specific metrics used for this function or service, and where does the e-commerce vendor stand in comparison to the competition?
- What are the acceptable service levels for mission-critical vs. non–mission-critical applications?
- What will the escalation process be if a product or service is not meeting predetermined levels?
- What provisions will be made for testing the effectiveness of the outsourcing deal during the contract?

By addressing these issues, managers can begin to think about all the potential problems that could ensue during the relationship with the company's e-commerce technology vendors. To address some of these e-commerce purchase-negotiation risks, here are some steps that managers can consider taking that are particularly relevant to the purchasing of outside services such as e-commerce network service providers. These suggestions are also broadly applicable to many of the other components of the e-commerce architecture:

- Call in a consultant to evaluate the situation, define the scope of the project, help in the Request-for-Proposal process, and aid in drawing up a contract.
- Make the contract as specific as possible.
- Develop a responsibilities matrix in the contract to

avoid unproductive efforts in assigning responsibility for the sources of problems.

- For e-commerce services and some product vendors, include the right to use third parties, termination conditions, the right to adjust service-level agreements annually, and periodic industry benchmarking to ensure technology is up to date and that pricing remains competitive.
- Do not sign a ten-year service agreement. Instead, take advantage of the greater flexibility inherent in shorter deals of three to five years.
- Understand what the costs are and what the penalties may be if the vendor's actual performance does not progress as outlined in the contract.
- For system components that are particularly critical to the successful operation of the e-commerce architecture, enlist an outside law firm to help in contract negotiations, even when in-house counsel is available.
- Define the scope of the project. Retain control of the pieces of the e-commerce architecture that are strategic to the business.
- Make sure the company has a single point of contact with the vendor. Work in partnership with the person from the outsourcing company who is managing the project.

In purchasing software for e-commerce architectures such as databases and Web front-end software, there are other suggestions that can help managers to control the risks inherent in the e-commerce contract negotiation process:

- *Establish a formal proposal evaluation methodology.* A formal evaluation methodology provides a structure for the decision process. It also minimizes the possibility that arbitrary factors and political pressure will be used to select a vendor. This document should outline the contract negotiation approach and the criteria used to establish the final award.

- *Avoid purchasing unproven software.* Although the e-commerce software market is new, organizations should purchase proven solutions as opposed to software in development. Some vendors may contend that specific parts of their software is being developed and will be completed before it is included in that module in the implementation plan. Under such circumstances, it is better to ask vendors to propose proven third-party solutions for these modules or provide deep discounts for using "beta" versions of the software.

- *Include vendor responses to Request-for-Proposal (RFP) business requirements in the contract.* Organizations often expend considerable resources on developing an RFP. Yet as selection proceeds, the RFP requirements often are forgotten. Moreover, without carefully analyzing the requirements, vendors tend to respond affirmatively in an effort to meet the RFP deadline. Including the requirements as part of the contract reduces the organization's risk and costs by minimizing expensive on-site development of the software through customization.

- *Avoid purchasing the lowest-performing/lowest-purchase price software.* In theory, e-commerce software could have a useful life of several years. The value of the software is extended by installing upgrades. Organizations should purchase the solution with the highest value (benefit/cost ratio) because purchasing the lowest-performing/lowest-purchase price software is likely to lead to requiring the company to purchase software again in a relatively short period of time. For this reason, the vendor's corporate strategy for the particular e-commerce application should be an important consideration in system selection.

- *Involve legal assistance at the end of the process.* Legal assistance in the e-commerce contract negotiations is an expensive but necessary undertaking. Fees for lawyers with expertise in intellectual property rights and software contract negotiations are considerably higher than other legal assistance. Consequently, waiting to bring the lawyers in until after the Statement of Work (SOW) is complete, and selecting one vendor as a finalist, is an effective way to reduce costs for both the organization and the vendor.

• *Negotiate contracts for e-commerce software with only one party in order to avoid subsequent unproductive blaming.* Many e-commerce software procurement processes typically involve two agreements: one for software and the other for consulting services. Organizations can prevent further contract management fragmentation by telling the prime software vendor that it is responsible for third-party software. This prevents the need to negotiate contracts with multiple parties, which only diffuses accountability in an already complex setting.

• *Use outside expertise in negotiations.* In having negotiated with many companies, vendors often have an advantage over a company's negotiation team. Outside expertise can help balance a company's bargaining power, especially on larger transactions. For outside consultants to generate a return for a company, however, it is especially important that they have knowledge of how companies are using e-commerce and technology trends. Most importantly, contract negotiation consultants should have no history of, or future plans for, doing business with vendors with whom they are negotiating.

• *Avoid overpaying for annual maintenance and support fees.* In order to keep a company's e-commerce software current, it is important to pay for maintenance and support. However, fees should only begin after the software has been installed. Furthermore, future-year rate increases should either be capped or tied to an index such as the consumer price index (CPI).

• *Link vendor compensation to the e-commerce software implementation time line.* Vendors should not be paid simply on the basis of hours used in the contract. To whatever extent possible, payments should be tied to deliverables and milestones in the project. Holding back say 10 percent, of the milestone payment is also considered reasonable as a way of encouraging vendors to meet deadlines.

Case Studies

Four small case studies illustrate some of the pitfalls that can be overcome through effective contract negotiations. These cases deal with the hiring of network service providers for intranets. The cases illustrate techniques for performance management and control of mission-critical applications. When companies negotiate with network service providers to offer "extranets," which provide access to external customers over the Internet, the companies must deal with the same issues.

The four mini cases that illustrate ways of handling these issues are summarized below:

1. The Horizon Healthcare case illustrates how a well-drafted contract can make it easier for a company that outsources e-commerce services such as network management to replace a vendor that is not performing effectively.
2. The Children's Hospital of Los Angeles case demonstrates the benefits of bringing in lawyers with expertise in high technology to help negotiate the terms of certain types of e-commerce services contracts, such as network management.
3. The Whirlpool case demonstrates the benefits of selectively outsourcing certain parts of an e-commerce network, and maintaining in-house control of specific elements of the network that are particularly strategic.
4. The Toronto Hospital case illustrates the pitfalls of not setting performance standards for the most mission-critical applications.

Horizon Healthcare

Horizon Healthcare was able to change its network vendor by virtue of a loophole in its outsourcing contract. According to *PC Week*, Ken Cole, network services manager at Horizon Healthcare in Albuquerque, was able to terminate a business relationship with a difficult outsourcing partner due to a loophole in his contract. Cole had handed over the management of Horizon Healthcare's computer network, a frame-relay Wide Area Network (WAN), that connected fifty-nine sites to a large communications carrier (which he declined to name). About a year into the three-year contract, the relationship began to deteriorate when the outsourcer's support for monitoring, reporting, and fixing network problems began to slip.[1]

Cole was able to monitor the specific problems within the network. According to Cole, Horizon Healthcare maintained a view into the network using software from Hewlett-Packard called OpenView. OpenView tested each router to see if it was reachable. Cole would see a router stop working (which could have been due to a circuit failure or a router failure), but it would take hours before Horizon Healthcare heard anything from the carrier about the network outage.

Terminating the contract would have cost a significant amount of money. Instead, Cole and his advisers analyzed the contract, and found a way to relieve the carrier from some of its responsibilities. By declaring that the carrier was not fulfilling its obligation in network management, Horizon Healthcare kept the overall contract in place, and dropped the network management portion.

Cole then hired Lucent Technologies' NetCare division to manage the WAN. This time, Cole looked to Lucent's own technicians. According to Cole, many carriers say they can support any router, but typically what they mean is that they will try. Ultimately, Cole noted that a company needs to know it can depend on the people employed by the outsourcing company. Cole recommended visiting the management sites of the providers. He suggested meeting the vendor's employees so Horizon Healthcare would be comfortable with the vendor's understanding of the technology and their ability to support Horizon Healthcare.[2]

Hiring an outside consultant can help identify false claims such as the ability to provide service for a device that they cannot actually support. A specialized consultant or law firm can also help outline a contract that clearly defines the roles and responsibilities of each party. Consultants attempt to negotiate the rights for companies to use third parties in case they want to give a piece of the network to a particular vendor. Consultants can also help companies determine ahead of time causes for termination. These contract provisions would have helped Cole deal with his carrier.

Children's Hospital of Los Angeles

In early 1997, Children's Hospital of Los Angeles was in the RFP process for an extensive outsourcing deal that encompassed a data center, desktop computing, telecommunications, and network services. According to *PC Week*, when Dean Campbell, the hospital's CIO, meets with a potential partner, he has a legal expert sitting next to him. Campbell praises his internal counsel, but uses the services of a specialized high-tech counsel rather than his healthcare–oriented internal counsel.[3]

Campbell's contract negotiations will be the final phase of a lengthy process. He has already done an initial trial of an outsourcing transaction when he hired Systems Management Specialists of Santa Ana, California in March 1997 to manage the network on a temporary basis while he fixed the hospital's internal infrastructure, including the e-mail system, desktop upgrades to Windows 3.1 and Windows 95, and server consolidation. Since relieving his staff from the day-to-day WAN and Local Area Network (LAN) management in 1997, Campbell has a better grasp of his network requirements.

Campbell suggests formalizing the reporting of network technical problems and follow-up calls to gain a clear understanding of the scope of the problem, and how an outsourcing partner can help. Based on his experience, Campbell was able to develop a comprehensive responsibility matrix. Regardless of the partner he chooses, Campbell will retain the right to approve the network equipment and any network decisions made.[4]

Campbell's experience provides useful insights for other compa-

nies that are seeking to contract with providers of e-commerce products and services. For example, many companies will choose to
outsource their network operations to outside companies. As I noted
in earlier chapters, setting performance standards for the network is
an important responsibility for senior managers. In order to enforce
these standards, executive like Campbell are increasingly negotiating contracts with network services providers that allow their organizations to shape the decisions that will affect the network services
providers' ability to meet these performance standards.

Whirlpool

Jim Haney, Director of Global Network Services at Whirlpool in Benton Harbor, Michigan, also retains final network architectural control
in outsourcing network management. In early 1997, Whirlpool entered into a five-year contract with AT&T's European arm, which will
set up frame-relay services for Whirlpool's global network. AT&T
will be responsible for managing and maintaining the Cisco Systems
routers and WAN connections. But Haney's staff controls the applications running over the network from Whirlpool's own data centers
in Benton Harbor and in Stuttgart, West Germany.

Haney notes that an outsourcer would need to know which applications work for the business, and how to adjust the network for
the application that needs the highest priority. Haney believes that
it would be difficult for an outsourcer to do that without being inti-
mately familiar with Whirlpool's core business.

It is also important, according to Haney, to build a relationship.
Regardless of how an executive may feel during the negotiation process, Haney believes that it does not make sense to make an outsourcing provider angry. Haney notes that if a company wants the
outsourcing relationship to work, it should create a partnership with
the outsourcing vendor. He also points out that if an organization
looks at the outsourcing company as simply a vendor, the organization will encounter problems.[5]

The Whirlpool case indicates the delicacy of the relationship between the company and the outsourcer. For companies negotiating e-commerce services contracts, the Whirlpool case has great relevance. Companies that end up purchasing network services may need to engage in tapered backward integration. This means that some companies will end up maintaining control over specific networking functions such as setting priorities for which applications will receive the most networking resources at a given time, while outsourcing less strategic activities such as maintaining the operations of the routers. In order to conduct such a relationship in a way that produces the best performance for the company, it is essential to build a good working partnership with the outsourcer.

Toronto Hospital

The value of having a third party along during outsourcing discussions is now clear to Toronto Hospital. According to *PC Week*, executives at Toronto Hospital had entered into an outsourcing agreement with an unnamed company in 1995 for a wide variety of IT support services for its 4,000-seat network in the areas of help desk, desktop computer support, e-mail, and server and network management. By 1997, it was obvious that Toronto Hospital needed a change.[6]

Karalee Miller, Director of Corporate Planning at the 1,000-bed teaching hospital in Toronto, recognized that the outsourcing agreement was a bad situation on both sides. The outsourcer was losing money, and Toronto Hospital was not receiving the services it needed.

While Miller and her colleagues were reluctant to assign blame, they say they learned valuable lessons from the poor performance of their first outsourcing agreement. Specifically, the first deal suffered from poorly defined service-level agreements and poor communication. Analysts from a consulting firm, Compass America, were brought in to help create an arrangement that would ensure those pitfalls were avoided the second time around with outsourcer Digital

Equipment of Canada, a division of Compaq Canada. Miller noted that Compass America had Toronto Hospital ask questions that it did not ask during the first outsourcing agreement.

The case of Toronto Hospital involved clearly defining mission-critical service levels and non–mission-critical service levels. The new agreement differentiates between acceptable downtime between the help desk application servers (where a sixty-minute downtime is not a real problem) and the patient care servers (where even thirty minutes of downtime could be life-threatening). This was not done with the initial outsourcing arrangement.

The new deal, a five-year contract signed in June 1998, also has special provisions in place to ensure that specific support levels are met. Along with having 15 percent of the fees directly tied to performance, Toronto Hospital also has the right to terminate the agreement at any time and without penalty after three years. Scheduled benchmarking tests are also part of the contract to make sure the service and costs stay competitive.

This improved service *does* come at a price. The new agreement, with all of its carefully crafted service levels and benchmarks, will cost Toronto Hospital 40 percent more than the first agreement. While this may seem like a huge jump, Miller and her team said it is worthwhile since Toronto Hospital's information technology department can now concentrate on building new services rather than reacting to outsourcing emergencies.[7]

The Toronto Hospital case offers an important lesson for e-commerce vendor contract negotiators. There is real value in distinguishing between levels of service required for mission-critical and non–mission-critical e-commerce activities. The performance levels of mission-critical activities must be articulated clearly, and linked to vendor compensation. In the case of mission-critical activities, it is worth paying a premium to make sure that the performance of the activities is at a sufficiently high level to assure that the application will operate in a way that satisfies customers.

These case studies suggest a number of important lessons for the e-commerce contract negotiation process. First, it is important to establish specific performance standards to which all vendors will be held. These performance standards should be set at the level of individual activities such as system installation, system operating performance, and matching network capacity to specific applications. Once these standards are set, it is important to articulate a method of linking vendor compensation to performance on these standards. An important corollary is that companies must make it clear how vendors will be penalized—and the terms under which contracts can be terminated—if vendors do not perform according to the standards.

Methodology for Successful E-Commerce Purchase Negotiation

While the cases focused on specific operational problems that reinforce the importance of following the right negotiation practices, they do not provide the answer to how best to negotiate e-commerce purchases.

Best negotiation practices are part of the answer. Such practices include:

- Asking questions about the license, including how licenses beyond the current contract will be priced, and if licenses can be freely moved among sites
- Maintaining a constructive relationship with the vendor even during tense negotiations
- Asking for benchmarks from previous customers to understand licensing and support arrangements of sites with similar installations
- Looking for nonfinancial ways to influence negotiations, including agreeing to be a reference site

Of course, these best practices, while useful, are not comprehensive or systematic enough to help managers who are starting from scratch. The remainder of this section details a methodology that will help managers conduct an e-commerce contract negotiation that is most likely to achieve the vision outlined earlier in this chapter.

e **_Develop an internal consensus on the objectives and business requirements for the e-commerce system._** Managers should describe their companies' e-commerce architectures, and articulate their business requirements. The discussion should result in a document that focuses on areas such as:

- _Applications and Business Processes the E-Commerce System Will Support._ This section should focus on topics such as which services are most mission-critical; whether the company is global, national, or regional; identification of critical time periods during which the network must be particularly stable.
- _Current Network Service Levels._ This section should focus on current goals and performance in such areas as network availability, mean time to system restoration, capacity utilization and speed of response; methods for gathering and reporting these performance measures; and areas in which improvements could be realized through investment in automation.
- _Network Architecture._ This section should focus on whether there are any overdue network design changes; which network protocols the network supports; plans to add, remove, or change locations, protocol support, or speed; and a description of any major problems with the network architecture.
- _Technology._ This section will include items such as specific hardware and software running on the network; any equipment or software modifications to support nonstandard protocols or systems; plans to migrate from routers to switches, and other network devices such as 14.4K bit/sec modems, V.90, or ISDN to digital subscriber line (DSL).
- _Help Desk._ This section should describe who handles application and network problem calls, and a description of the help desk's problem resolution responsibilities.

- *Current Budget.* This section should describe how much the company is spending on people, hardware, software, telecommunications, and net management. The company should also understand specific budget areas that outsourcing will not reduce or change, such as management salaries.
- *Contractual Obligations.* This section should articulate any of the company's IT contracts, which have exclusivity clauses, and the contracts' term commitments. This information could be important if the company chooses a carrier or ISP instead of its current service provider.

Once the company has documented the vision for its e-commerce system, it must decide which portions of the system will be purchased or outsourced to vendors. Such system components might include database software, Web front-end software, middleware, and network services. To develop a list of potential vendors in each category, managers can visit vendors' Web sites, and review analyses of the different categories provided by industry publications. Next, managers should meet with the vendors that appear to be able to meet their company's needs. Based on the results of these meetings, managers should cut the list of vendors to between three and five with whom they will work during the RFP process.

Draft the RFP. If the company develops an RFP that is comprehensive and honest, the proposals that vendors provide for the company are also likely to be comprehensive and honest. However, e-commerce purchasing relationships fail when the customer and vendor are discovering information about each other after they have signed the contract. Therefore, companies should share as much information as possible with prospective vendors.

While the following RFP outline is specifically targeted toward the consideration of one type of e-commerce network service, a virtual private network (VPN), it provides a useful framework that can be tailored to the specific needs of particular e-commerce system components. The RFP should include all of the following sections:

Section 1—General Information

This section should include the following items:

- *Executive Summary.* This section should describe the company's business, market position, and revenue. It also outlines the business and technical reasons for the e-commerce system.
- *Scope.* This section should outline the organization of the RFP document.
- *Schedule of Events.* This section should provide a time line for the vendors, including the date of the RFP release, proposal deadline, vendor presentations, contract award, and letter of intent. This section also lists the company's evaluation procedures and criteria.

Section II—Proposal Specifications

- *Introduction.* This section should define the expected proposal format, to whom and how the proposal should be delivered, and how questions regarding the RFP will be handled.
- *Letter of Transmittal.* This section should define the content of each responding vendor's cover letter. The letter of transmittal requires an officer of the company to sign the letter so the company knows that the vendor's bid has management approval and backing.
- *Content.* This section of the report should define the section layout of all vendor proposals. Ensuring consistent proposal format and content saves the company time in evaluating and comparing proposals.

Section III—Technical Requirements

The technical requirements of the RFP should ask detailed questions in an effort to gain a comprehensive understanding of each vendor's service offering. While this section will vary depending on the particular system component, this section should include:

- *General Considerations.* This section should provide an overview of the company's current system environment. For example, this section might cover the number of telecommuters, geographic dispersion, applications, equipment, software, security, network infrastructure, network management, help desk, and network service levels.
- *Equipment Specifications.* This section should outline the specifications for the equipment that the vendor will supply or manage. It should articulate a particular vendor standard. For VPN requirements, for example, this section might include details of equipment such as ISDN terminal adapters, DSL equipment, various sized routers, remote access concentrators and firewalls.
- *Software Specifications.* This section should list the specifications for the software that the vendor might supply or manage.
- *Installation and Project Management.* This section should outline the company's expectations for installation and project management. It will specify how long the project will last, the qualifications of the vendor's personnel, the availability of personnel in the geographic regions that the company requires, and the implementation time frame for new users.
- *Configuration Management.* This section should outline the company's expectations for configuration management. It should detail how often changes are implemented, the vendor's "back-out" procedures should a configuration change go wrong, and the locations in which configurations are stored.
- *Performance Management.* This section should outline the company's performance management requirements and reporting needs. In particular, it should include what management expects from the e-commerce system manager. These requests should be reasonable, yet meet the needs of the company's business users.
- *Fault Management.* This section should define the faults for which the company expects the vendor to assume responsibility. Defining boundaries of responsibility is critical; otherwise, the company and the vendor will engage

in unproductive blaming throughout the contract. Responses to this section will provide the company with insight into how a vendor manages networks, its network management infrastructure, and the number and experience level of its network management personnel.

- *Security Management.* Along with protecting the company from intrusion, security management is essential to understanding how the vendor manages the security of the company's network. For a VPN RFP, companies should make sure they understand the exact level of security. Security technologies provided normally include encryption, key management, authentication, and token cards.
- *Asset Management.* While this section is specific to network services outsourcing, it is worthwhile to note that outsourcing implies giving up control of the company's network. Therefore, companies should make sure vendors have a plan for managing and tracking companies' assets. Poor asset management can lead to extended network outages.
- *Help Desk.* Managing help desk support is challenging. Most vendors will only supply level two and level three network support, which means the company's help desk needs to take the initial call, diagnose the problem, and notify the vendor if the problem originated in the network. But it could be difficult to diagnose whether a remote user is having a network problem or an application problem, so the company may want to consider outsourcing first-level help desk services as well.
- *Maintenance.* The company should find out who will actually provide hardware maintenance. Vendors often use a subcontractor for these services, so a company should understand the service-level agreements (SLA) between the vendor and its subcontractor.

Section IV—Contract Terms and Conditions

This section should include the company's standard contract terms and conditions, and repeat the service levels that the company expects the vendor to meet.

e **Develop the vendor assessment framework.** While the company waits for vendors to submit their proposals, the company should construct an evaluation assessment form. The criteria should have been stated already in the RFP. Examples of such criteria include cost, reliability, management capabilities, and account support.

The easiest and most comprehensive method is to construct two spreadsheets to perform side-by-side comparisons. Managers can use one for quantitative assessments and the other for qualitative assessments.

Prospective vendors must understand the evaluation criteria. The quantitative assessment spreadsheet should include every section and question that the company has asked, along with a rating system weighted by the company's criteria. Managers can use this matrix to track vendors' scores.

A qualitative assessment is equally important. Although subjective, this spreadsheet helps determine the company's overall feel for vendors' responses. It helps address questions such as how well vendors understand the company's business, how well they understand the e-commerce system's business requirements, and their level of flexibility.

e **Evaluate vendor bids.** Once the proposals arrive from vendors, managers should read them and complete their assessment forms. Generally, managers should grade the vendors, and then re-read the proposals to re-grade them after a few days. Managers should also test the proposals for answers that appear unrealistic, such as promising 100 percent network availability.

The company should also give vendors a chance to clarify their proposals. This clarification may involve the company submitting questions to each vendor, and requesting a written response. The company may also choose to have vendors address the its managers at a proposal presentation. The vendor presentations should be used as a final qualitative assessment of the candidates.

If none of the proposals meet the company's requirements, the RFP efforts can help guide the company to outsource the components of the RFP that vendors can easily handle. For example, if the RFP pertains to outsourcing of network management, and the company often needs to change its WAN addressing structure or router configurations with little notice, it might not be feasible to outsource router management. However, the company may still want to outsource dial-up remote access to a provider that will handle hardware, software, dial-up access, and security.

In any case, the RFP exercise will give the company a comprehensive understanding of the network functions that are strategic to the company, and *cannot* be outsourced, as well as the tactical functions that *can* be outsourced.

 Finalize the contract. Before signing the contract with the company's chosen vendor or vendors, the following details must be addressed:

- *Review the processes.* Managers should take a final look at the vendor's implementation, escalation, management, customer service management, and billing processes. Managers should feel comfortable that these meet the company's requirements.
- *Meet the people.* Managers should visit the outsourcer's management center, and meet the people who will manage the company's network, or install and maintain the software or hardware. Managers should determine whether they seem overworked, properly trained, etc.
- *Get it on paper.* Managers should review the contract, paying special attention to performance measurements such as Service Level Agreements (SLAs), and how the vendor's reporting will indicate compliance.

Conclusion

Negotiating e-commerce purchasing contracts is an important management responsibility that can determine how effectively the vision for e-commerce is implemented. In order to conduct a successful negotiation, managers should develop a clear vision for how the process will work, and communicate that to vendors and the employees who will negotiate the e-commerce purchase contracts. Once the process is underway, it is essential that managers develop an RFP that is comprehensive and realistic. Managers must also communicate openly and frequently with vendors who participate in the process. Managers must also develop a clear set of criteria for evaluating vendors, and make sure that they have all the available information from vendors before making their final decisions.

Notes

1. Stephanie Neil, "The Outsourcing Ring Takes More Than Guts," *PC Week,* December 31, 1997 [http://www.zdnet.com/zdnn/content/pcweek/15011/266558.html].
2. Ibid.
3. Ibid.
4. Ibid.
5. Ibid.
6. Aileen Crowley, "Taming the Ferocious Outsourcing Beast," *PC Week,* February 15, 1999 [http://www.zdnet.com/pcweek/stories/news/0,4153, 389098,00.html].
7. Ibid.

12

Managing the Implementation

O nce the company has chosen its e-commerce vendors, and negotiated the purchase contracts, the company's executives must face one final challenge before they can make e-commerce a reality. E-commerce's ability to create value for customers and shareholders depends heavily on how well executives manage its implementation. In order to implement e-commerce effectively, however, managers need to address a number of critical issues:

- What elements of project management are unique to e-commerce?
- What project management principles work most effectively for implementing e-commerce systems?
- What methodology should executives follow to implement e-commerce projects successfully?

Chapter 12 helps to address these issues. The chapter begins by outlining the most important elements of successful e-commerce project management. It continues by presenting four cases of companies that have managed e-commerce projects (United Airlines, Allied Signal, American International Group, and Homebid.com). Chapter 12 continues by highlighting several principles that managers can follow to increase their chances of success in managing e-commerce projects. It concludes by presenting a methodology that managers can follow to implement e-commerce projects successfully.

Elements of Successful E-Commerce Project Management

The ability to implement an e-commerce system depends less on mastering the new technologies of e-commerce, and more on learning new ways of managing the people who have a stake in the success of the e-commerce system. According to *Computerworld*, e-commerce has changed the rules of information technology project management. To succeed in the new environment, project managers must redefine the customer, redefine the project, and embrace youth, according to Ralph Szygenda, CIO at General Motors (GM).[1]

GM's experience, while unique in many ways, is more broadly applicable to other industries. For example, Szygenda notes that e-commerce has attracted him to the car buyer. Unlike the systems-development process for previous technologies, e-commerce means that the IT department's customer is no longer an internal customer. Everything that GM's IT department does now affects GM's external customer. In this sense, GM's experience is typical of other industries where e-commerce is increasingly placing new demands on CIOs.

GM's traditional goal of optimizing manufacturing to beat the competition is no longer useful. GM now focuses more on understanding the end-customer than worrying about what Ford or Chrysler is doing. In the past, Szygenda noted, GM treated each sale separately, and had no way of knowing if a sale was a customer's first Cadillac or tenth. Now GM collects and consolidates twenty databases of customer information so that a customer's entire car-buying history will be linked to every order.

In the past, GM built cars first, shipped them to dealerships, and then tried to entice customers to buy what was in stock. Now customers come from the Internet knowing the cost of vehicles. GM no longer conducts negotiations with cus-tomers.

So GM is moving to build-to-order and Internet direct sales, starting with fifteen major pilot programs. Szygenda said he hopes to integrate the direct-sales channel throughout the company by the end of 2000. If Szygenda does not meet or beat that timetable, he believes that GM will hire an outside firm to implement the customer-facing front-end. He also anticipates that the outside firm would end up dictating to GM's IT de-partment how the IT department's end of the system will op-erate.

Szygenda believes that anyone involved in e-commerce must be become a "sixty-day business." Szygenda concluded that the ability to move swiftly is essential because competi-tors Autobytel.com, E*Trade Group, eBay, and Priceline.com can change the way they market, and change distribution channels very rapidly.

As a result, IT project managers must redefine projects. Rather than having ambitious, long-term goals, today's proj-ects need to deliver value very quickly, and then build on that. To move at that speed, Szygenda believes that project manag-ers must use their intuition. He concedes that making those kinds of changes is difficult. In fact, Szygenda acknowledged that every GM sector is resisting e-commerce because they are generally afraid.

Szygenda believes that one way to advance GM's e-com-merce efforts is to embracing youth. He thinks that the people who understand the Internet are people who were born and bred on new technology. He added that most people over the age of 40 lack the intuitive grasp of the younger generation.[2]

The GM case highlights some of the most important man-agement challenges facing an e-commerce project manager. To implement e-commerce, managers must understand how the new system will create value for customers. Managers must also be able to adapt their e-commerce business model very rapidly in order to keep up with changing competitor strate-gies and customer needs. In addition, managers must be able to address and overcome the enormous internal resistance to e-commerce that they may encounter during the implementation process. Finally, managers must try to hire relatively young individuals at all levels of the company to improve the likely acceptance of e-commerce within the organization.

The e-commerce project manager must also deal with an issue that is of importance to managers of any type of project: the budget. As a company is experimenting with e-commerce, the magnitude of the budget may be small in comparison to other IT projects such as ERP systems. As a result, the e-commerce project manager may have an easier time obtaining an adequate project budget when a company is in the earlier stages of e-commerce systems development.

However, as the magnitude of the e-commerce system expands to incorporate more of the company's operations, the size of the e-commerce budget will expand as well. Despite this budget expansion, the cases we are about to review suggest that for most companies, the limiting resource in e-commerce systems development is not dollars, but the availability of qualified people who can develop the desired system rapidly enough to keep the company from falling behind in the race for market share.

E-Commerce Project Management Cases

E-commerce project management depends heavily on the ability to work effectively with outsourcers. In fact, *Internet Week* estimates that 60 percent of current e-commerce projects are being outsourced by Fortune 1000 companies. Companies outsource e-commerce implementation to accelerate time to market, to offset a lack of internal Web and e-commerce expertise, and to control the cost of going online. Often an IT organization will turn over application development that requires Web and Java expertise to a specialist in that field. Yet corporate managers retain control by keeping project management and architectural decisions in-house, often teaming their developers with the outsourcers working on-site.[3]

Here we will examine four brief cases that illustrate the complexity of managing the implementation of e-commerce when outsourcers are involved:

1. The United Airlines case illustrates how a large company worked with outsourcers to accelerate its time-to-market and to bolster the lack of e-commerce expertise of its internal staff.
2. The AlliedSignal case demonstrates how large companies whose IT staffs include individuals with mainframe and client/server knowledge (but little Java and Web skills) used systems integrator GE Information Systems to implement its e-commerce applications.
3. The American International Group (AIG) case illustrates the benefits of teaming internal Web technologists with those from outside companies in order to make the best use of available internal resources while accelerating the e-commerce development process.
4. The Homebid.com case illustrates how it is cheaper and faster for Internet startup firms to hire a systems integrator to implement the e-commerce application completely. Such companies may intend later to bring their e-commerce development in-house once they get big enough to afford a capable staff.

United Airlines

United Airlines is an example of a large company that chose to work with outsourcers to accelerate its time-to-market. With an annual IT budget of $550 million and 1,500 IT professionals, the $18 billion United Airlines concluded that it could not move quickly enough to develop e-commerce on its own. Specifically, United Airlines wanted to give its 28 million frequent fliers the ability to redeem mileage for free flights, to check account status, and to receive other third-party travel discounts.[4]

Susan Fullman, a United director of e-commerce initiatives, said that United outsourced due to concerns about time-to-market and the lack of internal resources.

United worked with Internal Travel Network, in which it owns an unspecified stake, to develop advanced flight booking, and to run United's infrastructure and back-end systems. This required creating a transaction server—based on BEA Systems' Tuxedo running on an HP-UX server—that is linked to United's Mileage Plus database running on an MVS version of IBM's DB2 database.

United also worked with Sapient, a consulting firm focused on developing e-commerce software, to add navigation features to its online reservation system, which was launched in May 1999. United worked with Sapient to develop software that integrates customer profiles with tools to let users choose seats, hotels, and rental cars.

Like many enterprises, United recognized that outside experts could complete a project in roughly half the time that the internal staff could. The early results of the project were encouraging. The number of Mileage Plus passengers accessing the site was 200,000 daily in June 1999, an increase of 25 percent over the May 1999 levels.

In June 1999, Fullman was optimistic that the site would generate additional online sales of tickets because it offered personalized travel discounts and reservations. The airline projects online sales of $500 million in 1999 were more than double 1998's $200 million. While that amount represented less than 3 percent of sales, United hoped that 20 percent of its sales would occur online by 2002.[5]

The United case demonstrates that working with systems integrators can achieve important objectives such as completing an e-commerce application very rapidly in order to maintain a company's competitive position. As this example illustrates, teaming with multiple outside companies—one for network services and one for application development—produced an e-commerce system for United that has contributed to a doubling of its online ticket sales in a year.

AlliedSignal

AlliedSignal demonstrates the tremendous value of using systems integrators to close the skill gap needed to implement e-commerce applications in a timely fashion. According to *Internet Week*, Allied-Signal is the aircraft engine manufacturer that planned to merge with Honeywell in 1999 to form a $25 billion company. Allied had 2,000 IT employees with expertise in legacy programming languages such as COBOL, as well as in the client/server architecture.[6]

AlliedSignal wanted to build a Web site that would enable pilots who want to purchase electronics for private planes to design the planes' cockpits. To build the Web site, Allied worked with GE Information Services (GEIS) to start the project. Allied hopes this project will serve as a launching pad for a broader business-to-business e-commerce initiative.

Allied CIO Larry Kittelberger's goal is to move 50 percent of AlliedSignal's business and customers to the Internet by 2004. Kittelberger chose GEIS because Allied had a tremendous amount of work to be done in a short time, and the company did not have all the expertise in-house.

Allied needed front-end and back-end systems development capabilities. The company needed the front-end skills to build the customer front-end and the back-end and extranet links so that customized orders could be forwarded to distributors that sell the electronics.

Allied hopes to bring more of its application development in-house. However, since hiring e-commerce developers that earn six-figure salaries would be prohibitive, Kittelberger is training all Allied Signal's IT people in Web technologies.

American International Group (AIG)

Some users implement their e-commerce systems by mixing internal and external resources. American International Group (AIG), a $37 billion (1998 revenues) insurer, has some in-house Internet experts, although not enough for its online insurance applications and claims-processing applications under development.

Robert Guido, Senior Vice President, Global Internet Technologies, noted that in 1999 AIG had an Internet staff of forty people out of the company's total IT department of 1,500 people.

Guido pointed out that AIG's core team of architects and strategists had to be augmented by using outside consultants. In this case, AIG worked with SGI, a New York consulting firm, to gain access to creative skills for activities such as Web site design, graphics, and the general appearance of the company's Web site. AIG also outsourced its HTML (HyperText Markup Language) coding and less mission-critical applications such as AIG's corporate online directory. In addition, AIG hired Icon, a company owned by Qwest Communications, to create the front-end Web design for its Trade Credit Web site, which went into operation in June 1999.

Guido suggested three important factors that he uses in dealing with outsourcers. First he suggested always choosing a reputable outsourcer such as IBM Global Services. Guido recommended that if a company uses a small systems integrator, it should make sure that the principals have a good performance record and ample experience. Second, Guido suggested that a company should make certain that it owns the code that the outsourcer has written. Third, while the company should define the deliverables and dates in the contract, it should put some flexibility into the outsourcing contract to accommodate changes in business needs.

Guido did not outsource all AIG's applications. In particular, AIG did not outsource applications that were critical to its corporate operations. AIG manages its back-end systems (e.g., connecting to general ledger) and managing corporate assets (e.g., secure online insurance buying over its extranet).

AIG is a relatively sophisticated consumer of external resources for the implementation of its e-commerce system.

While it is too early to tell whether AIG's work with its systems integration partners will result in the success of its e-commerce projects, Guido's confidence in a positive outcome appears high. His confidence suggests that tapered backwards integration for different e-commerce applications can achieve a favorable outcome for many organizations.

Homebid.com

Some startup companies are using systems integrators to complete the implementation of e-commerce applications while they build their business models. Homebid.com, for example, conducted its first online home auction in May 1999, after having its site completely developed by Scient, an e-commerce integrator.

Jean-Luc Valente, Chief of Marketing and Operations, noted that Homebid.com needed to build a site that could handle thousands of bidders, and that was capable of checking background information for buyers. To save money and time, Homebid.com built its e-commerce system by partnering with Scient.

Valente said that the outsourcing contract was for $1.5 million, much less than the cost that would have been incurred if the company had hired the twenty to thirty IT people needed to launch the site. Valente noted that future enhancements will be brought in-house as the company is able to hire its own IT staff.

Principles of Successful E-Commerce Project Management

Rather than rehash the principles of successful project management, most of which apply to e-commerce development, let's focus here on principles of project management that are unique to e-commerce. Before describing these e-commerce principles, it is worth reminding the reader of some of the most important general principles of project management:

- *Assign clear accountability.* If accountability for completing a project is diffused, it is very likely that the project will not be completed. Only if one individual is ultimately held accountable for the success of the project can there be a reasonable hope that the inevitable obstacles to project completion will be addressed and overcome.
- *Build a team that includes all stakeholders.* The project team must include systems people, business managers, and system users. Whoever is not included in the process could ultimately delay the project, or undermine its success. Therefore, it is generally better to err on the side of inclusion.
- *Provide senior management support.* Senior management must communicate (at the risk of over-communicating) the importance of the project to the company's future. This verbal support must be backed up with the allocation of sufficient capital and people to complete the project.
- *Set firm deadlines and concrete budgets.* The project manager must commit to achieving the project by a specific time and within a concrete budget. For the project to succeed, it is essential that these deadlines and budgets are tight, yet realistic. When a gap emerges between the plan and the delivery of results, it becomes very difficult for the project manager to reestablish credibility.
- *Plan for contingencies.* Despite the best intentions of all involved, events can take place during a project that make it impossible to adhere to the original project time line. Managers should anticipate such problems in their project planning.

Bearing in mind these general project management principles, here are six e-commerce project management principles that managers should follow for successful e-commerce implementation:

e ***Identify the capabilities needed to make the e-commerce project successful.*** E-commerce projects demand a broad range of capabilities including new technologies such as HTML and Java, as well as the ability to link these technologies with "back-end" systems in order to provide customers with a fully integrated e-commerce experience. Furthermore, e-commerce projects often involve people with creative skills to design Web front-ends, and more traditional engineering skills to make the network operate effectively.

e ***Analyze the company's capability gap.*** When large organizations embark on e-commerce projects, they often have IT people who are very capable in traditional technologies such as COBOL and mainframe computers. These same organizations are weak in the Web technologies. Such organizations are often quick to recognize—depending on their sense of urgency—that the best way to close the capability gap is to rent the capabilities needed for the project.

e ***If necessary, hire an outside consultant with a compelling track record and experienced people.*** If the company chooses to hire a systems integrator to help with the project, it makes sense to take a careful look at the company's prior record of e-commerce projects. Companies should work with a systems integrator that has previously developed e-commerce systems that are similar in scope to the company's project. Companies should also seek out systems integrators who have a reputation for delivering high-quality work on time and within the budget. Finally, companies should pick systems integrators who will assign experienced individuals to their projects. It generally is not a good practice for companies to train the systems integrators' inexperience staff.

e ***Anticipate the effort of integrating back- and front-end systems.*** In setting these deadlines, it is imperative that companies are aware of the need to integrate the back- and front-end systems. If a company sets up a Web site that is not linked effectively to back-end fulfillment systems, then it becomes very difficult to create a superior customer-value proposition. E-commerce systems have this unique element that often requires a higher budget and a different set of skills than may have been required in a traditional systems-development project.

e ***Fix the time and cost of the e-commerce development process.*** There are systems integrators who are willing to work on a fixed time/price basis. These companies are generally the most desirable ones to hire because they are willing to take on projects and commit to finishing them within the deadline and budget that the company requires. In order to hire such systems integrators, the companies themselves must be willing to commit the internal resources necessary to achieving deadlines and budgets that are sufficiently realistic so that the systems integrator is willing to undertake the project.

e ***Be prepared to modify the e-commerce system after it goes into operation.*** E-commerce systems generally come with a built-in feedback mechanism from customers. The ability of customers to complain about the system directly to the company via e-mail and indirectly through newsgroups and chat rooms creates a tremendous challenge for companies to solve problems quickly, and to adapt the e-commerce system to changing customer needs and changing competitor strategies. This rapid rate of change means that companies must be prepared to build the first version of their Web site very quickly, and then continue to reinvest in it in order to stay competitive in a very rapidly changing environment.

E-Commerce Project Management Methodology

To apply these principles effectively, managers must follow an approach that provides specific benefits that are unique to the e-commerce environment. As I noted earlier, companies often work with systems integrators to complete their e-commerce systems development projects. The methodology outlined below enables companies to work with outsiders to achieve the following benefits:

- *Respond dynamically to feedback.* The proposed approach is designed to make the e-commerce system adapt quickly to feedback from customers, and to changes in competitor strategies and technology.
- *Produce measurable results.* The proposed approach defines and delivers specific economic benefits such as lower costs or faster order processing—as well as less tangible benefits such as increased levels of customer satisfaction.
- *Meet project deadlines, and adhere to budget.* The proposed approach is intended to help managers meet their time and cost budgets.

The e-commerce development methodology has four stages:

 Define business objectives. During the first stage of the methodology, the company defines the initiatives, strategy, and the expected results for the e-commerce systems development project. This stage occurs in two phases: strategy and technical.

1. *Strategy.* In this phase, the company develops a high-level e-commerce strategy that uses technology to innovate and support the company's overall business strategy. This phase is a recapitulation of the e-commerce strategy development process that we explored in Chapter 5.
2. *Technical.* In this phase, the company examines its current technology infrastructure and organization to target and define strategic initiatives.

At the end of this stage, the company should have the information necessary to define key business success factors, and to prioritize the potential e-commerce projects based on a clear understanding of its e-commerce objectives.

Develop system scope and design. In the second stage, the company defines the scope of the e-commerce applications to be developed and designs applications to enable the company to achieve the objectives articulated in stage one. During this stage, the company scopes and designs the underlying infrastructure to integrate the software, network, and hardware components necessary to support the applications. This stage includes the evaluation of any third party software.

This second stage occurs in two phases: scope and design.

1. *Scope.* The goal of this phase is to collect application and process requirements to develop a baseline for the design phase. This phase is accomplished by following the process addressed in Chapter 10.

2. *Design.* During this phase, the company defines the processes, components, and time line necessary to achieve the business objectives of the e-commerce system. The goal of this phase is to create a complete plan that allows the applications to be constructed, tested, and implemented on time and within budget.

After the second stage, the company has a blueprint for its e-commerce system development. This blueprint identifies in detail the tasks necessary to meet the objectives and overall strategy goals as defined in the first stage of the methodology.

Code, test, and deliver the system. In this stage, the company builds and delivers the e-commerce applications, which may include the incorporation or integration of third-party software. Within this stage are three phases that are focused on successfully implementing the applications defined during the second stage: detailed design, implementation, and testing.

1. *Detailed Design.* In this phase the company adds more specific details to the requirements, including the user interface and key technical designs.

2. *Implementation.* In this phase, applications are built and refined until they are ready for testing. This phase is aimed at producing the tangible results for the company that were identified in the earlier stages of the methodology. During the implementation phase, the company also trains both internal and external users on newly built applications.

3. *Testing.* In this phase, applications are tested to ensure they meet all functional, technical, and user requirements. This phase is intended to ensure that the engineered applications perform in accordance with the requirements defined in the second stage of the methodology.

Upon completion of the third stage, the e-commerce application is ready to operate.

e *Plan for future enhancements.* In the fourth stage, the company establishes a plan for ongoing application development and content management designed to sustain the its market leadership. The fourth stage is delivered in five distinct phases: definition, transition, management, infrastructure evolution, and application innovation.

1. *Definition.* During this phase, the company assesses its established e-commerce system, and defines future objectives.
2. *Transition.* Transition activities focus on the technical, process, and user-oriented aspects of further transforming the company's e-commerce system.
3. *Management.* The management phase involves the ongoing management of the e-commerce systems, including application management, performance management, and system security management.
4. *Infrastructure Evolution.* During this phase, the company identifies and innovates new technology infrastructure and capacity, along with performance specifications on an ongoing basis.
5. *Application Innovation.* During this phase, the company incorporates new features into its e-commerce system.

Conclusion

The growth of e-commerce depends on the ability of companies to achieve dramatic improvements in economic performance by using Internet technology to change the way they work with suppliers, employees, and customers. Achieving these potential economic performance improvements can only happen if companies are willing to lead fundamental change in their organizations. This change process may involve re-thinking the company's competitive strategy, and changing the organization structure and compensation system. If the company can make these fundamental changes, then it is prepared to develop the e-commerce architecture, and manage its implementation effectively.

Notes

1. Kathleen Melymuka, "E-Commerce: Driving a Redefinition of GM; CIO: Focus Must Be on Customers, Youth," *Computerworld*, June 28, 1999, p. 20.
2. Ibid.
3. Saroja Girishankar, "In Focus: E-Commerce Outsourcing—Internet Time Forces Anxious Enterprises to seek Outside Help," *Internet Week*, June 28, 1999, p. 1.
4. Ibid.
5. Ibid.
6. Ibid.

Index